Reflections of a Radical Moderate

By the same author

The Creative Balance

The Uses and Limitations of Law

ELLIOT RICHARDSON

Reflections of a Radical Moderate

Pantheon Books
New York

320.97309 ̄MAY (1) 2000
Ric

Grateful acknowledgment is made to Henry Holt & Company, Inc., for permission to
reprint an excerpt from "The Death of the Hired Man" from *The Poetry of Robert Frost*,
edited by Edward Connery Lathem.

Library of Congress Cataloging-in-Publication Data

Richardson, Elliot L., 1920–
    Reflections of a radical moderate / Elliot Richardson.
        p.   cm.
    ISBN 0-679-42820-8
    1. Democracy—United States.   2. United States—Politics and government.
I. Title
JK1726.R53   1996
320.973'09'049—dc20
                                                            95-49346
                                                            CIP

BOOK DESIGN BY LAURA HOUGH

Manufactured in the United States of America
FIRST EDITION
9 8 7 6 5 4 3 2 1

ELLIOT RICHARDSON

Reflections of a Radical Moderate

Pantheon Books
New York

320.97309 [MAY (1) 2000
Ric

Grateful acknowledgment is made to Henry Holt & Company, Inc., for permission to
reprint an excerpt from "The Death of the Hired Man" from *The Poetry of Robert Frost,*
edited by Edward Connery Lathem.

Library of Congress Cataloging-in-Publication Data

Richardson, Elliot L., 1920–
    Reflections of a radical moderate / Elliot Richardson.
        p.   cm.
    ISBN 0-679-42820-8
    1. Democracy—United States.   2. United States—Politics and government.
I. Title
JK1726.R53   1996
320.973'09'049—dc20   95-49346
                                                                    CIP

BOOK DESIGN BY LAURA HOUGH

Manufactured in the United States of America
FIRST EDITION
9 8 7 6 5 4 3 2 1

*For
my beloved
wife*

*For
my beloved
wife*

If we could first know where we are, and *whither* we are tending, we could then better judge *what* to do, and *how* to do it.

ABRAHAM LINCOLN
JUNE 16, 1858

Contents

Acknowledgments

We all have the defects of our qualities, and so does this book. The qualities owe much to the comments and criticisms, knowledge and research of the many individuals whose contributions are acknowledged here. The defects are inseparable from the form in which, for better or worse, I chose to cast the things I wanted to say: breadth of subject and tightness of expression are a difficult combination to manage.

As for clarity and readability, you'd have to have seen the work in progress to appreciate how much I owe to thoughtful and generous friends. Foremost among them are Hélène and Ernest Sargeant. From punctuation and choice of words to substantive content, almost every page owes something to their abhorrence of obscurity and eye for accuracy. And if you come across passages that you think might better have been omitted, the chances are good that they would not have survived had I taken the Sargeants' advice. The book as a whole has also benefited from Christopher Perry's stylistic craftsmanship, James Pfiffner's broad knowledge of government, and Janet Brown's cheerful irreverence.

Many other people made valuable contributions to individual essays. The late Robert Carter gave me provocative ideas and warm encouragement at an early stage of the essay on peace enforcement. Ellen Guidera's intelligence and sensitivity were important to those on information, peace enforcement, and a sense of worth. In the case of several other essays, my brother George's structural suggestions, FitzGerald Bemiss's political insights, Jan Schneider's incisiveness, and Richard Darman's stress on accessibility all deserve special thanks. My children—Henry the philosopher, Nancy the psychologist, and Michael the journalist—drawing on their particular strengths, were also a great resource.

Throughout the book, often in a single sentence, are statements resting on a lot more inquiry than you might suppose. With regard to religious leadership in promoting respect for other faiths, useful information came from Lawrence Sullivan of the Center for the Study of World Religions at Harvard's Divinity School, David Little of the United States Institute of Peace, and others I met through the kindness of Nancy Ignatius, former president of the National Cathedral Association. Dwight Ink, Dona Wolf, Frank Cipolla, and Robert Schaetzel identified useful indicators of the current state of the federal bureaucracy and career services. Julius Katz, former deputy United States trade representative, and John Jackson, professor of law at the University of Michigan, clarified my understanding of the role of the World Trade Organization. With regard to the public welfare system, William Gorham, president of the Urban Institute, and his colleagues, Isabel Sawhill and Demetra Nightingale, supplied both corrective comments and statistical data. Robert Ball's unmatched knowledge of Social Security contributed significantly to my discussion of that subject.

The essays on peace enforcement and interaction were substantially strengthened by suggestions from Louis Sohn, Edward Luck, Jonathan Moore, Michael Stopford, and Sir John Thomson, each of whom is broadly experienced in the work of the United Nations and other international organizations. James Schlesinger on the Gulf War and Alphonse LaPorta on war crimes tribunals were also helpful. Bernard Oxman's careful review of the essay on interaction yielded numerous clarifications and corrections. Stephen Canner of the U.S. Council for International Business furnished data on the current state of the international investment scene. Finally, on the controversial subject of climate change, I've had the benefit of the balanced assessment of Aristides Patrinos, associate director of health and environmental re-

Acknowledgments

search at the Department of Energy, and the informed assistance of Elizabeth Poyck and Tiffany Elliott, my colleagues at Milbank, Tweed, Hadley, & McCloy.

And yet the foregoing acknowledgments by no means cover all the references, statistics, or factual statements in this book. Almost all of those not otherwise acknowledged have been ferreted out, dug up, verified, and/or summarized by Misty Church and her partner, Julie Altman. Their thoroughness and tenacity have been extraordinary. And if, despite their efforts, the text still contains erroneous statements, it's because I insisted on making them on my own authority.

I'm also grateful to several other Milbank, Tweed colleagues. Our librarian, Gabriele Zsebi, devoted expert knowledge to supplying references and tracking down quotations. Her assistant, Ryan Rupe, quickly located key research documents. Dean Manson, usually at short notice, was an efficient exploiter of Lexis and Nexis. And Christiane Van Hout, whose conscientiousness and good humor surmounted numerous tight deadlines, was extremely helpful in transferring the final changes to the galleys.

But the only person who has given this book almost as much time and effort as I have is Marguerite Ziccardi Randolph. She became my secretary at the State Department in 1977, and since then we've been through many things together. From beginning to end Marguerite has had to turn my handwritten drafts into readable type. She has also been responsible for maintaining the files, finding miscellaneous notes and clippings, keeping track of correspondence and phone calls, and helping me stay abreast of other commitments. Throughout all this she has been cheerful, encouraging, and, when necessary, candid. I can never thank her enough.

I've been fortunate as well in the stage beyond the best that Marguerite and I could do. Pantheon Books has been constructive and considerate in every way that an author could hope for. I'm especially grateful to Erroll McDonald, my editor, and to his unfailingly helpful assistant, Nara Nahm.

There is, finally, one other person whose indispensable contributions cannot be tied to any particular part of the process from which this array of words has come. That person is my wife. To her I owe an immeasurable debt for patient understanding, steady support, and rare good sense. But that has been true for all of nearly forty-four wonderful years.

Preface

If I knew how to make it so, this book would sound like a radical tract. For I am a radical—a radical moderate.

I believe profoundly in the ultimate value of human dignity and equality. I therefore believe as well in such essential contributors to these ends as fairness, tolerance, and mutual respect. In seeking to be fair, tolerant, and respectful I need to call upon all the empathy, understanding, rationality, skepticism, balance, and objectivity I can muster. These are the attributes of moderation.

For me, moderation is not a fighting faith but a faith worth fighting for. My commitment to it is passionate, uncompromising, and deep-rooted—hence, radical.

Moderates have ideals, but they are not starry-eyed idealists. Moderates perceive clearly the ugly aspects of human behavior, but they are not hard-bitten cynics. Moderates try to see the world clearly and see it whole. They are realists.

As everyone knows, moderation is not colorful or dramatic. Its deliberations tend to come across as dull. Moderates seldom get headlines, and their utterances cannot easily be reduced to sound bites. All this is unfortunate. It would be better for the health of the democratic process if moderate centrism could get itself at least as much attention as right-wing conservatism (left-wing liberalism has almost disappeared).

Preface

Being problem solvers, moderates put a premium on solutions. It takes much more than split-the-difference, down-the-middle compromise to work out a sensible accommodation among valid competing claims. To achieve and maintain a creative balance you have to be resourceful and inventive. Take, for example, constitutional conventions, bills of rights, and means of curbing abuses of private power that leave adequate room for private initiative. These are among the moderate tradition's most durable inventions. Similar resourcefulness has more recently found ways of advancing civil rights, protecting the environment, and strengthening the federal-state partnership.

For a long time now it has been my good fortune to occupy one or another well-situated perch from which to observe the interplay of government and politics. The scenes I witnessed provided a fascinating display of human behavior. Watching the actors perform reinforced my awareness that our conduct is only partially accessible to reason and never fully controlled by it. Our most pathetic and amusing actions, as well as the noblest and most inspiring, are driven by the need to endow our identities with enduring significance. The former include both the compulsive pursuit of recognition and shallow attempts to stave off oblivion. To ask a status-seeking young person, Why knock yourself out for a fleeting reward? would be like asking a salmon why it hurls itself upstream. But just as the salmon's spawning helps to perpetuate its species, so society's approbation acknowledges some benefit to itself.

The examples of noble and inspiring conduct that I've also seen have in common the pursuit of some good end for its own sake. Some of these examples have involved unselfish devotion to the public interest, some unswerving adherence to the merits, and some conspicuous courage under pressure. Countless individuals whose performances I watched neither sought nor expected recognition but nevertheless felt the desire to play a meaningful part in dealing with broadly shared concerns. What else would explain their speaking so feelingly of the desire "to make a difference"?

It would have been impossible in the circumstances not to accumulate a considerable store of insights and opinions, and as time went on I began to think about putting them on paper. What got me started was my growing concern that burgeoning complexity, rampant distrust, and cynical appeals to narrow interests were threatening to extinguish the spirit of moderation. At first I assumed that all I had to do would be to take already well-formed thoughts, put them in order, and find the right words. I was wrong. The "well-formed thoughts" turned out to be riddled with gaps and inconsistencies. That was the bad news. Yet from the filling in and straightening out that went into correcting these flaws gradually emerged a much clearer understanding of the subjects I wanted to discuss. Indeed, it has occurred to me that the more successful I have been in communicating this clarity, the more likely you will be to say, "Surely this is obvious!" Perhaps. But it may also be profound.

For me, in any case, the effort that has gone into this book has more than paid off. I've learned a lot. If, in addition, these essays persuade you of the wisdom of this nation's moderate tradition, I will be doubly rewarded.

Reflections of a Radical Moderate

Reflections of a Radical Moderate

Power in Washington

Do you believe that the pursuit of power is the national capital's favorite form of exercise? That wielding power is Washington's most gratifying occupation? That skill in its manipulation is the key to effectiveness? That to get to the top of the Washington heap you have to have a streak of ruthlessness, even meanness?

If your answers are affirmative, you share a set of widely held beliefs. That they happen to be wrong should not embarrass you. It's quite understandable, in fact, that you and so many others should think this way. Events that are "newsworthy," which is to say exciting or dramatic, are more likely to seize your attention than those that are merely important. Power, in any case, has an exciting aura (while still new to Washington Henry Kissinger called it "the great aphrodisiac"). There is drama in its capture, manipulation, curtailment, or loss. These are things we all read about in the morning paper and watch on the evening news. No matter how conscientious, we could not possibly give proportionate attention to the remainder—89 percent perhaps—of what the Washington complex is actually chewing away on day by day.

History has scarcely more time than journalism for the ordinary and undramatic. Just as good news is no news, uneventful times have no

3

history. And while Washington's history has not been uneventful, its hardest-fought struggles have been over purposes and policies rather than power. By comparison with that of other great capitals, Washington's past has been tame. Every national election has been held on the appointed day. Every transfer of power from one administration to the next has proceeded without incident. No American politician has ever gone to the chopping block, forfeited his estates, or been sent into exile. There has never been even a hint of a conspiracy to take over the White House and oust the president. And only one president has been forced to resign.

Machiavelli would be confused by Washington. He would find it hard to believe that it is in reality a city of cocker spaniels more eager to be loved, petted, and admired than to wield power. He would wonder where the pit bulls are. And while Machiavelli might see encouraging signs that the nation's capital is on its way toward becoming a place in which he might eventually feel at home, he would encounter little immediate use for his skills. The reason for his disappointment, of course, would be that our system has throughout its history been strikingly successful in cutting down to size those who seek personal aggrandizement. It has also done very well in harnessing political power to the security and welfare of the American people.

But past success is small solace for future failure, and the system is indeed coming under increasing strain. It is important, therefore, for us to try to understand how and why it has worked so well up to now. This essay records the outcome of my own efforts to reach such understanding. What I have to report will, I hope, help us stay the course.

One clue to the system's success that struck me early on is a clue like that of the dog that *didn't* bark in the Sherlock Holmes story: it is the scarcity in Washington of individuals who are recognizably driven by the pursuit of power for its own sake. Your typical cynic will, of course, reject this observation, but that need not trouble us; cynics are not distinguished for their realism. Journalists and fiction writers (the difference between the two is not always clear) would also have us believe that Washington is full of power-hungry monomaniacs, but they have, after all, a certain interest in encouraging this belief.

In the real Washington, even the most ambitious people I know would insist that they seek power only for the sake of worthy ends. It goes without saying that they want to win as well as to achieve recognition, enjoy respect, and make a comfortable living. They realize, however, that being perceived as too aggressive or too self-seeking could jeopardize these aims. Besides, in Washington as elsewhere, success seldom confers esteem unless it appears to have been won in accordance with the rules. Why otherwise would those who are known to have broken them on the way up later feel compelled to try to cultivate social acceptance?

The truth about power in Washington is that no individual has much. The system works, not in spite of that fact, but because of it. The dispersal of power has from the outset been a source of vitality and resilience. The system is constantly renewed, indeed, by the perennial necessity both to combine the efforts of people who share an objective they cannot accomplish on their own and to head off the opposition of people any of whom could block it on their own. You see these processes going on at every point around the circle linking voters with interest groups with the presidency with executive branch agencies with Congress with voters and so around the circle again.

Let's break into the circle at the presidency. The president is, of course, much more powerful than anybody else in the system. But what does he actually do with his time? Mostly, he tries to build support. When Theodore Roosevelt referred to the "bully pulpit," he was not exulting in the power of his office but making the point that the White House is a good platform from which to win converts and rally the faithful. The later Roosevelt's "fireside chats," JFK's press conferences, Clinton's town meetings, and every recent president's nationally televised speeches have all been means not simply of explaining presidential policies but of building broader support. This has to go on continually and on many levels: with the general public, interest groups, members of Congress, businessmen, religious leaders, educators, the medical profession, heads of other governments, and on and on and on.

The president has to have his own pollsters to tell him what the people want and how to get across to them what he thinks they should want. He has to have his own lobbyists to track developments on the Hill, sell his programs, and spot the senators and congressmen who need his personal massaging. The president has to answer critics, mollify interest groups, and cultivate the media. He has to be image-conscious twenty-four hours a day. His fellow citizens' dislike or distrust can reduce him to impotence.

The people who work for the president at high levels in executive branch departments and agencies have to operate in the same kind of way, although of course on a smaller and narrower scale. Making decisions and issuing orders won't cut it. For every important initiative it is essential to seek and win support. Indeed, this conspicuous difference between the day-to-day roles of government managers and corporate executives may explain why success in business is no guarantee of success in government.

From the president on down, people in the executive branch used to take what advantage they could of a limited supply of carrots and sticks. Both the sticks and the carrots were fashioned from the same material—government grants and contracts, presidential appointments, bills or appropriations of special interest to a constituency, pork-barrel projects, and the like. Where inducing congressional cooperation was concerned, the carrot held out support for some such interest; the stick warned of opposition to it. These carrot-and-stick combinations, however, are of limited utility. For one thing, there were often larger public interests at stake that inhibited their use. For another, there was at any one time only a limited number of interests unique to an individual senator or congressman that the executive branch could legitimately advance or impede. Moreover, any given carrot or stick could be used only once. The risk of making a permanent enemy also had to be weighed.

The executive branch's lobbying resources, in any case, had to be spread thinly over a very broad agenda. The White House had first claim on the valuable items. Those left over were useful only for secondary issues. Back in the days of President Eisenhower's second term, when I was responsible for the Department of Health, Education, and Welfare's legislative program, the goodies at my disposal were so insignificant that to mention them would have been more likely to derail my appeal on the merits than to win a congressman's support. That experience set a precedent for all my later contacts with Congress.

The only situation I can recall where a show of readiness for some sort of deal might have made a difference was in the effort to induce Senator Russell Long, the all-powerful chairman of the Senate Finance Committee, to let the Family Assistance Plan, President Nixon's welfare reform program, go to the floor. It was a good program—much better than the one now being pushed—and the House passed it twice, both times by comfortable margins. Senator Long kept the bill bottled up for reasons that were never entirely clear, and though I kept looking for some approach that would persuade him to let it move, I never succeeded in finding one. Bob Haldeman's diary for July 13, 1970, supplies a shockingly duplicitous explanation: "About Family Assistance Plan, [Nixon] wants to be sure it's killed by Democrats and that we make a big play for it, but don't let it pass, can't afford it."[1]

In the decades since the Eisenhower administration the demands on the president have continued to grow even while his ability to meet those demands has been shrinking. The growth is an inescapable consequence of developments discussed in subsequent essays: the increase of complexity, the need to address systemic interconnections, and the inseparability of domestic and foreign concerns. The shrinkage, as Adam Clymer, chief congressional correspondent for the *New York Times*, pointed out in a 1994 *Times* piece, is a by-product of "reform":

> Before there was a Common Cause, before logrolling and offering or withholding favors became incorrect (or even illegal), politicians regarded them as serious work tools for the business of passing legislation. For better or worse—worse for Mr. Clinton—those days are long past.[2]

Also undercutting presidential initiatives is the pressure on the Senate calendar that, by enabling the mere threat of a filibuster to block action on any legislation, effectively imposes a three-fifths requirement for the Senate to do its business.

The weaker the executive branch's bargaining position, the more important is the help of sympathetic national organizations. Throughout the three years of my HEW legislative job during the Eisenhower administration, I met regularly with the Washington representatives of about a dozen such organizations ranging from the American Legion to the American Association of University Women. When it came to our most important and most controversial initiative, the National Defense Education Act, I asked my chief assistant to leave the government and set up

---

[1] H. R. Haldeman, *The Haldeman Diaries: Inside the Nixon White House* (New York: G. P. Putnam's Sons, 1994), p.181.

[2] *New York Times,* "Week in Review," June 19, 1994, p.1.

an "Emergency Committee for the National Defense Education Act" with a membership of about a hundred organizations. All such an effort can achieve, of course, is to reach the folks back home. Whether or not they then do anything is up to them. Anyway, the bill narrowly passed in the summer of 1958—a result, I still think, that was greatly in the national interest.

Every new Congress reconfirms the saying "The president proposes and Congress disposes." The House's exclusive power to originate revenue bills, the Senate's tolerance of unlimited debate, and both bodies' delaying tactics can be maddening to a president who thinks he knows what he was elected to accomplish. Given these frustrations, it's easy to see why presidents have been so anxious to get the line-item veto and why the present Congress has not yet let them have even a watered-down version of it.

Despite all the time and money that other people give to winning their support, senators and congressmen have no time to enjoy the possession of power. Other than butlers and firemen, they're the only people I know of who are constantly being summoned by bells. An executive branch supplicant is surprised only the first time when a committee chairman suspends a meeting in his office to take a call from an important constituent. And no matter how often you've testified at committee hearings you don't get used to being stopped in midsentence so that members can answer a roll call.

But the surest way to lose one's awe of congressional power is to expose oneself to the apparatus that Congress has assembled to handle communications with constituents. The audio and video facilities, the computerized files, the mail-handling machinery, and the copying, faxing, and word-processing equipment—all these show whom Congress holds in awe.

Most House members have between four and ten staffers who do nothing but sort and answer mail and another three or four who do nothing but handle casework. Most members spend an average of fifteen to twenty hours a week meeting with constituents, taking them to lunch, or showing them around the Capitol. All members have local offices at which citizens can make their requests and voice their complaints, and most have regular office hours and town meetings back home on weekends. Even the unremitting necessity of raising money pays homage to people power. According to a *Congressional Quarterly* study of all reported expenditures in the 1992 House and Senate campaigns, the share that went into communicating with the electorate was 44 percent for House incumbents and 56 percent for House challengers, 53 percent for Senate incumbents and 62 percent for Senate challengers.

And what about the constituents themselves? Do they feel good about all the attention lavished on them by the suitors for their support? Not if you can believe the opinion surveys. The proportion of the adult public who think that people running the country don't really care what happens to them has risen steadily year by year for a long time. So too has the proportion who think that most people with power try to take advantage of people like themselves. This is a deeply disturbing development. It reflects a sense of inefficacy and helplessness which, though the product of factors quite different from those to which it is attributed, is meat for a demagogue like Ross Perot.

The designers of our constitutional system would be astonished and perhaps dismayed by the scale and complexity of the society to which their inventions are being applied. Showing them Washington would be like showing a Boeing 747 to the Wright brothers. But the framers would surely be gratified to learn that, thanks to their devices for limiting, dispersing, and checking the use of power, ours is the only major country in the world which, in the last two hundred years, has never been ruled by a dictator or an oligarchy.

At this point the cynic breaks in. Though almost always wrong, he can be astute. He observes that the dispersal of power, rather than supporting my view of its limited motivating force, proves nothing more than that the game engages a great many players. Knowing my weakness for constitutional history, he then throws in my face *The Federalist*, no. 51's famous dictum on the separation of powers: "The great security . . . consists in giving to those who administer each department, the necessary constitutional means, and personal motives, to resist encroachments of the others. . . . Ambition must be made to counteract ambition." Following up this thrust, the cynic then goes on to cite Madison's exposition in *The Federalist*, no. 10, of the manner in which groups and interests ("factions") are bound to struggle for advantage.

The cynic has a point. The framers, however, did not assume that self-interest alone would assure outcomes in the general interest of everyone. Self-government could not succeed unless, as Madison put it, there were "other qualities in human nature which justify a certain portion of esteem and confidence." "Republican government," Madison added, "presupposes the existence of these qualities in a higher degree than any other form." Were it otherwise, "the inference would be, that there is not sufficient virtue among men for self-government . . ." (*The Federalist*, no. 55). As to factions, "a multiplicity of interests" would tend to make "a coalition of a majority of the whole society" unlikely "on any other principles than those of justice and the general good" (*The Federalist*, no. 51).

If it were not for the common bonds of human decency, ours would be a far nastier society—and Washington, D.C., would be a far less tame capital—than they actually are. Not to acknowledge these facts would be palpably unrealistic. Indeed, it is just such a lack of touch with reality that discredits cynicism. My conception of our system, in any case, is not confined to the self-adjusting mechanisms of its constitutional machinery and the psychological insights that inspired its design. The dispersal of power has never been the only contributor to the prevention of its abuse. To account for the survival of our system of government in essentially unchanged form for more than two hundred years it is also necessary to grasp the indispensable role of certain uniquely American ways of looking at and approaching things. What I have in mind aren't traits or characteristics exactly, or values, though they're related to values. I call them "attitudes."

The first and most basic of these attitudes is the demand for accountability. The generation that shaped the constitutions of the first thirteen states and then gave birth to the Federal Constitution did in fact ordain and establish governments of a new kind: governments that derived their just—and limited—powers from the consent of the governed. "We the People" are the continually renewed body of citizens of the United States of America who hold accountable those of their fellow citizens who at any given time occupy elected or appointed public offices.

The second attitude is almost equally basic. An offshoot of the first, it is our insistence on openness and transparency in the conduct of governmental affairs.

The third attitude keeps us focused on what works and on what really matters. The result is a blend of idealism and practicality. This attitude explains why few Americans have been drawn into struggles between competing ideologies.

Partly contributing to and partly generated by the system shaped by the framers' genius, these three attitudes have throughout our history held government to the service of the American people. They made it adaptable to change, resilient in surmounting adversity, and resourceful in accommodating clashing interests. Little by little they transformed the system into a democracy. And, perhaps above all, more than "supplying the defect of better qualities," these attitudes called forth better qualities.

The attitudes I have identified were, I believe, the keys to the ability of our form of representative democracy to disperse and limit power while at the same time making possible the practical resolution of contentious issues. It seems to me important, therefore, to expand on my reasons for holding this view.

First, then, accountability. To understand the force of this demand, we have to go back to the early 1760s when Great Britain arbitrarily imposed the writs of assistance and the stamp tax on its American colonies. It was fundamentally wrong, argued the protesting colonials, for such measures to be foisted on them by a government in which they lacked representation. "Taxation without representation is tyranny," they cried, but not even James Otis could demonstrate that the Parliament sitting at Westminster lacked plenary power.

A few years later the Declaration of Independence, by breaking all ties with Great Britain, disposed of this dilemma and enlarged the claims of accountability. With a bow toward Hobbes's and Locke's concept of the "social compact," the Declaration proclaimed that governments derive their just powers from "the consent of the governed." Where Hobbes and Locke assumed that revolution was the people's only remedy against abuses inflicted on them by a government created by such a compact, Jefferson attributed to the people the inherent "right to alter or to abolish" the offending government "and to institute new government." This, as John Adams later pointed out, was the real American Revolution.

The ex-colonists now faced unprecedented issues. By what means were they to grant their consent to a new government? How could it be made clear that this government had only such powers as the people saw fit to give it? And if, moreover, the people wanted to alter their government, how should they go about doing so?

It was essential, above all, to make inescapably clear that the legal instrument defining the new government's powers originated with the people. The citizens of Massachusetts were the first to find a way of doing this. When in 1778 the Massachusetts legislature, known to this day as the General Court, submitted a proposed constitution to a vote of the towns, the towns rejected it by a margin of 5 to 1 in large part on the ground that the General Court had no business putting forward any such proposal. How, they asked, can the legislature limit its own powers? In June of 1779, responding to a call from the General Court, the people in every town chose respected fellow citizens to represent them at a statewide convention charged with framing a new constitution. Farmers, doctors, merchants, artisans, shopkeepers, and lawyers debated the provisions of a new constitution and, having come to agreement, delegated the drafting to a committee of thirty. The final draft, principally the work of John Adams, was sent out to the towns in March 1780. Throughout that spring town meetings all over the Commonwealth deliberated on this unprecedented document and voted one by one to adopt it. On June 16 the constitution was declared ratified, and in October 1780, the government thus created came into existence. The Massachusetts constitution is to this day the oldest such instrument still in effect.

The other states soon followed the Massachusetts example, and the American people's crowning act of delegation took place in 1787 when their representatives in Philadelphia specified the powers to be conferred upon a new federal government. And lest anyone later question that this and only this was what the people had done, the Tenth Amendment (added at the same time as the Bill of Rights) made the point doubly clear: "The powers not delegated to the United States by the Constitution, nor prohibited by it to the States, are reserved to the States respectively, or to the people."

During the 168 years in which the citizens of thirty-seven more states became beneficiaries of the Tenth Amendment there has been unimaginable growth in the scope and complexity of the dealings between governments at all levels and between citizens and their governments. The fundamental relationships, however, have not changed. We the people, taking it for granted that government at every level belongs to us, also take it for granted that it is accountable to us.

As so often happens to travelers, it took a revealing exposure to a very different culture to give me insight into my own. In the summer of 1949 my friend David Ives and I were staying in a pensión on the main street of Guatemala City a couple of blocks from the Plaza Mayor on the day a coup attempt was launched. By late afternoon rebellious air force units had seized the principal military air base, and the president of Guatemala had taken refuge in the Honduran embassy.

Shortly before sunset David and I walked to the Plaza, a rectangular space with a fountain in the center. On one side was the Palacio Nacional. A light tank was going round and round the perimeter of the Plaza, and every time the tank passed the palace it let go a burst of machine-gun fire. We found ourselves in the company of a couple of youths who, like us, kept moving around the fountain so as to keep it between us and the tank. Finding no other excitement in the deserted square, we went back to our pensión.

Early the next morning a civilian on the street outside our window was shot by a sniper. We stayed put the rest of the day. The shops we could see were shuttered. No traffic moved. We could hear occasional shellfire, and from time to time a handful of militiamen carrying rifles would go by. The pensión proprietor told us that at such times the populace at large would remain barricaded in their homes.

What we took to be apathy puzzled us. Why weren't people taking sides? Why weren't they outraged? Was it because they regarded a contest for control of the government as none of their business? Talking about these questions during the course of the day drove home the realization that Americans, being incapable of regarding such a struggle as being not ours but somebody else's, would have felt obliged to become involved.

The best evidence of the American perspective toward government is that nothing makes us angrier than public officials who seem to have forgotten that they work for us. One reason why the outside world finds it so difficult to understand the American system is that it underestimates or altogether fails to comprehend this attitude. When the people of other countries read phrases like "ordain and establish," "separation of powers," "checks and balances," they understand the words, but they can't hear the music. This tone deafness, presumably, explains the failure of our European friends to understand why Americans got so worked up about the odd array of petty crimes we call "Watergate."

From the "second-rate burglary" of Democratic Party headquarters and the plumbers' break-in of the office of Daniel Ellsberg's psychiatrist to the "enemies list" and the ultimate cover-up, Watergate gradually exposed Richard Nixon's cynical contempt for his fellow citizens' feelings about accountability. On Saturday, October 20, 1973, the day when

Richard Nixon ordered the firing of Archibald Cox, the Watergate special prosecutor, Cox declared: "Whether ours shall continue a government of laws and not of men is now for Congress to decide and, ultimately, the American people." Professor Cox was right, with this difference: it was the American people first, and only then the Congress, who made the decision. Three million of them sent angry messages to their senators and representatives. Many more would have done so if the circuits had not been clogged. No such enormous outpouring of public protest had ever been seen in this country. The American people could not have made plainer the continuing force of their demand for accountability.

We come now to insistence on openness, the second distinctive attitude that has enabled our system to survive. Openness is essential to accountability. It prevents public officials from forgetting that they work for us. Even though this awareness may on occasion promote timidity, tempt headline-seeking, or prompt the faking of ethical behavior, its observance is almost invariably to the net benefit of the American people.

Openness allows us to know what our governments are doing and thus to decide whether or not they are meeting our standards and serving our purposes. By allowing us to stay in touch with and have a voice in the formulation and execution of government policies, openness is vital to the ultimate aim of the democratic process. The framers, were, of course, well aware of this, as evidenced by the priority they gave to protection of freedom of speech and the press in the Bill of Rights. And though publishing and broadcasting are, as Supreme Court Justice Potter Stewart observed, the only private businesses that have been given explicit constitutional protection, there is no way in which government could be given responsibility for administering standards of fairness and accuracy that would not do more harm than good.

Openness strengthens the hands of people in public office who want to do things right. Luckily for me, I learned this lesson at an early stage of my education in bureaucracy. One day in the spring of 1958, when I was acting secretary of Health, Education, and Welfare, I got word that the Food and Drug Administration had rejected the offer of an Atlanta warehouse for conversion into a laboratory despite the fact that it was the cheapest available space. The FDA justified the rejection on the ground that, to be usable as a laboratory, the warehouse would require the installation of false ceilings which, allegedly, could harbor rodents that might contaminate laboratory specimens. As it happened, the warehouse was owned by the state chairman of the Republican Party of Georgia. According to Georgia Republicans, this was the real reason why those left-leaning FDA bureaucrats didn't want the building.

Secretary of Commerce Sinclair Weeks of Massachusetts, a former U.S. senator and chairman of the Republican National Finance Committee, took me aside at a cabinet meeting in order to warn me not to let the FDA cheat a good Republican. He later sent over an arrogant young aide to reinforce the message. Senator John Sherman Cooper of Kentucky, explaining that he was the closest thing to a Southern senator the Republican Party had, came to see me on the Georgia chairman's behalf. I also received an appeal for the FDA side from a Democratic congressman from Atlanta who happened to chair a subcommittee important to HEW. Senior career people throughout the department were watching closely to see which way I would move.

There was only one thing to be done: get all the facts and try to come up with the correct answer. I concluded that the FDA was right. The building was unsuitable. New bids should be sought. I sent copies of a memorandum explaining this conclusion to the secretary, the senator, the congressman, and the Georgia state chairman. I never heard another word from any of them.

The realization that doing things openly and doing them right is the easy, lazy way has served me well over the years, but never more so than in December 1976. Gerald Ford was a lame-duck president; I was his lame-duck secretary of commerce. Awaiting departmental action was the guarantee of a $750 million private loan, the largest ever to reach that stage. It would be for the construction of liquefied natural gas (LNG) tankers at the General Dynamics shipyard in Quincy, Massachusetts. The tankers would be used by Burmah Oil under a contract to carry LNG from Indonesia to Japan.

The surrounding facts were not that simple. There was reason to suspect that Burmah Oil may have won its original contract by bribing foreign officials. Burmah Oil now had a new contract, but this had to be bulletproof because there was a worldwide glut of LNG tankers; but for the existence of the contract the new tankers would not be built at all. Although constructed in the United States, the ships would be manned by non-American crews, and this added to questions about whether the loan could legally qualify for a government guarantee. Tong Sung Park, a notorious Washington wheeler-dealer, was rumored to have a finger in the transaction. On top of all that it was also being said that I wanted the deal to go forward so that, later on, as a candidate for governor in the upcoming Massachusetts gubernatorial election, I could point to the jobs I had brought to the state. The *New York Times, Washington Post,* and *Wall Street Journal* had each reported all this in several extensive front-page stories and were following the situation closely.

But perhaps the new administration would want to deal with the matter. I asked the Carter transition team if they would like me to defer it until President Carter took office. "Hell no!" they said. So I got my most experienced advisers to go over every aspect of the whole thing very, very carefully. They found nothing significantly wrong. "Let's go ahead, then," I said, "but we need a memorandum anticipating all the questions that are likely to be raised." We attached this memorandum to a statement announcing my approval of the loan guarantee. The papers that had been following the story ran short pieces on the announcement, mostly in the back pages. That was all. The story was dead. And the moral? In public life the most transparent shield is also the toughest.

But with respect to openness as well as accountability the best example is Watergate. Indeed, Richard M. Nixon could have saved the country and himself a lot of grief by practicing more openness. His personal demons had to have been behind the interlinked series of attempts to subvert openness that ran through Watergate: the stealing, distorting, fabricating, misusing, misrepresenting, concealing, or suppressing of information. These attempts included bugging the Democratic National Committee headquarters, tampering with the CIA's intelligence-gathering role, pretending that the Watergate break-in was being thoroughly investigated, announcing that all previous statements on Watergate were "inoperative," paying hush money, erasing damaging portions of tapes, shredding documents, suborning perjury, and invoking executive privilege.

In a remarkable turn of the wheel, Watergate's betrayals of openness were redressed by the tenacious pursuit of openness—digging out information, leaking it, confessing it, revealing it, publishing it. Disclosures, indeed, marked both the turning-point of Watergate (Alexander Butterfield's almost casual reference in congressional testimony to the routine taping of Oval Office conversations) and its denouement (the publication in August 1974 of the tape in which Richard Nixon ordered a halt to the investigation of the Watergate break-in).

But the height of irony was that even a belated display of openness could have saved Nixon from the consequences of his own evasion of it. Yet from the beginning of Archibald Cox's investigation, the White House resisted the production of documents. "That doesn't make sense," I said to Fred Buzhardt, counsel to the president. "You ought instead to tell Archie Cox to send over a truck and load it up with all the material he and his staff could possibly want." In that event, if anything damaging was found, Nixon could issue a public apology and couple it with a convincing expression of penitence. The American public, I thought, would be more than likely to forgive and forget.

But accountability and openness would not by themselves have been sufficient to keep this nation on course for so long had they not been accompanied by the American people's steady focus on what works and what really matters. This third characteristic has often been remarked upon by observers of America. Its philosophical counterpart is pragmatism, itself a distinctively American idea. The pragmatic attitude sees issues as problems to be solved, not doctrines to be debated. In day-to-day civil life, this problem-solving approach transcends prejudice and promotes mutual respect. In government, it encourages realistic accommodations between the branches, across party lines, and among competing interests.

The resulting combination of practical problem solving with political necessity tends both to narrow the range of the national debate and to reinforce the preexisting distaste for ideology. The habit of focusing political debate on practical issues converts the dispersal of power from a potential source of conflict into a means of creating awareness of the necessity for broad-based compromise. American tinkering has thus accomplished by common consent what other nations have achieved only through strong leadership or centralized authority.

Again and again throughout our history, practical good sense has salvaged situations that looked to be hell-bent for foolhardy action, irreconcilable hostility, or permanent deadlock. Even the one exception—the Civil War—may by its tragic example have strengthened the hand of moderation for subsequent generations.

In my own dealings with executive branch colleagues over the years, ideological differences rarely got in the way. Indeed, I can't at the moment think of a single example. If ideology had intruded itself it would have been because I wore a "liberal" or "moderate" label and my likeliest antagonists were "conservatives." The effective conservatives I've known, however, have invariably turned out to be what I call "rhetorical conservatives." They sound like ideologues until confronted with a real problem. Then, without skipping a beat, they put the rhetoric aside and go directly to the practicalities of the situation. William E. Simon, Gerald Ford's secretary of the treasury, is like that. You'd think, to hear Bill Simon talk, that he must be an ideologue. I learned otherwise through seeing him in action in the Ford administration, when I served under his chairmanship of the Economic Policy Board. He might at any of our daily meetings start off sounding like Adam Smith or Friedrich Hayek, but as soon as we got down to business he became as pragmatic as any of us.

An earlier secretary of the treasury, George Humphrey, was another "rhetorical conservative." I happened to be at a cabinet meeting in Eisenhower's second term at which Humphrey inveighed against pouring good American foreign-aid money down India's socialist rathole. When Humphrey ran out of steam, Eisenhower, with an air of polite inquiry, said, "That's very interesting, George, but tell me, if you were in charge, how would you raise the standard of living in India?" Taking the bait, Humphrey started talking about things like building infrastructure, financing rural development, and expanding technical education. When Humphrey paused again, Eisenhower asked, "Do you see much difference, George, between what you're advocating and what they're trying to do?"

It was my good fortune that I was spared the necessity of having to deal with real ideologues until late in my government service. My first such encounters did not occur until the Carter administration, when I became the special representative of the president for the UN Conference on the Law of the Sea. This involved me in negotiations on the creation of an International Seabed Authority that would have certain supranational powers. Such a multilateral body is anathema to the rabid right, and I soon learned that one of the two definitive field marks of an ideologue is that he (the only ones I know are "he"s) would rather hold to his ideological course and let the ship pile up on the rocks than take a tack offshore. The other field mark is an astonishing imperviousness to rational persuasion. You can demonstrate to an ideologue that one of his arguments is just plain wrong, even factually wrong, but he will invariably repeat the same argument the next day in exactly the same words.

By the grace of God and/or the attitudes I've been discussing, ideologues have seldom played a significant role in this country. Jesse Helms, I suppose, comes closer to meeting the definition than anyone on the national scene today. For the most part, clashes of economic interest and questions of integrity, not ideas, have dominated the American political process. Although sometimes associated with the aims of social justice, as in the case of slavery or free silver, such battles as those between merchants and manufacturers, farmers and railroad barons, tycoons and trustbusters, free traders and protectionists were mainly contests over sharing the wealth.

There was, to be sure, a brief period during the worst of the Great Depression when left-wing radicals were able to attract a following. My Harvard class (1941) had a small Communist cell as well as a vocal band of idealistic socialists. Although Franklin Delano Roosevelt ran on the promise of a balanced budget, not a social philosophy, the New Deal had a strong ideological tinge. Since then the American left has almost disappeared. There is no counterpart in the United States of the Socialist Parties of Europe and Japan. Even one of the more liberal members of the U.S. Senate—Ted Kennedy, for instance—would be uncomfortable in the British Labour Party, much moderated though it has been of late.

The uniquely American attitudes that I have been discussing—the demand for accountability, insistence on openness, and a pragmatic approach—have had a combined influence on government and politics in many ways not specifically traceable to any one of the three. If, putting aside preconceptions, you look closely at what the people caught up in governmental affairs actually do and don't do, you will see the consequences of this influence. You will also see why the common assumptions about power in Washington cannot be squared with the way our system of government really works.

To illustrate what I mean, let's take the sort of plot that I think a believer in these assumptions is ready to suspect. We can skip over such cozy but unambitious initiatives as, say, a move to protect a subsidy for toupee makers or to secure a tax break for a bankrupt chain of funeral parlors. A better example would be a scheme cooked up by Washington lawyers and lobbyists in collusion with corporate and trade association executives to induce the Pentagon to procure a new but nonfunctioning version of an existing weapons system. That just such a combination might be formed is, of course, conceivable. That it could operate behind the scenes is not. The scrutiny mandated at every stage from the Pentagon's own procurement procedures through Office of Management and Budget review and congressional hearings to General Accounting Office evaluation is not easily circumvented. All along the way, moreover, competitors and opponents would be ready to blow the whistle.

A conspiratorial approach to influencing the outcome of a major public issue would be totally impractical. In the executive branch even a medium-sized issue like wetlands protection engages half a dozen departments or agencies from Agriculture and Interior to the Environmental Protection Agency, the Office of Management and Budget, and the Corps of Engineers. Scores of civil servants have to be involved. A really big issue like the Clinton administration's health-care program engaged an executive-branch cast of thousands.

As soon as the legislative process begins, a lot more people get into the act. Even a modest bill can be referred to as many as half a dozen subcommittees in the House and four in the Senate. If its implementation will cost money, still other staffers will be deployed by the committees and subcommittees on appropriations.

Generally speaking, nothing in Washington can be kept confidential for long: someone's ego, a disagreement with official policy, or a personal grudge is sure to precipitate a leak. And since different issues produce differing combinations of players, no one who intends to be around for a while can safely treat a partner in an ad hoc coalition with the unqualified trust appropriate only to a permanent ally.

The one area where the American public has been willing to scale back its insistence on accountability and openness is, of course, that of national security. During the Cold War the need for this exception was clear and convincing. Some justifications for secrecy still persist, notably in combating international terrorism and drug trafficking. For the very reasons, however, why openness has been vital to the health of the system, Americans see risks in altogether suspending openness even for activities whose secrecy is vital. We have, therefore, imposed substantial accountability requirements on our intelligence services. The House and Senate Select Intelligence Committees are watchdogs even of their most secret operations. This, by the way, is in marked contrast with Great Britain, where not even the name of the head of MI5, roughly the counterpart of our CIA, was publicly disclosed until 1992.

Having been reassured by these oversight requirements that covert operations would not be allowed to get out of hand, many of us were shocked by the Iran-Contra revelations. The central fact was that William J. Casey, director of the Central Intelligence Agency, had set up an ingenious scheme for evading congressional oversight. The proceeds of illegal sales, whether of arms, software, or narcotics, would be deposited in a fund available at any time to pay for covert operations under his personal control. In the Iran-Contra case, the funds came from the sale of arms to Iran, and the proceeds were used to support antigovernment forces in Nicaragua known as Contras despite a law, the Boland amendment, specifically prohibiting the use of American tax dollars for that purpose.

Casey was convinced that he knew better than the intelligence committees what was good for the country. So far as he was concerned, the less anyone else, including the president and the vice president, knew about what he was up to, the better U.S. national interests would be served. This, of course, was the same brand of arrogance that had so thoroughly outraged the American people in the Watergate affair barely more than a decade earlier.

The cause of accountability and openness, however, has gained valuable allies from an unexpected source. These watchdogs are the lobbyists who play such a prominent part in the Washington scene. How so? Well, to begin with, every significant issue has more than one side, and each side is represented by its own lobbyists. Each group of lobbyists has an interest in making sure that its rivals do not gain an unfair advantage. When, therefore, one group detects another's dirty dealing, the former will find a way of seeing to it that the skulduggery comes to light. Again, the possibility that today's opponent may be tomorrow's ally is an additional factor helping to keep things on the level. Lobbyists have a large stake, moreover, in protecting their reputations for trustworthiness. Congressional staffers often have to phone lobbyists to get factual information for their boss's immediate use on the floor. I well remember having to make such calls when I worked for Senator Leverett Saltonstall. Woe betide the lobbyist who furnishes inaccurate information!

First required to register under a law passed in 1946, lobbyists have acquired considerable respectability since Walt Whitman, as quoted in Bill Safire's *Political Dictionary,* called them the "lousy combings and born freedom sellers of the earth." Opprobrium has lately shifted to their principal employers, the so-called interest groups. Political analyst Kevin

Phillips's recent book[3] blames almost everything he finds wrong with the current Washington scene on the influence attributable to the campaign contributions generated by the groups representing financial interests. That strikes me as pretty far-fetched. All of us have interests, and most of us belong to organizations dedicated to advancing or protecting those interests. But in 1993–94, eight of the ten biggest PACs represented gainful occupations—doctors, teamsters, schoolteachers, trial lawyers, automobile dealers, and the like. (The other two were United Parcel Service, Inc., and the National Rifle Association.) Campaign contributions are only one factor in an interest group's influence. The popular appeal of an organization's cause and the number of voters for whom it speaks are more significant.

If individuals didn't have professional associations, labor unions, veterans organizations, Audubon societies, taxpayers' federations, the American Association of Retired Persons, and a host of other groups to champion their interests, how would they have a chance of being heard? Madison, as noted earlier in this essay, had it right: interest groups are inevitable, and the very competition among them yields "a coalition of the majority of the whole society." The only thing new about the current scene is the sheer multiplicity of interest groups, which not only creates confusion, but also diminishes the influence of any one group. But these are inescapable consequences of the overloading of the system, and I do not know of any way of offsetting them that is not discussed later on in "Overload," my essay on that subject.

The same factors that keep lobbyists publicly accountable also compel other Washington competitors to rely on affirmative means of getting what they want. For reasons of prudence, if not of principle, they would rather hold out carrots than apply sticks. Persuasion, publicity, honors, and economic rewards are safe. Backstabbing, character-assassination, and dirty tricks are risky. How often negative devices of the latter sort are used is, of course, unknowable, but my guess is much less frequently than the cynic supposes. Generally speaking, the most practical ways of applying negative pressure involve some form of blocking action. In the legislative branch, such opportunities can include

---

[3] *Arrogant Capital: Washington, Wall Street, & the Frustration of American Politics* (Boston: Little, Brown, 1994).

threatening to hold up a colleague's most urgent pork-barrel project, sitting on the confirmation of her nominee for a judgeship, or withholding a coveted committee assignment. In the executive branch, you can put something at the bottom of the pile, refer it to a study group, or marshal evidence that it costs too much.

Looking back over the forty-five years in which I've observed the Washington scene from a series of good perches, I can recall only a handful of individuals who made a habit of using negative power. One was Wayne Hays of Ohio, a fourteen-term member of the House from 1948 to 1976 and later chairman of the House Committee on Administration. Hays seemed to want to make people crawl at least as much for the fun of it as for the sake of anything he sought to gain. He would, for instance, withhold parking space from a colleague in retaliation for a fancied slight. But in 1976 it emerged that he had been keeping on the payroll an ex-beauty queen who boasted that she couldn't even answer the telephone. This disclosure led to a widening scandal that resulted in Hays's attempted suicide and eventual resignation from the House.

The great majority of successful Washington operators are decent, friendly, honorable people. The frequency with which such individuals are chosen for key roles tells you a lot about Washington. Two recent examples are the former Speaker of the House of Representatives, Tom Foley, and the former minority leader, Bob Michel. Despite having become the highest-ranking Democrat in the nation (before the election of Bill Clinton), Tom Foley remained a thoughtful, honest, fair-minded man, never harsh or overbearing, and no more partisan than he had to be. Bob Michel has the same fine qualities, and, notwithstanding the frustrations of perpetual opposition, he too—he was first elected to the House in 1956 and served as minority leader from 1981 to 1995—was a restrained partisan. Both put the national interest first and both had a highly developed instinct not only for the issues and situations in which competition between the parties would do the system more good than harm but also for those in which the opposite was true.

An elusive and impalpable lubricant of congressional business is "comity." The word stands for the blend of understanding and respect, courtesy and affection with which rivals in an established institutional setting conduct their dealings with one other. In the congressional case its source is mutual regard for the public interest. Comity exists within and between each body of Congress and, to a lesser though significant extent, between the executive and legislative branches. Comity contains problems that could otherwise become unmanageable, moderates over-weening ambitions, and disciplines passions that might otherwise get out of control.

It would be interesting to try to specify the role of comity in situations where the outcome of a major issue hung in the balance. Possible candidates for such analysis might be the one-vote margin by which the draft was extended in 1941, the authorization in 1991 of the use of force in the Persian Gulf, or the squeaky margin by which Bill Clinton's economic program scraped through both branches in 1993. It would take a lot of careful work to trace the contribution of comity in these cases, and even when the experts had completed their analysis they probably wouldn't agree. The effort would be worthwhile, nevertheless, if only to confound cynicism by creating greater awareness of comity's role.

But perhaps the most telling clue to the qualities needed for success in Washington is the kind of person you find handling governmental affairs for big companies. For many years one of the most successful and respected of this elite group was Clark MacGregor, senior vice president of United Technologies. Clark MacGregor was hired in 1972 by the CEO, Harry Gray. Now, if there has been a more hardheaded aerospace and defense company boss in the past forty years than Harry Gray, I haven't heard of him. If it had been smart to hire a manipulative backroom type to handle government relations, Harry Gray would have done it. But he knew better. He knew that he needed someone who had substantial Hill experience, understood the executive branch, and could deal with the media. Anyone who could meet these requirements would meet the additional requirement of being universally liked, trusted, and respected: no one who isn't so regarded would have survived long enough to acquire the necessary knowledge and experience.

Clark MacGregor had everything Gray was looking for. A Dartmouth graduate, MacGregor had been a congressman from Minnesota, a candidate for the U.S. Senate against Hubert Humphrey, and had served as Richard Nixon's counsel for legislative affairs. His integrity was—and is—beyond question. In the course of his fourteen years in the United Technologies job, he was in full charge of government relations at all levels both here and abroad.

Every big company or trade association looking for a head of its Washington office tries to find someone like MacGregor. John Eden specializes in the recruitment of trade association executives for a large head-hunting firm. "We look for certifiably decent people," he told me. But being a decent person doesn't mean that you have to be stupid. On the contrary, the individuals that John Eden searches for know when and how to go after what they want, how hard to press, and when to back off. They're masters of their briefs as well as of the procedures—bureaucratic, regulatory, and legislative—that define the routes to their objectives. They're good at making friends and equally good at keeping them. They also keep their word. Intending to be around a long time, they are loath to make enemies and would rather leave some chips on the table than a sore loser sitting at it.

It wouldn't be hard to demonstrate that the average member of Congress, vice president for public affairs, and trade association executive are at least as competent and honorable as their fellow citizens. We can readily agree, moreover, that straightforwardness and decency are not uncommon among the latter. We find these qualities in people we deal with every day. Indeed, I would guess that most of us—certainly those with any experience of the world—are able to discern them in other people's expressions, the way we're greeted, the manner in which our remarks are received, and in lots of other little signs. It would help a lot if we credited the people who make our government work with the same qualities.

Later essays will argue that what we're seeing is the product of a self-reinforcing cycle whose driving forces are discontent with the status quo and disillusionment with the failures of government to correct what is widely felt to be wrong. Excessive expectations, the alarmist language used by interest groups in their fund-raising appeals, tabloid journalism, and polarizing politics have all played a part in stirring up anger and insecurity.

It is also disturbing that some of the very things that have served us well in the past are now being pushed to excess. Watergate's and Irangate's insults to accountability and openness have encouraged the assumption that if a lot is good, a lot more is even better. Open-meeting laws, investigative reporting, inspectors general, General Accounting Office audits, congressional oversight—each a good thing in itself—have cumulatively sapped confidence and eroded trust. The word "ethics" no longer refers to moral principles but to rules of conduct aimed at preserving the appearance of propriety. With these developments has come a decline in public understanding of the meaning of public service, and a corresponding decline in its attractiveness. While I cannot judge the true extent of the spirit of meanness that President Clinton's despairing friend and counsel Vincent Foster thought he saw, it worries me. I'm concerned that what the cynic already thinks may yet become true.

Ironically, the infrequency with which flagrant malfeasance is discovered has shifted attention to secondary offenses: conflicts of interest, appearances of conflicts of interest, employment of illegal immigrants, sometime pot-smoking, lapses of political correctness, and so on. Not only petty but unsubstantiated charges get picked up and passed around, gaining velocity in the process. Since small-bore wrongdoing is common and media coverage can make it look serious, the incessant flow of stories about it adds to the impression that decay is well advanced.

Meanwhile, a number of other developments are straining the system. The unprecedented crunch between claims and resources prevents adequate responses to critical needs. The inexorable increase of complexity is overloading the capacity of government agencies. Moreover, by making it seem hopeless to try to keep up with an ever-expanding litany of difficult issues, the growth of complexity has narrowed everyone's focus. Other people's concerns come to seem less and less real, and more and more people tend to judge politicians solely in terms of what the politician has done for them lately. Even the dispersal of power, which has served us so well, threatens to get out of hand.

In the off-year election campaign of 1994, resentment against those in power swept through the status quo like a wave breaking through a barrier beach. One of its most dramatic results was a radical shift in the manner in which power has heretofore been exercised in the House of Representatives. Speaker-presumptive Newt Gingrich served notice within days after the 1994 votes had been counted that he intended to make major changes in the way the business of the House was conducted, and he has carried out this aim with great panache. He saw to it, for instance, that committee chairmanships went to individuals whose loyalty and support he could count on. He enforced discipline among the backbenchers by making it clear that they would be sorry if they broke ranks. He simultaneously served notice on the Democratic minority that he would give no quarter on partisan issues. The success of these initiatives was dramatically demonstrated by the speed and efficiency with which the Contract with America, the budget resolution, and the appropriations process were pushed through the House with minimal defections on his own side and significant support from the other side.

Does the Gingrich leadership of the new Republican majority in the House of Representatives give reason to question the continued relevance of comity? The Gingrich revolution will have been under way barely more than two years when this book goes to press. That is much too short a period on which to base a firm prediction. It may take a long time, moreover—a decade or more, perhaps—for the forces now in motion to play themselves out. But the process will be fascinating to watch, and for me that's a major incentive to stick around a while longer. I can't wait to find out whether or not I'm right in thinking that Gingrich's approach to the use of power cannot work over the long term. Here, for the record, is how I reached that conclusion.

Under our Constitution a political party has to have the support of a broad-based coalition. This is an inevitable consequence, though not one likely to have been foreseen by the framers, of the requirement for the election at fixed four-year intervals for a fixed four-year term of a head of state who is also the head of government. Rather than take a chance on forming a coalition government with the help of splinter parties, as in a parliamentary system, the backers of an American presidential candidate have to appeal to a wide spectrum of public opinion. That necessity leads to the formation of large, inclusive political parties. Anyone who wishes to do so can join such a party. No one can be expelled for heresy. As a consequence, no political party under our system can for long maintain a set of policies and principles sufficiently unambiguous to be the subject of rigorous party discipline. Witness the fact that Jesse Helms and I are both Republicans!

In the legislative branch, the independence of senators and representatives is constitutionally guaranteed. With geographical bases of their own, they can and, to save their political skins, sometimes must, defy party discipline. But that aside, it would in any case be impossible for either party's House or Senate members to hammer out and reach consensus on a concrete set of principles and proposals comprehensively addressing the nation's most urgent concerns. While the Contract with America did to a remarkable degree succeed in enlisting consensus, it could by no stretch be regarded as a serious national agenda. That awareness soon began to sink in, and may in due course be followed by disillusionment with mean-spirited partisanship. At that point the need for comity will once again assert itself.

Much of what I shall be saying later on deals with threats to the processes that have up to now enabled this nation to channel and control the uses of governmental power. For the moment I will only say this: our constitutional system has again and again demonstrated its powers of self-correction and renewal. We, its masters, being both optimistic and otherwise occupied, are slow in reacting to a developing threat and even slower in coming to a consensus as to how to deal with it. Like a spring whose power to recoil increases with the pressure exerted against it, the distinctively American attitudes discussed in this essay can reassert themselves. But whether or not they do so must not be left to chance. Subsequent essays will tell you what, to my mind, needs to be done to improve the odds that they will rebound.

A Place in the Sun

The first time I ran for statewide office in a general-election campaign was as a candidate for Lieutenant Governor of Massachusetts. In the course of that campaign I made an amazing discovery. It was that even after I had met thousands and thousands of people, the next new face did not merge into an indistinguishable blur. On the contrary, the more hands I shook and the more faces I looked into, the more strongly I felt the uniqueness of each new person. To this day, whenever I walk along a busy street or ride the subway or go to a baseball game, I still look at people one by one. Both their individuality and their similarities are to me equally striking.

From the uniqueness and common humanity of each human being follows the inherent significance of all human beings. All of us have equal claims to respect, and for each of us respect plays an essential part in sustaining and enhancing the conviction that our existence matters, that we have value. Indeed, the need for a sense of worth is as integral to our existence as food, sex, or scratching an itch.

Some part of our sense of worth comes from the coupling of our own unique traits with the instincts of survival and procreation. But where these basic elements of individuality leave off, our imaginations come into play, for it is by way of the imagination that we are introduced to the reality of other human beings and made aware of our own uniqueness. Curiosity also plays a part through enlarging our perception of the world around us and helping us to find our places in it. But the sense of worth thereby developed can never be quite sufficient. Some support for the feeling that we matter is given to us without our asking—growing up in a loving family, for example. We have to strive for the rest. The mix of components that contribute to a sense of worth varies widely from individual to individual; what counts is the aggregate.

The good society enhances its members' sense of worth and democracy is an important means to this end. While this is not a new idea, it struck me with special force when, in 1988, I served on a commission that monitored the United Nations–supervised elections in Namibia and, in 1989, as the personal representative of the UN secretary-general for the Nicaraguan elections. In places named Oshakati, Keetmanshoop, and Rundu, and Matagalpa, León, and Puerto Cabezas, long lines of people waited patiently for the chance to register to vote. They had walked for hours under a hot sun and through choking dust, enduring risks of intimidation and who knows what apprehensions of violence for the sake of that opportunity. I saw the way they walked and the way they held themselves as they came out of the registration places carrying the cards that attested to their right to vote. Their pride was unmistakable. On election day I could sense the quiet satisfaction felt by the people I talked with. They had exercised their right to a voice in choosing their leaders, and they knew that with the granting of this right came official recognition of their dignity and worth.

In Manila a few months later, the president of the Philippine Senate, Jovito Salonga, told me that he had talked earlier that year with Lech Wałęsa in Poland. Wałęsa movingly expressed his own sense of indebtedness and that of the members of Solidarity, and perhaps all Poles, to the Filipinos, whose "People Power" had overwhelmed the Marcos dictatorship in 1986. As Salonga and I spoke, other waves of people power were sweeping away the hollowed-out structures of failing communist regimes in East Germany and Czechoslovakia, Bulgaria and Hungary, and in the Soviet Union itself.

History's most important revolutions have been inspired by new and powerful ways of affirming human worth. The New Testament is a momentous example. Others are the Declaration of Independence and the *Communist Manifesto*. Although utterly different in origin, purpose, style, and philosophy, all three changed the course of history because each in its own way lifted the spirits of ordinary people everywhere by telling them in words never before spoken that they were important.

The most fundamental teaching of the New Testament is compressed in the words with which the disciples of Jesus Christ interpreted the meaning of his life: "God so loved the world that He gave His only begotten Son, that whosoever believeth in Him shall not perish, but have everlasting life." Whosoever believeth in Him—slaves, commoners, countesses, kings—*whosoever* believeth in Him and observes His sacraments shall be deemed worthy of the greatest conceivable reward. The Christian response to the aspiration for individual worth reaches out to all humanity, but especially the poor, the weak, and the neglected. And because the Christian promise can be fulfilled only in an afterlife, it can never demonstrably fail.

The Declaration of Independence proclaims the equal worth of every member of human society here on earth. Its familiar words deliver this message with unmistakable clarity: "We hold these truths to be self-evident, that all men are created equal, that they are endowed by their Creator with certain unalienable Rights, that among these are Life, Liberty and the pursuit of Happiness." Having launched the American struggle for freedom and democracy, the Declaration of Independence has ever since inspired the creation of the political means by which individuals are given a voice and a share in shaping the forces that govern their destinies. And never, surely, was its liberating power more dramatically demonstrated than in the late 1980s, when in quick succession it toppled one totalitarian regime after another and brought an end to the Cold War.

Ironically, the *Communist Manifesto* set in motion the forces that led to the imposition of those very regimes. When in 1848 the *Manifesto* called upon working people to unite in overthrowing all claims to superiority or special advantage for one human being over another, it too spoke to the aspiration for a sense of individual worth. The revolution for which the *Manifesto* appealed would be the prelude to the reign of liberty: "In the place of the old bourgeois society with its classes and its class antagonisms, there will be an association in which the free development of each is the condition for the free development of all." From this free development would emerge a just society whose governing principle Karl Marx later summed up in the words "from each according to his abilities, to each according to his needs." But no regime that acquired power in the name of this ideal could pretend for long to be engaged in the task of creating a heaven on earth. The necessity for coercion in carrying out the abolition of private property opened the door to dictatorships not of the proletariat but of brutal oligarchies. Having suppressed human rights in the name of equal shares of poverty, communism's eventual but inevitable collapse was brought about by long-suppressed yearnings for the freedom and dignity it had originally promised. And so, in the end, the *Manifesto* failed because it promised too much.

But if I'm right in thinking that the history-making impact of these three messages came from their responsiveness to the universal aspiration for a sense of worth, I can't avoid asking whence that aspiration derives its strength. Why should the individual need to be told that she or he has worth? Why aren't we featherless bipeds self-sufficient like cows or tigers? We start, after all, at the same place: with the need for air, water, food, and sleep. We have the same basic instincts: self-preservation, procreation, and protection of our offspring. We share at least one distinctive attribute with a variety of other creatures: for instance, territoriality with bears, the herd instinct with caribou, nest-building with birds, hoarding with squirrels, command and control systems with baboons, a love of water sports with sea lions, and with our best friend, the dog, a hunger for approval.

We are, of course, smarter than any of these creatures, but it is certainly not our intelligence that impels us to seek a sense of worth. The answer, I think, can be found in two distinctive characteristics that humans do not share with any other species. The first is that reaching physical maturity does not complete our growth. In varying degrees we continue throughout our lives to work toward the development of our talents and abilities. The U.S. Army holds out to volunteers the developmental value of its training with the slogan "Be all you can be." What this really means, of course, is *"Become* all you can be."

Harvard president Neil Rudenstine in his 1993 baccalaureate address gave this developmental process a new dimension when he urged each member of the graduating class to "imagine and reimagine the possibilities of your life." In choosing among the imagined possibilities of our lives we commonly come to terms with the reality of our limitations but seldom impose comparable constraints on our aspirations. We choose, moreover, not simply the role we want to play but the kind of person we want to be. A paramount goal of our development is increased self-esteem. The pursuit of this goal demands some combination of effort with discipline and sacrifice. In the midst of our striving, we seek, even if we do not require, assurance that the goal is important.

A second relevant difference between humans and other species is that the range of our relationships is much wider and more demanding. As individuals, we humans have more responsibility toward our fellow creatures and are more dependent on their taking responsibility toward us than is true even of ants. Like us, cows and tigers have to feed themselves and keep themselves tolerably clean. Our responsibilities, however, for feeding ourselves and keeping ourselves clean and clothed and for earning our keep are complicated by the knowledge that if we do not meet these responsibilities, we will become dependent on other people. Although many other species take care of their offspring until they can take care of themselves, the mutual interdependence among the members of a human family can last a long time and embrace several generations. Robert Frost's classic definition of home makes the point neatly: "Home is the place where, when you have to go there, / They have to take you in."

We know as love the bond that ties us to those for whom we care most deeply, as patriotism our attachment to the country of our citizenship, and as compassion the tug of sympathy we feel for the faraway victims of famines and floods. We feel needed when we fulfill our responsibility to others; we feel cared for when others respond to our dependency on them. Both feelings satisfy as well as attest to our need for a sense of worth. So integral to this sense are our relationships with other people that we cannot even define ourselves except in terms of those relationships. Our ties to others extend outward in ever-widening circles from ourselves and our families to our communities, our nations, and—ultimately—all humanity. Though attenuated by distance and time, these ties never completely disappear. "No man is an island, entire of itself," wrote John Donne, and therefore ". . . any man's death diminishes me, because I am involved in mankind."

Just beneath the surface of our conscious connections with other people are the instincts we share with less complicated animals. These instincts are constantly on the alert. Self-preservation is a psychological imperative that needs no conscious prompting. Only some very powerful motive can overcome it—for the soldier, a disciplined sense of duty; for the fanatic, all-consuming zeal; for the suicide, despair. A threat or a wrong to anything we hold to be ours—freedom, self-esteem, personal possessions—can arouse a similar reaction. Thus, an extension of self-preservation is the protective instinct that attaches to the family. It is equally alert, and, in defending the well-being or self-interest of a family member, this instinct can be fierce. Similar challenges arouse similar reactions throughout the whole range of relationships that evoke responsibility and dependency, though diminishing in intensity as the circle widens. Indeed, who has ever doubted that if threatened by invaders from another planet, human beings everywhere would immediately join forces against the common enemy?

Since 1953 when James D. Watson and Francis Crick first described DNA's intricate double helix, we have learned quite a lot about the molecular mechanisms that transmit instincts. The human genome project is now revealing the structure of these mechanisms in all its exquisite detail. Individual uniqueness is more than adequately accounted for by the billions of possible recombinations among the genes that determine such inheritable characteristics as hair color, mathematical ability, nose shape, or a tendency toward obesity. It now appears, indeed, that all of our instincts—self-preservation, sex, courtship, parental love, and competitiveness, for example—are indentured servants of a genetically programmed drive to transmit our individual traits. And if, by direction of our genes, our instincts commit us to the perpetuation of our own identities, it is understandable that this commitment would be expressed in terms of an insistent need for a sense of worth. Just such a genetic rationale no doubt accounts for the perverse pride that almost any form of uniqueness can inspire. One of the most appealing real-life characters in *McSorley's Wonderful Saloon* by Joseph Mitchell (one of my favorite books) is Lady Olga. Lady Olga had a thick, curly beard measuring thirteen and a half inches. "In an expansive mood," wrote Mitchell, "she will brag that she has the longest female beard in history and will give the impression that she feels superior to less spectacular women."

My focus up to now has been on the universality and strength of the aspiration for a sense of worth. I have also suggested reasons why it is a distinctively human attribute. Let us now look at ingredients of a sense of worth that come from sources outside ourselves. The number and variety of these ingredients is staggering, touching, and endlessly astonishing. Some, like promotions and bonuses, are both economically valuable and socially esteemed, and for these we ordinarily have to compete. Some are the product of assiduously maintained conventions—lifestyles, perks, medals, titles, uniforms, and the like—whose function is to enlist all of us in furthering the attainment of self-esteem by some of us. But by far the most widespread and accessible—and in many ways the most successful—means of enhancing a sense of worth is religion, which speaks to us from beyond and above society. I shall have more to say about religion later on.

Arguably, the most important component of our belief in ourselves is a sense of identity. Formed in part by self-awareness and in part by the ways in which others see us, our sense of identity is at the same time reinforced by a sense of place and belonging. I saw this at Camp Pickett, Virginia, in the summer of 1942, when, together with four other basic trainees, I was assigned to a pyramidal tent in the Medical Basic Training Center. The youngest of my tent-mates was a nineteen-year-old farm boy from East Corinth, Maine. The oldest—a stonecutter born in Italy who had spent most of his life carving gravestones in Brooklyn—was forty-five. The third was a second-generation Italo-American from New London, Connecticut, who looked like a model for a Botticelli angel. Murray, the last, was a young man in his late twenties from Lawrence, Massachusetts. He had always lived at home, working, when there was work, in a textile mill and helping his mother take care of the house.

We soon began to create identities for one another. My favorite Louis Armstrong record was "Bye and Bye." One night I tried to sing what I could remember of it. After that Murray insisted that I sing it every night. To the rest of us the Brooklyn stonecutter was an old man, and he did his best to play up to the part, reminiscing about his childhood in Italy as if it had been seventy years earlier. The boy from Maine was the unfooled innocent; the Connecticut youth was the ladykiller. I, of course, was "the Harvard man."

The more secure we are in our own identity, the less need we have for the approval of others. A fortunate few are outstanding in this respect. Comfortable in their own skins, they're friendly and outgoing. They seldom try to impress other people, and they're never petty, spiteful, or mean. Faced with a tough situation, they size it up quickly, figure out what to do, and do it. No wasted motion. No wasted emotion, either—no self-castigation, no recriminations, few regrets. Both admirable and enviable, such people remind me of a hymn we sang in school when I was a boy. It begins:

> *How happy is he born and taught*
> *That serveth not another's will;*
> *Whose armor is his honest thought,*
> *And simple truth his utmost skill.*

The neglected African-American children who grow up in drug-infested inner-city neighborhoods are not so lucky. Their situation is powerfully described in an *Atlantic Monthly* article by Elijah Anderson.[1] Having literally to fight for their place in the world, these children give searing proof of the innate force of the need to be somebody. Playing in groups from which they derive their primary social bonds, they are "initiated into a system that is really a way of campaigning for respect."[2] By their late teens "Many feel that it is acceptable to risk dying over the principle of respect. In fact, among the hard-core street-oriented, the clear risk of violent death may be preferable to being 'dissed' by another. . . . Not to be afraid to die is by implication to have few compunctions about taking another's life."[3]

The damage to self-esteem wrought by the gnawing tooth of prejudice and discrimination is not confined to the most deprived. Claude Steele, a professor of sociology at Stanford, has uncovered a revealing answer to the question of why African Americans score significantly lower on standardized tests than whites. As reported by Ethan Watters in a *New York Times Magazine* article, Professor Steele and Joshua Aronson from the University of Texas "gave two groups of black and white Stanford undergraduates a test composed of the most difficult verbal-skills questions from the Graduate Record Exam. Before the test, one group was told that the purpose of the exercise was only 'to research psycholog-

---

[1] *The Atlantic Monthly,* May 1994, p. 81.

[2] Ibid., p. 86.

[3] Ibid., p. 92.

ical factors involved in solving verbal problems,' while the other group was told that the exam was 'a genuine test of your verbal abilities and limitation.' . . . The blacks who thought they were simply solving problems performed as well as the whites (who performed equally well in both situations). However, the group of black students who labored under the belief that the test could measure their intellectual potential performed significantly worse than all the other students."

The explanation, Steele suggests, is "stereotype vulnerability," a phenomenon attributable not to the acceptance of the stereotype but to the burden of having to contend with the whisper of inferiority at a moment of intense mental stress. Additional experiments conducted by Steele and Steve Spencer of Hope College indicate that stereotype vulnerability can negatively affect women and white men who believe, respectively, that math test scores will reflect "gender differences" or that Asians outperform whites.

Most of us play out our lives somewhere in between these extremes. Although needing continual reinforcement of our self-esteem, mere attention may suffice. How many of us males have ever wholly outgrown the ten-year-old who shouted "Lookit me!" as he launched himself into a gigantic bellyflopper? How many graduating high school students did not relish being congratulated on their election as class valedictorian? How many middle-aged achievers are so detached or so self-denying as to let it be known that they want no part of society's compulsive attempts to stave off oblivion: the awards, the testimonials, the gifts in our names, and, to be savored only in anticipation, the commemorative plaques and eulogies?

But the rewards of approval and appreciation need not be trivial. Liking, admiration, gratitude, and respect are valuable returns on an investment in the effort to be understanding, honest, fair, and helpful. When resourcefulness and courage are added to integrity in the pursuit of this effort, society's highest forms of recognition may follow. So also may criticism, envy, and neglect. Either way, these are yesterday's headlines. At the end of the day there remains the enduring kind of satisfaction that no one else can give and no one can take away.

While never so foolish as to let the enjoyment of my work depend on how widely my performance was noticed, I'm also sure that the desire for recognition had a lot to do with my deciding while still in college that I wanted to go into politics. Could it have been the tension between this ambition and the ideals of my secondary school (its motto is "Dare to Be True") that prompted me to choose for declamation in Harvard's annual Boylston Prize competition the passage from Ecclesiastes that concludes, "Vanity of vanities, saith the Preacher; all is vanity"? (Speaking of vanity, this was the Preacher who also said, "Of making many books there is no end.")

Hunger for esteem and hunger for food are much alike. Most people moderate their appetites. Among those who don't, the range from pushy self-promotion to naked self-aggrandizement is roughly that between overeating and stuffing yourself. In most societies throughout history the majority have tacitly conspired to keep the top dogs happy by letting them gorge on privilege and place. At the elbows of the mighty have been the Machiavellis and mandarins who, in exchange for scraps, have schemed to keep their patrons in power. Meanwhile, down through the layers to a level short of the most downtrodden (but not necessarily excluding the poor), the hierarchy fed its members' sense of identity by giving them roles in an established social order. But an authoritarian structure can maintain its grip only as long as it can hold in check the voracity of its greediest individuals and factions. It is not surprising, therefore, that history records few situations in which a breakdown of the established order did not bring in its wake a new period of conflict. Examples of this breakdown can be found in the "new world disorder" that followed the end of the Cold War.

For multitudes of people, nevertheless, society's identity-reinforcing devices can never supply an adequate sense of worth. For those people the irremediable flaw in every such device is its lack of external validation. They are not satisfied, therefore, by the self-invented expedients we employ to convince one another that we really do matter. They cannot be fully convinced of their own importance just because their colleagues and compatriots assure them of it.

If everyone had the same uneasiness, society's identity-building machinery would lose much of its efficacy. To be sure, not even a thousand Jeremiahs denouncing the entire apparatus for a decade could bring it to a halt. But neither, on the other hand, will the seekers of certainty ever succeed in suppressing their doubts about any merely human certification of personal worth. Even when supported by all the other things we depend on for this purpose—recognition, status, and prestige; belonging to a clan, tribe, lodge, or club; language, culture, and custom; familial, communal, regional, and national ties—the certification will still remain inadequate.

In order to be wholly convincing, the message assuring us of our own significance has to come from a source regarded as possessing ultimate authority. To be so regarded, the source must be perceived as divine, not mortal; spiritual, not temporal; eternal, not evanescent. What it communicates must, in short, be capable of compelling faith. The only messenger that can fulfill these requirements is religion. Religion, by definition, is a transmitter of final answers to questions about our place in a comprehensible scheme of things. While our readiness to accept these answers is no doubt augmented by what William James called "the will to believe," attainment of a secure faith has more to do with *need* than with will.

The need to believe is opportunistic. Drawing sometimes on tradition, at others on invention, it will also embrace revelation if revelation there be. But it is belief that matters. We are told that in 1827 the angel Moroni disclosed to Joseph Smith the place on the Hill Cumorah in Palmyra, New York, where he would find plates of gold inscribed in mysterious characters. We are also told that Joseph Smith translated those characters into English with the aid of a pair of crystals set in a silver bow. The belief that Joseph Smith did indeed do this is a cornerstone of the Mormon religion. Appropriately, therefore, one of the most prominent memorials in Temple Square in Salt Lake City is the one honoring the Three Witnesses who solemnly swore that these were the means by which the Book of Mormon became accessible.

The best evidence, of course, of the universality and strength of the need to believe is that throughout history virtually every known society gives evidence of having practiced one or more religions. Out of about 5.8 billion people now alive, 80 percent, according to the *International Bulletin of Missionary Research,* are affiliated with one or another of the world religions. And all of these religions relate human beings to a universal scheme of things. There is evidence, moreover—for example, the spread of evangelical groups in the United States and the rise in Islamic fundamentalism—that the hold of religion is gaining worldwide.

The aspiration to a sense of worth has many paths to fulfillment. One who possesses an ultimately satisfying religious faith has little need for less authoritative reassurance. With complete faith comes humility because the believer's sense of worth owes nothing to himself. But the average churchgoer whose religious beliefs are not fervent and whose inner sources of self-esteem are not sufficient to make up for this deficiency can round out a sense of worth through cultivating the esteem of others. Such a person can also draw as necessary and as opportunity permits on the society's manifold identity-building devices. One way or another, humanity's aggregate demand for a sense of worth is passably well satisfied.

That is the good news. The bad news, unfortunately, is the direct and inevitable consequence of the good news. The bad news is that the same human attributes that create craving for a sense of worth are for that very reason the principal instigators of human conflict. More elementary needs, to be sure, can account for conflict arising from competition for a limited supply of a desirable thing. But where competition involves the pursuit of status, recognition, or power as distinguished from a necessity—food and shelter, for example—a sense of worth is at stake. At the top, according to some, comes winning for its own sake—a goal that Vince Lombardi is supposed to have called "the *only* thing."

Groups, no doubt because they tend to speak for the most vociferous and narrowly focused of their members, tend to be more quarrelsome than individuals. Nations mainly reflect to other nations only the common denominators of their people's interests. National behavior, consequently, tends to be more prickly, peevish, arrogant, and selfish than that of a mature adult (not redundant: many conspicuously successful adults are arrested adolescents). Slights to national pride, prestige, or hegemonic influence evoke immature reactions that can quickly escalate to all-out war. This explains why I concluded during my first State Department tour that the best preparation for a career in foreign policy would be a sound grounding in child psychology.

But the ugliest and most intractable conflicts are those aroused by threats or wrongs to a group whose members' sense of worth is identified with the group. Any challenge to such a group can provoke hostility. Where such threats are frequent or continuing, they generate hatred. When the threats are followed by violence, they generate war. Since a shared religious faith is the strongest element of group identity, it has always been the dominant as well as the most unyielding factor in prolonged and recurrent conflicts. History teaches us that wars of this kind can be bloodier, nastier, and less amenable to some form of rational accommodation than wars fought over territory and resources.

On the other hand, it is futile to hope for some sort of fundamental improvement in human nature that would neutralize our combativeness. Charles Darwin, to be sure, believed that "man in the distant future will be a far more perfect creature than he now is." It is not clear, however, whether he was talking about both human character and human physical capacity or only the latter. He was, in any case, referring to the "distant future." Besides, it is not easy to identify a way of "fixing" human nature that would be more likely than not to improve human behavior.

To make clear the elusiveness of this aim, let's take a look at some of the components of individual worth. The ones most apt to precipitate conflict are also those most integral to our relationships with and responsibilities toward our families, our communities, our cultural traditions, and our spiritual heritage. To reduce conflict, we would have to diminish the importance of these things. In addition to diluting our sense of worth, this would radically transform human society as we know it. Would we want to do that? Or, take the pursuit of status and esteem. Given the benefits to society deriving from the competition and emulation thereby stimulated, it is not obvious that the resulting reduction in conflict would be worth the price. Religion, moreover, though a chronic source of conflict, responds to the need for a secure sense of worth in a way that nothing else can. If the power of religious faith were somehow to be diminished, any diminution of the conflict caused by religious differences might be more than offset by the increase in quarrelsomeness generated by the more aggressive pursuit of socially conferred self-esteem.

And what about the instincts associated with the perpetuation of our own uniqueness? Suppose hypothetically that a true believer in creationism were to petition God to adjust these instincts so as to eliminate their ugly side effects. The creationist would be wise to assume that the problem is not so much with the instincts themselves as with our imperfect discipline of them. On that assumption he could ask God to equip human beings with an automatic control mechanism. But suppose that the mechanism switched on moments before an orgasm? To prevent the inhibition of healthy drives the mechanism would need to be capable of injecting just the right amount of self-discipline at just the right moment. Failing this, God would by the next century have to keep on adjusting and readjusting the self-disciplinary levels of ten to fifteen billion human beings round the clock every day. While conceivable that an omnipotent and immanent Being might manage such a feat, for us humans it is at the same time unimaginable.

But if our defects are irremediable consequences of the attributes that compel us to seek a sense of worth, what about our qualities? Must not these too be products of the same attributes? As I pointed out early in this essay and as I think we can all agree, a secure sense of self-esteem is commonly associated with a high degree of self-discipline. And self-discipline is linked in turn to such other good qualities as generosity, tolerance, and magnanimity. These good qualities are also the ultimate constraints on conflict. Fortunately for humanity, they are not in fact uncommon. Were it otherwise, this would be a dog-eat-dog world that not even a cynic could enjoy.

To be sure, humans, like other animals, seek to fulfill their own needs. Unlike animals, however, we are endowed with the gift of imagination. We cannot help being aware that we share with our fellow humans needs and instincts similar to our own. I may assert my own demands in preference to yours, but I am bound to acknowledge that yours are no less real. I cannot escape, therefore, the awareness not only that you matter just as much as I do but also that your needs have an equal claim to fulfillment. The moral dimension emerges the moment I recognize these realities.

The most enduring expression of this insight is the commandment "Thou shalt love thy neighbor as thyself." This precept first appears in Leviticus, the third book of the Bible. Dating from at least as far back as 500 B.C., it is embedded in a code of laws communicated directly, we are told, by the Lord God to Moses. Preceding it are laws regulating sacrifices, requiring kindness toward the deaf and blind, proscribing talebearing, and other such ordinances. Immediately following it are the words "Ye shall keep my statutes."

The same words, minus their original context, reappear in the gospels according to Matthew and Mark, the letters of Paul to the Romans and Galatians, and the letter of James to the twelve tribes scattered abroad. In none of these writings, however, are we told how we should receive this utterance. Is it an injunction to be obeyed? An admonition to be observed as best we can? Or is it an ideal too lofty to be taken literally? But perhaps what matters is not how we receive the message but how we act on it, for down through the millennia it has remained an inspiring standard of morality.

The proof that this standard or something like it does in fact influence the conduct of most people most of the time is that good behavior, like good news, gets no headlines. Passably moral conduct must therefore be the rule rather than the exception. If treating our neighbors as we treat ourselves were exceedingly hard, how could that be? A partial answer, I think, can be found in a combination of three factors: early influences, parental, educational, and religious; the desire for social approval; and the practical necessity for maintaining order. But this explanation calls for further explanation. What is the origin of the early influences? Why is social approval deemed desirable? Why isn't a minimal level of order, once achieved, regarded as sufficient?

As previously noted, moral obligations spring from our awareness that other people have the same needs and desires as ourselves. When the affirmative obligations that stem from this awareness are denied or disregarded, the result is behavior we regard as immoral or unethical. In every such case the wrong being done—the immoral or unethical act—consists in some failure to treat another person as having significance equal to our own. The real origin of the moral impulse is thus not teaching but feeling, not law but love. It is demonstrated every day in the way human beings relate to each other. That we do love each other—though not always, not universally, not unreservedly—is an undeniable fact. "Thou shalt love thy neighbor as thyself" can thus be read not as an admonition but as a statement of fact. You will love your neighbor because you can't help it: you feel with and for him or her. Exactly that, after all, is the root meaning of the words "compassion," "sympathy," and "empathy."

Whether we owe the awareness of other people that sparks our moral sense to divine revelation, a social instinct like that of an ant or a bee, or, as I've suggested, our uniquely human capacity for imagination, is a question I don't have to pursue, at least not now. It is clear, in any case, that our grasp of the reality of other people leads us to respect in them the shared attributes I spoke of earlier: their individual uniqueness, the equality of their significance with that of every person, and some degree of dependency for self-esteem on sources outside themselves. The more secure our own individual self-esteem, the more open we are to appreciation of the worth of other people. And the sooner in childhood a foundation of self-esteem is laid, the likelier it is that it will become secure. Loving care and the encouragement of self-expression coupled with firmly established limits are the building blocks of this foundation. Upon it rests, in addition to self-esteem, the framework of our moral values.

Translated into ethical principles and guidelines, moral values can be applied to concrete situations. But no manual on ethics can resolve a tough moral dilemma. As Oliver Wendell Holmes, Jr., observed, "General propositions do not decide concrete cases." And here again imagination is the key. The teaching of ethical principles that does not enlist the imagination is next to useless.

Wait a minute, someone may say. To imagine is to understand. To understand is to forgive. That way lies relativism and the eventual abandonment of all moral standards. At the bottom of the slippery slope "because I couldn't help it" is a defense for almost anything. At that point evil has become impossible to define. But this reductio ad absurdum is plainly wrong. Like many such exercises, it exposes its own absurdity. To understand is not necessarily to forgive and to forgive is not necessarily to condone. Besides, in the absence of moral standards there is nothing to forgive and nothing to condone.

But I agree that evil is hard to define. I looked the word up in a fat book called *The International Dictionary of Thoughts*[4] and found vacuous pronouncements like Nietzsche's "What is evil?—Whatever springs from weakness" and Pascal's "Whatever hinders man's perfecting of his reason and capability to enjoy the rational life, is alone called evil." With encouragement like that I have no hesitancy in offering my own definition. Here it is: evil is the willful disregard for other people that leads to treating them as less than human, as lacking in significance, or as unworthy of respect.

And so we come back to the link between imagination and morality. The person whose imagination cannot encompass the reality of other people is trapped in a narrow world of ego-centered desires and gratifications. He can cheat others, steal from them, or hurt them with no fellow-feeling for their loss or pain. The combination of isolation and alienation eventually produces an antisocial predator to whom other people exist only for purposes of exploitation. At its extreme, disregard for other people reveals itself in such ugly forms as bigotry, intolerance, hatred, perse-

---

[4] John P. Bradley, Leo F. Daniels, Thomas C. Jore, eds. (Chicago: J. G. Ferguson Publishing Co., 1969).

cution, and violence. It would be hard to think of a sicker example than the car bombing of the federal building in Oklahoma City in 1994.

Where moral constraints are not sufficient we call upon a variety of approaches to preventing and resolving conflicts. One is democracy itself. That democracies do not fight each other has often been remarked upon. Democracy can also help to contain domestic conflict. By giving representation and a voice to all groups, democracy diminishes their need to preserve their identities by isolating themselves. This is an insight I first heard expressed shortly after the end of the Gulf War at a meeting in Iraq between representatives of the Kurdish minority and a United Nations humanitarian mission of which I was a member. "We have come to realize," said the senior Kurdish leader, "that for us democracy is more important than autonomy." And certainly we in the United States can take legitimate pride in the degree to which our own democratic values and institutions have taught just this lesson.

When a quarrel begins to escalate, individuals with no stake in the outcome can sometimes lead both sides to see the merits of practical and equitable considerations to which their biases had blinded them. Such time-tested procedures as conciliation, mediation, and arbitration are often successful. Supplementing these procedures is an array of recently developed tools for promoting "win-win" outcomes. As my friend Roger Fisher, founder of the Negotiation Project at the Harvard Law School, has pointed out, "In every significant conflict each party is reasonably saying 'no' to what others are demanding. The challenge is to look behind those demands for underlying interests and to confront each party with a new choice that meets enough of its interests for 'yes' to be a reasonable response."

Backing up all these modes of dispute resolution are the resources of the law. Thousands of years of experience have gone into shaping its rules and principles. Despite jokes like "I always bury lawyers four feet lower than anybody else," said the undertaker, "because deep down lawyers are nice people," deep down we all know that life without lawyers would be ugly. I chanced many years ago to hear an admirable, if legocentric, one-sentence tribute to them in a speech by Francis T. P. Plimpton, one of this century's wisest American lawyers and diplomats. "The history of civilization," he said, "is the history of myriads of solved conflicts." Implicit but unspoken was the addendum, "which is to say, the history of the contributions of legions of good lawyers." From these contributions have in fact emerged safeguards of liberty, guidelines for the governance of commercial transactions, definitions of crimes, guarantees of due process, and a creative balance between rights and obligations. In the wonderful phrase perennially addressed to law-degree recipients at Harvard commencements, these are "the wise restraints that make men free."

But none of these means of dealing with conflict resolution has thus far had much success in stopping the violence stemming from deep-rooted ethnic, cultural, and religious differences. The religious component of conflict is intrinsically resistant to conciliation. By its very nature, total belief in one's own religion is irreconcilable with acceptance of someone else's religion. In the eyes of the true believer, the nonbeliever is bound to appear wrong, benighted, or in need of being saved. If he can't be converted, he deserves to be pitied, perhaps even condemned. But such an attitude on the part of the believers in Religion A is all too likely to be seen by the believers in Religion B as a threat to their sense of identity, and vice versa. Hostility turns into hatred when a group whose religious beliefs are an important part of their lives perceives another group as not only despising those beliefs but as aiming to impose their own. Hatred begets more hatred, and soon it no longer matters which side posed the first threat.

We are and should remain appalled by Northern Ireland, an integral part of a country that has long been a maker as well as a model of civilized standards. But for a British occupying force, God knows what the Protestants and Catholics might have done to each other. Only now, after decades of effort, is there a realistic prospect of a healing solution. In Bosnia, whenever in the past five centuries strong external rule has broken down or been removed, deep-seated rivalries among Catholics, Muslims, Bogomils, and Orthodox Christians, all of whom are Slavs, has led to new outbreaks of violence. And in Sudan, the civil war between the Islamic north and the Christian south has since 1983 exacted an enormous toll.

When in addition to religious beliefs such other contributors to a sense of identity as ethnic traditions and cultural values are also attacked, any chance of reconciliation is further diminished. Personal rivalries and territorial disputes embitter the antagonism, and the wrongs done by each side seep more deeply into the memory of the other side.

The perpetration of these wrongs, moreover, loses none of its frightfulness in the tales handed on to the next generation. And thereby is accumulated and kept ready the volatile fuel of violence.

Given this self-perpetuating cycle and the inadequacy of existing means of dealing with it, the world community badly needs to develop better options. Emil Payin, director of the Center for Ethnopolitical Studies for the Foreign Policy Association in Moscow, is pursuing this goal. The limited value of traditional approaches, he suggests, is explained by their reliance on "the psychological aspects of communication between representatives of the conflicting parties." These work well for minor conflicts like those between seller and buyer, management and union, or municipality and community. But for large-scale "ethno-ideological" conflicts like those in Central Asia, the Transcaucasus, and the Crimea, which involve "the irrational veneration" of "sacred historical rights" and "tribal ideologies," new kinds of control levers are required. These, Payin believes, should include economic incentives and sanctions, public education, the organization of talks between the parties, and laws prescribing ethnic policies.[5]

The world community will in time treat the senseless killing that results from ancient enmities as a crime against humanity. It may by then have developed effective sanctions against this crime. But stronger moral sanctions against inflicting harm on the believers in another religion need not await the law's evolution. Every religion should recognize as one of its most fundamental obligations the teaching of respect for nonbelievers. Indeed, this is an obligation implicit in religion itself. How so? Because moral values are intrinsic to religion.

Until recently I was not convinced of this. Although aware, of course, that religious institutions taught moral precepts and dealt with moral judgment, these lessons were subordinate to their true ministry, which spoke to the meaning of our lives, not the morality of our behavior. Many pious and even saintly religious leaders over the centuries seem to have believed that man's inhumanity to man was simply to be expected; it was an inevitable consequence of our flawed nature. Besides, ethical principles, unlike religious dogmas, are not peculiar to any particular re-

---

[5] *The Woodrow Wilson Center Report*, vol. 5, no. 3 (November 1993).

ligion. They are shared, rather, by believer and nonbeliever alike. Indeed, countless millions who do not accept Jesus of Nazareth as the Son of God nevertheless revere him as a uniquely inspired teacher of moral values.

The realization that I had been wrong—that morality is an inseparable part of religion—became clear to me in the course of my effort to understand the moral implications of respect for other human beings. This change of view traced the following path: A religion that is prepared to welcome new adherents thereby shows its respect for all potential believers. Its very hospitality to nonbelievers attests to their equal value. And since this affirmation is at the base of all moral obligations, religious leaders should teach their followers that disrespect for nonbelievers is morally wrong.

This responsibility rests to a unique degree on sects that promise a blissful afterlife to some, at least, of their own members while also teaching that nonmembers have no hope of salvation. The believers in such a faith, convinced that it is their duty to save nonbelievers from hell, can easily be induced to carry the pursuit of converts into the territory of other religions. On the other hand, Hinduism and Buddhism, which do not hold out the prospect of individual immortality, are less fervent proselytizers, and Judaism, which was bestowed on a chosen people, does not proselytize at all. Not surprisingly, the sects that have most aggressively sought converts have tended to be the most frequent instigators of conflict, and those least inclined to do so, its victims. And since a hostile reaction is an all-too-frequent consequence, the world community has good reason for encouraging the proselytizing sects to restrain their followers' enthusiasm.

A front-page story in the *Birmingham News* for September 5, 1993, highlighted the problem. Under the headline BAPTISTS CONVERT THE LOST, the story disclosed that the Southern Baptists had done a survey which estimated that 46.1 percent of Alabamans risked going to hell. Jews, Hindus, Buddhists, members of other non-Christian religions, and everyone not belonging to a church congregation were counted as "lost." Estimates of the unsaved from other Christian denominations were based on how closely those groups' beliefs matched Southern Baptist doctrine. Many faithful adherents of the other denominations were incensed. Southern Baptist leaders expressed surprise at all the fuss. "The survey has a good motive behind it," said one, "and that is not one of judging but of reaching." No doubt. But "reaching" is a seed from the same stock that produces the rank weed of Islamic fundamentalism.

In one way or another every religion addresses the eventual destiny of the human soul. So far as I have been able to discover, however, not since seventeenth-century Calvinism promised salvation to "the elect" has any religion assured its followers that their earthly behavior would have no bearing on their afterlives. On the contrary, most religions teach that the dead will be judged in some manner on the morality of their behavior while alive and rewarded or punished accordingly.

Christianity holds that judgments on the dead not only determine their destination—heaven, hell, or purgatory—but also, as Dante tells us in searing detail, prescribe for the damned the precise forms of punishment that will best fit their crimes. In the religion of ancient Greece (its beliefs did not become "mythology" until they ceased to have believers), three judges chosen for their inflexible integrity passed sentences on the dead. Rhadamanthus judged the souls of Asiatics, Aeacus those of Europeans, and Minos had the deciding vote. In Islamic doctrine the dead will be resurrected on the Last Day and a judgment will be pronounced on every person in accordance with his deeds. The condemned will burn in hellfire and the saved will experience both physical enjoyment and spiritual happiness. And Hinduism, broadly speaking, teaches that the soul goes though successive incarnations, rising from pig to ape to man, for example, or falling back down, depending on one's deeds. The final reward of the highest virtue is emancipation from impermanence into oneness with God.

Morals are the common concern of the Roman Catholic confessional, the Confucian Analects, and Buddhism's Eightfold Path. Islam has a legal system of its own, whose purpose is to regulate moral behavior. Every major religion enjoins regard for the person and property of all humans. In reaching verdicts, therefore, should not the ultimate tribunals regard as a serious transgression of moral law the brutalizing of another person on the ground of religious difference? And in that case, should not all religions be eager to protect their adherents from condemnation on this account?

Although to serve its purpose a religion must speak with authority, that does not excuse a lack of regard for other religions. Against the bloody backdrop of today, religious leaders would seem to have a clear obligation to condemn fanaticism and to find ways of neutralizing their own tendency to encourage it. There is an urgent need as well for their vigorous leadership in teaching that mutual tolerance and respect are moral imperatives intrinsic to the very concept of religion.

Benjamin Franklin's address on the last day of the Philadelphia Convention turned out to be the single most influential appeal for the adoption of the U.S. Constitution. Urging his fellow delegates to "doubt a little of [their] own Infallibility," Franklin referred to the Protestant who, in a dedication, "tells the Pope, that the only Difference between our two Churches in their Opinions of the Certainty of their Doctrine, is the Romish Church is infallible, and the Church of England is never in the Wrong." Nearly two centuries later John XXIII, the first pope since the fourteenth century to receive the archbishop of Canterbury at the Vatican, saw no need either to renounce his own infallibility nor to ask the archbishop to admit that he might sometimes be wrong. The significance of Pope John's invitation to the archbishop lay in its implicit acknowledgment that the members of another church are also real and therefore entitled to respect. Pope John made the same point even more engagingly when he said to a Communist diplomat, "I know you are an atheist, but won't you accept an old man's blessing?"

The only religious body I know of that proclaims its own fallibility is the Unitarian-Universalist Association, but that, presumably, is because it has no formal catechism. As Ted Sorensen, the only non-Catholic on the staff of freshman Senator Jack Kennedy, has observed, the advantage of being a Unitarian is that it doesn't interfere either with your politics or your religion. But note: The UUA credo puts first "The inherent worth and dignity of every person." This could well be the reason, therefore, why the UUA, though a small denomination, has from the outset had a prominent role in the World Conference on Religion and Peace. First assembled in Kyoto in 1970, the conference has on five subsequent occasions brought together about a thousand leading representatives of the major religions. The most recent assembly took place in Rome and Riva del Garda in 1994 and adopted a declaration that squarely addresses the above-mentioned issue:

> As religious peoples, we are particularly saddened that religion is misused at times to legitimize violence and wars and stir hatreds. We strongly condemn destructive religious nationalism and religious extremism as crimes against religion. In response, we call

not for uncompromising secularism but for authentic religion, which we believe must be a powerful force for human rights, freedom and non-violent political transformation; the impulse of religion must be toward peace, not war.[6]

And yet for a religious body no less than for a nation, a community, or an individual there is no escaping the necessity for balancing internal obligations against external claims. Pope John Paul II, speaking for the Roman Catholic Church in a recent book, discusses the essential components of such a balance. The church is bound, to begin with, to proclaim the truth of its own fundamental doctrines. This requirement gives rise to a "clear need for a new evangelization" that will carry out Christ's injunction: "Go, therefore, and make disciples of all nations." His Holiness affirms, nonetheless, the church's "high regard" for other faiths and suggests that "instead of marveling at the fact that Providence allows such a great variety of religions, we should be amazed at the number of common elements within them."[7]

But surely the commonality of these elements can be accounted for on the basis that every religion speaks to the common denominators of the human condition. All religions, though in a great variety of ways, affirm the significant worth of each human life. On this foundation the World Conference on Religion and Peace, the United States Institute of Peace, the Center of the Study of World Religions at the Harvard Divinity School, and many other organizations are striving to build mutual tolerance and respect among religious groups whose adherents have all too often been at each other's throats.

From these initiatives are beginning to emerge new approaches to preventing ethnic and religious conflicts. Awakened by modern telecommunications to the suffering of the victims, the world community may before long make effective use of these approaches. Now there would be a *real* giant step for [hu]mankind!

---

[6] The Riva del Garda Declaration (World Conference on Religion and Peace, Sixth Assembly, November 3–9, 1994), p. 2.

[7] *Crossing the Threshold of Hope* (New York: Random House Large Print in association with Alfred A. Knopf, Inc., 1994), pp. 77, 78, 105, 113.

Overload

My father was a professor of surgery, and as a boy I heard stories about his awesome diagnostic skills. Both my brothers are doctors. So I learned early on that before the treatment comes the diagnosis, and before the diagnosis come the thumping, the palpating, the scanning, and the lab tests. And starting it all off are the patient's complaints.

Democracy in America today is at the complaining stage. We don't have a prescribed course of treatment because we don't have clear diagnoses, and we don't have clear diagnoses because we haven't yet looked closely at the causes of our complaints. On the other hand, we do have all kinds of data on what the complaints are about: anecdotal material, public opinion surveys, journalistic analyses, scholarly studies, and think-tank papers.

All these sources confirm that the number one target of complaint is government—government in general, but especially the federal government. And bracketed with government in public disesteem are the people, both bureaucrats and politicians, who work in government. According to a *Washington Post* survey in early 1994, only 14 percent of Americans think that politicians generally tell the truth. A later poll by

Time-CNN found that 91 percent of the people surveyed had little or no confidence in government's ability to solve problems. Attitudes toward government and government people range from frustration through resentment to outright anger, and spreading outward from these attitudes is the corrosive acid of cynicism. Meg Greenfield, the *Washington Post's* editorial page editor, whose witty and incisive observations occasionally appear on the op-ed page, wrote a column in 1995 viewing this phenomenon with considerable equanimity. The recent manifestations of cynicism were consistent, she thought, with the established tradition of American irreverence for government. And while it's true that American humorists have always delighted in skewering politicians, the cynicism has a bite now that it didn't used to have; the humor has a nasty edge.

Cynicism, Meg Greenfield suggests, may be our "only sane and prudent response" to the world around us. As justification for this response, she cites the HUD scandals, the S&Ls, the indictment of Dan Rostenkowski, and other examples of alleged sleazy behavior on the part of public officials. But official wrongdoing is not new, and there is no evidence that it has recently become more common. The realist recognizes that betrayals of the public trust, though inevitable, are exceptional. The cynic assumes that they're routine features of everyday political behavior.

There are at least two reasons why we should be seriously alarmed by the accelerating rate at which the cynic's assumption has been gaining ground. One is the indispensability to democracy of trust in those to whom we have delegated responsibility for things that concern us in common. The second reason, more pertinent here, concerns the consequences of letting ourselves believe that whatever goes wrong must be the politicians' fault. The more convinced we are of this, the less we feel the need to seek out the real causes of our complaints. Moreover, blaming the politicians also prevents us from recognizing that some of the blame—quite a lot of it, in fact—belongs to us.

Our insistence on quick cures of resistant and even untreatable ailments is making it harder and harder for politicians to tell us the truth. We turn against those who try to warn us that simplistic remedies won't work. And when they don't work, we get angry at government's failures to deliver on its promises.

To illustrate what I mean, let's take a look at some of the problems that show up year after year in public-opinion surveys of the "ten most serious issues." Among these perennials are crime, drug abuse, welfare reform, teenage pregnancy, and erosion of family values. For each problem the demanded remedies are clear, simple, and ineffective. Here is a quick look at the matchup:

Crime—longer jail sentences, "three strikes and you're out," and increased reliance on the death penalty.

Drug abuse—interdiction and mandatory minimum sentences.

Welfare reform—work requirements without adequate provision for job training, placement services, or day care.

Teenage pregnancy—exclusion from welfare benefits oddly coupled with the denial of tax dollars for abortions.

Erosion of family values—school prayer and denunciation of Hollywood.

The consequence of our insisting on nonsolutions for chronic problems is that we make no progress toward solving them, and that lack of progress adds both to our complaints and to our insistence on bigger doses of the nonsolutions. Sadly, we're now at the point where only an exceptionally courageous, charismatic, or foolhardy politician would dare to challenge these demands.

Once we get a grip on our impatience, one large fact will stand out. This is the constant increase in the number and difficulty of the tasks being heaped upon government and politics. All or almost all (I can't think of an exception, but maybe you can) of our current complaints are traceable to the overloading of the system. My purpose here will be to lay bare the factors contributing to this overload, examine their consequences, and suggest ways of limiting, if not repairing, the damage they do.

The most conspicuous of the factors contributing to overload is everywhere visible. It is growth, all forms of growth. Every significant increase in number, volume, scale, or knowledge feeds other increases: The larger the population, the more it consumes, the more numerous and widely scattered must be the sources that supply this consumption, and the larger must be the transportation and distribution system that links these sources. As the growing population's disposable income goes up, it can afford more diversified products manufactured by more sophisticated methods and requiring a wider variety of materials. Techno-logical evolution has moved faster in two decades than biological evolu-tion in twenty million years. As industries, jobs, and products are born, flourish, and decay, wastes accumulate, pollution worsens, and forests recede. We wake up one morning and find that first-graders are playing with computers, cardiac-bypass operations have become routine, giant corporations have gone global, and the planet is beginning to be seen as an ecological whole.

All these and countless other manifestations of growth and change produce complexity, and complexity must inevitably increase faster than any of the several exponential trends contributing to it. Indeed, it should eventually be possible to feed these trends into an equation that would yield the annual rate of increase in complexity. In the meantime we shall have to make do with such indicators as the rates of increase in data-pro-cessing capacity, securities trading, air-passenger miles, and jail occu-pancy.

Measurement aside, the difficulty of the choices confronting the democratic process is bound to increase in rough proportion to the in-crease in complexity. As to that, it is relevant—and disturbing—to recall a useful rule of thumb. Known as the "rule of 72," it tells you that a quan-tity growing at a given annual rate will double in the number of years you get by dividing the rate into 72. Thus, if the annual rate of increase in complexity is, say, 6 percent, it will take only twelve years for complexity to double.

The interaction of growth and complexity has driven the expansion of government at all levels. One example is the federal highway program launched under Eisenhower. Others are the National Aeronautics and Space Administration, also created under Eisenhower, the Occupational Safety and Health Administration and the Environmental Protection Agency, both created under Nixon, and the Resolution Trust Corporation created under Bush. Resistance to big government may have influenced the roles of these agencies, but it could not ignore the realities that brought them into being.

In the case of the environment, the realization that the federal gov-ernment would have to act began to sink in soon after World War II. In most places tanneries, chemical plants, and paper mills were free to dump their wastes into the nearest stream. I still recall the disgust I felt during a 1957 visit to Cincinnati's Robert A. Taft Sanitary Engineering

Center on being shown vials of black, viscous stuff distilled from the water of the Ohio River. The possibility that sulfur dioxide carried downwind from public utility smokestacks might be poisoning distant lakes had not even been suggested. And while most of the hunters crouched in the blinds dotting the central flyways accepted the need for bag limits, few had focused on preserving the wetlands that supported the ducks they were shooting at.

And what about automobile safety? Consumer protection? Occupational safety and health? The integrity of private pension funds? The bailout of savings and loans institutions? I don't hear many conservatives saying that government should not have "intervened" in these matters. The inevitable result, nevertheless, was to bring about more intrusive contact between people and their government, some of it time-consuming, annoying, or, in the eyes of those being regulated, burdensome. These reactions swelled the chorus of complaint. Meanwhile, it would not have occurred to the majority who benefited from these intrusions to lift their voices in a hymn of grateful praise.

The unabating flow of ever more complex legislation has put increasing pressure on the time available for hearings and debate. The Social Security Act of 1935 was only 32 pages long, and 36 pages were enough for the 1956 Interstate Highway Act. But Reagan's 1986 tax bill weighed in at 461 pages, and Clinton's health legislation was more than three times as long. While the House can adjust to these ballooning demands through tough scheduling and the restriction of amendments, the Senate's only remedy is the limitation of debate, and this requires sixty votes. As a result, the Senate suffered through some sixty-six filibusters from 1991 through 1994—more than in Congress's first one hundred and forty years. Floor time is now so precious that the mere threat of a filibuster can prevent an important issue from being debated at all.

Together with growth in scale and volume as well as in complexity, government has also had to adjust to even more widely ramifying systemic interconnections. A system, as I understand the term, is a structure whose components serve a single unifying aim. In some ways a system is rather like a balloon: if you poke it in one place, it will bulge somewhere else; if you put a strain on it anywhere, the strain will be transmitted throughout the whole. But a system differs from a balloon in being made of many interlocking and interactive parts. In that respect it's like the human body. The parts—heart, lungs, kidneys, muscles, brain, and all the rest—are individually differentiated but organically inseparable. The whole world is an ever more closely linked system of systems—ecological, economic, social, and political. So is the United States of America.

Among the systems internal to the United States the most intricate, perhaps, is the health-care system. Its single unifying aim is to keep and make people well, and its success depends on the efficiency with which all of its components contribute to fulfilling this aim. As in the case of all systems, it is a mistake to concentrate on one component without keeping steadily in view its functional relationship with the others. The failure to recognize such interrelationships can lead to unanticipated side effects that do more harm than good.

In the early years of my experience with the health-care system we did not question the utility of a piece-by-piece approach. When, for example, I was at the Department of Health, Education, and Welfare during the Eisenhower administration, we assumed that we could reduce the amount of money spent on acute-care hospitalization by increasing the accessibility of diagnostic and ambulatory services and convalescent care. It did not occur to us that encouraging patients to use less costly facilities would induce the hospitals to fill up their empty beds by accelerating elective surgery and expanding the use of life-prolonging procedures. As Dr. John Knowles, then general director of the Massachusetts General Hospital, said to me one day in the early sixties, "This hospital is turning into a giant vacuum pump pulling in people who used to die in community hospitals for six thousand dollars apiece so that they can die here for thirty-six thousand apiece."

When I returned to HEW in 1970, I found waiting for me a problem involving another component of the health-care system. The American Medical Association and the medical schools were sounding the alarm about an imminent shortage of doctors. Although a handful of analysts disputed this forecast, nobody had sufficient data on which to base a definitive estimate of the future demand for doctors. We concluded that it would be wiser to take a chance on training too many doctors than to risk a shortage that might not only restrict the availability of medical care but also drive up its price. HEW accordingly proposed and Congress enacted legislation increasing the number of students for whom the federal government would pay a "capitation fee" to medical schools. In the next ten years total medical school enrollment increased by more than 60 percent.

Looking back, we can see that the principal consequence of enlarging the supply of doctors was a rapid increase in the number of specialists. The availability of the specialists led to more referrals, more tests, more medications, and more operations than would otherwise have occurred. For doctors who completed their medical educations with a heavy load of debt, specialization, being more lucrative, was more attractive than primary care. The total cost of health care went up proportionally, thereby contributing to the need for cost-containment measures like performance review and managed care.

The criminal justice system is an organism rather like the health-care system. In place of the unifying aim of health, it has the unifying aim of law enforcement. To this aim is harnessed a huge apparatus extending all the way from the cop on the beat and in the patrol car through the crime lab and the grand jury to prosecution, sentencing, probation, incarceration, and parole. My first direct involvement with the system came when I left HEW in 1959 to become U.S. attorney for the District of Massachusetts. But it was not until 1967 that I had occasion as the newly elected attorney general of Massachusetts to look closely at the system's interrelationships and interactions. This came about because one of my first acts was to set up a commission on criminal justice. We got one of the very first grants from the Justice Department's newly formed Law Enforcement Assistance Administration, hired an extremely able staff, and began a top-to-bottom assessment of every aspect of law enforcement in the state.

As a result of my involvement in the commission's work, I came to understand why each piece of the criminal justice process is part of a system. I learned, for example, that if the only thing you do is improve the crime-fighting capability of police departments, this will lead not only to more arrests and more criminal charges but also to more criminals being turned loose to commit more crimes while the prosecutors and the courts fall further behind ever lengthier dockets. If to reduce the backlogs you hire more prosecutors, get more judges appointed, and convict more criminals, the already crowded jails become even more crowded, less capable of rehabilitating their inmates, and more practiced in graduating hardened criminals. If you improve the penal system's ability to perform its part in the rehabilitation process without also strengthening the probation system and helping discharged offenders to find productive jobs, you will largely nullify the value of all the antecedent improvements. And if, despite having achieved top-to-bottom reform of the system, you get no help from other agencies in an all-out assault on the social conditions that turn children into lawbreakers, the crime rate will continue to rise.

Experiences like this, not just in health care and criminal justice but in many other fields as well, eventually convinced policymakers that an essential step toward dealing with any serious problem is to get a handle on its systemically interrelated components. But once you start exploring the systemic ramifications of a problem that seems at first to fall within the province of a single agency, you soon find out that a number of other departments or agencies have legitimate interests in the same problem, can provide valuable input, or both. Issues that a cabinet member could once have decided independently may thus become "presidential," thereby leading to the formation of a slow-moving cabinet committee or working group on which all the concerned entities are represented. This further complicates the process by alerting each entity's cluster of national organizations and interest groups to their stakes in the outcome.

When the legislation produced by the interagency deliberative process is eventually sent to the Hill, it seldom fits within the mandate of a single committee or subcommittee in either body. It triggers instead a jurisdictional free-for-all engaging as many as a half a dozen subcommittees. The number of national organizations and interest groups that discover a stake in the outcome is correspondingly enlarged. At the end of the day, the need to deal with systemic interconnections has made the governmental decisionmaking process substantially more complicated and time-consuming than it already was. And this inevitably becomes still another factor adding to the public perception that government is top-heavy, slow-moving, and inefficient.

But if government backed into the systemic thicket, it hurled itself into the attack on poverty. As we shall see, it got no thanks for that either.

In 1961, when John F. Kennedy became president, the rising tide was, as he put it, lifting all the boats. The very growth that had compounded complexity also created confidence and encouraged compassion. Millions of Americans believed that their society had come into the possession of skills and resources sufficient to tackle and overcome scourges that previous generations had no choice but to suffer and endure. In this spirit the young president began to plan a war on poverty. In this spirit also, decent, caring Americans willingly, even gladly, supported the dedication of tax dollars to the eradication of poverty, disease, and deprivation.

Although JFK's life was tragically cut short, his initiatives were picked up and energized by Lyndon B. Johnson. To carry on the war on poverty, Congress at his urging passed the Economic Opportunity Act providing for community action programs. Johnson's Great Society, though ultimately sidetracked by the war in Vietnam, produced a flood of new legislation. Between 1959, when I left HEW, and 1970, when I returned, the number of departmental programs had grown from about a hundred to more than three hundred. In case after case these hopeful initiatives demonstrated the "don't just stand there, do something" syndrome. Almost any unmet need from more day-care centers to a cure for Lou Gehrig's disease could evoke this response. Moreover, almost any plausible-sounding combination of a slogan, a law, and a new bureaucratic entity, supplied with whatever amount of money the congressional appropriators were willing to provide, could qualify as a "program." The only requirements: that the unmet need be visible and appealing and seem capable of correction or cure.

Looking back, we can plainly see that the assault on poverty, disease, and ignorance launched with such high hopes in the sixties was no less foredoomed than Pickett's charge at Gettysburg. The later assault failed for much the same reasons as the earlier one: the forces deployed were far too small and inadequately armed to be capable of fulfilling their mission. But Robert E. Lee did at least have a battle plan: he thought the Union line would be thinly defended at the center, and that's where Pickett's charge was aimed. The assault on poverty, ignorance, and disease had no plan, and its objectives were numerous, scattered, and constantly increasing in number. It thereby stretched and subdivided the available resources, placing excessive demands on limited stores of knowledge and skill.

At least with hindsight it's not hard to reconstruct what happened. One factor, surely, was that LBJ, the commander in chief in the war on poverty, was eager for early results—and why not? So were the groups that would benefit directly. His supporters in the general public asked no questions. They, for the most part, were well-meaning people just enough moved by genuine compassion to join in calling for some kind of action but not so deeply concerned as to insist on being shown that the resulting "program" was capable of doing the job. Rather than face the fact that limited efforts like community action projects and corporate sponsorship of job training were incapable of exerting a lasting impact, they preferred to believe that the poverty cycle was about to be broken. And since the routes between their suburban homes and their usual downtown destinations bypassed the ugliest realities, their disillusionment would be indefinitely deferred.

Recalling that hopeful era (as lieutenant governor of Massachusetts at the time, I was trying to coordinate the state's human services programs), I'm reminded of a long-ago suggestion by my brother George. Ours, he said, should be named the "Silo-Flush society" (after a then well-known brand of "commode"): we want unpleasant things removed from our sensory orbit as swiftly and quietly as possible. The very word "commode," by the way, evokes some earlier examples of the "don't just stand there, do something" syndrome's disinclination to face unpleasant facts. Take the terms "house of correction" and "reform school." We began to give these names to jails late in the last century because we wanted to believe that these were the roles they would have. The words are still in use despite overwhelming proof that jails, far from being places that correct or reform, are kilns that put a hard glaze on criminal tendencies. Our daily discourse is full of terms that encourage the avoidance of reality. "Interdiction" cultivated the illusion that we were stemming the tide of drug shipments. "Urban renewal" permitted us to ignore the costs of destroying inner-city neighborhoods. A clear-eyed reading of any daily newspaper will turn up newer examples.

Our talent for avoiding inconvenient facts is particularly useful when we want to assert incompatible demands. Conspicuous cases in point are balancing the budget while cutting taxes, denouncing red tape while egging on congressional micromanagement, and boasting about the superiority of American science while reducing support for basic research. But I can't recall a more striking example than the public attitude toward business that I encountered as secretary of commerce in 1976. This attitude could have been summed up in one nonstop sentence: "We expect the highest-quality products at the lowest possible prices manufactured under conditions of maximum worker safety and minimal damage to the environment while conserving energy and generating capital both for developing the technology that will keep America competitive and for expanding production so that more and more people can be put to work at ever higher wages." Those who shared this attitude would have been hard put to say all this without pausing for breath, but they managed to think it all at once without stumbling over the built-in trade-offs among competing goals.

Our tendency to avoid unwelcome facts is the flip side of our natural optimism. When, therefore, the facts do eventually force themselves on our attention, the shock of disappointment is all the greater. This is what happened to the high hopes generated by the War on Poverty and the Great Society. It won't be long before a similar fate befalls today's less benign illusions. But each of these failures, when it does come to light, will deal yet another blow to confidence in government.

Signs of impending disappointment began to emerge during my second tour at HEW. When I returned to the department in 1970, the expectations generated by the War on Poverty and the Great Society were still at a high pitch. The attacking forces had not yet fallen back. The programs we took over continued to expand, and the Nixon administration introduced new proposals of its own, including the Family Assistance Plan, the most far-reaching welfare-reform program ever put forward. But the comprehensive health-care program was even more ambitious. Addressing everything from health-insurance coverage to HMO expansion, health education, malpractice, primary care, and inducements for doctors to locate in underserved areas, it also contained the National Health Insurance Partnership Act. This combined a federally financed substitute for Medicaid with a requirement that all employers provide a specified minimum level of health benefits. Ironically, the similar mandated-coverage component of the Clinton health-care plan was attacked as an extreme example of tax-and-spend liberalism.

While still believing at the end of my HEW tour that our new proposals were well conceived and much needed, I had grown increasingly uneasy about the growing gap between the promises implicit in the programs we were already administering and our ability to deliver on those promises. Many of these programs fell far short of reaching every eligible person. Head Start enrolled only 15 percent of the entitled children; the Community Mental Health Program helped about 20 percent of its intended beneficiaries; the nutrition-of-the-elderly program, even though fully funded, served only 5 percent of those who qualified. Concerned that similar shortfalls would be found in most of our other programs, I asked for an estimate of how much it would cost in fiscal 1972 to extend all of HEW's service-delivery programs to every eligible person. The estimate exceeded my wildest surmise: the additional cost for fiscal 1972 alone would be $250 billion—enough to double that year's *entire* federal budget!

I could get no comfort from the possibility that the numbers might have been inflated. In fact, they were quite conservatively calculated. Although there is a real correlation between cost and quality in the case of most services, the projections for programs that varied in cost from state to state used a benchmark two-thirds of the way up the scale from the lowest to the highest cost provider. In the case of Head Start, for example, the annual cost per child in 1972 ranged from $1,048 in Arkansas to $1,970 in New York; for the unenrolled children nationwide we used the Arkansas figure plus two-thirds of the difference between Arkansas and New York. Had we used the high end for every program, the aggregate annual shortfall would have been a lot more than $250 billion.

The more I thought about the implications of these numbers, the more concerned I became that the resulting disappointment would generate a backlash. In a paper circulated among my HEW colleagues at the time, I compared the expectations that our predecessors had awakened and that we were still encouraging to "a giant helium-filled balloon cast loose from its moorings, sailing beyond sight." The paper continued:

> We must somehow bring our expectations back to earth: we must
> level with each other. For either we shall understand the reality
> of what can and cannot be done over time, or we shall condemn
> ourselves to failure, and failure again and again.

In addition to fostering unrealistic expectations, we had allowed appealing but poorly conceived projects to soak up scarce resources, thereby diverting them from better uses. We needed clear and objective means of determining how well, if at all, our programs were fulfilling their purposes. All too often, I learned, we were employing "input" rather than "output" measures of evaluation. A "program" to combat juvenile delinquency, for example, could be evaluated as successful merely because the formula grants were being promptly distributed to the designated state agencies and spent on the specified purposes, because research projects were being funded at competent institutions, or because stipends were being awarded to suitable trainees—all without a dime's worth of evidence that the program was having any demonstrable effect in cutting down juvenile crime.

During my brief tenure as attorney general of the United States, I happened upon a truly classic example of this fallacy. Having been invited to speak at the dedication of the New York City's new police headquarters, I was met at LaGuardia by a deputy commissioner of police. On the way into Manhattan he told me that he was responsible for the city's battle against organized crime. I asked him how he was doing. "Great," he said, and proceeded to tell me how many Mafiosi had already gone to jail. "That's impressive," I said, "but has that had any effect on organized crime?" He continued in the same vein, detailing the grand juries that were in session, the number of indictments handed down, and the investigations still under way. I said, "That's impressive too. But tell me, have all these convictions and prosecutions had any impact on the volume of loan-sharking, drug pushing, or illegal gambling?" He looked at me disgustedly. "How the hell would I know?" he said. "We're fighting *organized crime!*"

From one perspective, choice is a luxury. The unluckiest of our fellow citizens are those who have the fewest opportunities for choice—the illiterate, the unskilled, the mentally ill, the homeless, the destitute. But choice can be a bleak exercise when it involves allocating limited resources among the needs of those very people. That's why, ever since leaving HEW, I've been an evangelist for the wider use of such aids to choice as more and better data, more sharply focused program evaluation, more precise program design, more rigorous cost-benefit analysis, and improved foresight capability. It's not a mission that fills stadiums. Not even Billy Graham, I suspect, could give it crowd appeal. Indeed, its only major protagonist in the two decades between my departure from HEW and the inauguration of the Clinton administration was the General Accounting Office.

With the enactment of the Performance Review Act of 1992 and Vice President Al Gore's recommendations for making government work, I felt a new stirring of hope. The Gore report, however, was primarily concerned with performance in the sense of carrying out a defined task efficiently and well. As chairman of the GAO's Quality Review Board for several years, I became somewhat familiar with the opportunities to enhance public confidence in government by raising the level of this kind of performance. The even more serious concern I'm addressing here, however, is performance in the sense of fulfilling commitments. The government's failures to deliver this kind of performance is one of the contributors to the erosion of trust in the democratic process itself.

But better management cannot tell us how to weigh the needs of the very old against the needs of the very young, research on AIDS against research on Alzheimer's disease, or jobs in the timber industry against protecting the spotted owl. These are choices that can be made only on the basis of values, feelings, and instincts. The very purpose of democracy is to give each of us a voice in making these kinds of choices. But the success of this process depends on the willingness and ability of a substantial fraction of the general public to develop a pretty good understanding of important issues. And this is where we come up against the limitations of human intellect and energy and the remorseless ticking of the clock. The more choices we have to deal with, the harder it is for us to play our individual parts. We are already perilously close to the point where even the most conscientious citizen feels overwhelmed.

As the competing claims that have to be resolved become more numerous and more impossible to satisfy, the elected officeholder's ability to deal with them is more and more thinly stretched. The means of coping are few and unsatisfactory. One option is to lean more heavily on staff support. Another option is to speed up the rate at which business is disposed of, but this adds to the likelihood of poorly thought out solutions. The only remaining option is simply not to act on some categories of problems despite the certainty that this will lengthen the litany of public complaints.

As indispensable links between the elected and the electors, the media (the plural of medium, "intermediate means or channel") also have to cope with overload. Held within inflexible limits on column inches and airtime, they have been able to track the political process only by resorting to more compression, more omission, more simplification, and a shorter half-life for any given story. Print's answer to TV's sound bites is USA Today. These are the journalistic counterparts of fast food, and we have similar reasons to complain about as well as to be grateful for both.

For the well-educated and the civic-minded, the New York Times and other national newspapers, Jim Lehrer, and Sunday morning's talking heads do an admirable job in distilling, analyzing, and interpreting the important events and issues. National Public Radio's Morning Edi-

tion and *All Things Considered* keep countless commuters like myself tuned into a rich variety of reports on the outside world. Meanwhile, CNN brings us the minute-by-minute unfolding of the crisis of the day, the talk shows remind us of just how opinionated some people can get, and Internet plugs those who know what they want to know into the vast storage capacity of digital information systems.

But even if the media were able to expand their coverage of the political scene just as fast as its complexity increases, few people could or would take advantage of this bonanza. Already beset by the increasing complication of our own lives, most of us do well to maintain, to say nothing of enlarging, the time we give to trying to understand the issues whose resolution ultimately rests with us. Our very awareness that so much more is happening than we can keep up with tends to narrow our focus even as it broadens our field of vision. Being unable to grasp or retain most of what we read or see or hear, we give our full attention only to things that particularly appeal to our interest or directly affect our interests. The groups that speak for the latter are encouraged in their shrillness by our support. Meanwhile, increasing self-absorption diminishes our awareness of the needs and problems of others.

The erosion of long-established standards and conventions has further complicated the task of political choice. That such erosion has occurred is clear. As to why this has happened, I have a theory which I think fits the facts pretty well. To begin with, conventions are like habits. They supply practical rules for governing our behavior toward things we don't want to have to stop and think about. In the course of time, however, change can eat away at the empirical base of a set of conventions, and suddenly they begin to slip. The weaker the conventions' practical justification—where they serve, in other words, primarily as rules for the sake of rules—the more vulnerable they are to the influence of change.

An example is the arts. Except as they decorate, move, or entertain, they have no pragmatic function. That could explain why long-established artistic conventions became vulnerable about a hundred years ago to such movements as postimpressionism in painting and atonality in music. Photography had by then largely taken over painting's purely representational function, and that freed the painter to experiment with any form of expression that pigments laid on canvas could produce. At about the same time recordings were beginning to make the established musical repertoire so familiar that an aspiring composer seeking a distinctive style was virtually forced to break with tradition. Similar guesses can plausibly explain the weakening of other conventions. The Pill, for example, must surely have been the "proximate cause," as lawyers would say, of the wholesale abandonment of constraints on premarital sex. For married as well as unmarried couples, pleasure rather than reproduction became accepted as the primary function of sexual intercourse. The pleasure principle has also made homosexuality easier to tolerate, although the mind-set conditioned by the functional differentiation of the sex organs has no doubt slowed down its acceptance. In both cases it seems likely that the weakening of the old constraints was accelerated by the slippage of other conventions.

As to the status of women, it is shocking in retrospect to realize that in the advanced industrial countries women did not win the right to vote until seventy or eighty years ago. Or that it was only after World War II that substantial numbers of professional females began to be admitted to the most prestigious American schools. But the exclusion of American women from occupations outside the home may well have been the result, not of failure to appreciate their abilities, but of awareness that they were critically needed at home. In one of his many insightful observations about America, de Tocqueville said, "If I were asked . . . to what the singular prosperity and growing strength of [the Americans] ought mainly to be attributed, I should reply: to the superiority of their women."

What was it, then, that at long last broke down the barriers to equal opportunities for women? A persuasive answer, I think, is that the labor-saving inventions which came into increasing use as the twentieth century progressed had a twofold effect. First, they relegated to the bottom of the heap jobs that formerly put a premium on physical strength, thereby wiping out the only basis for regarding women as inferior to men. Second, they diminished the time and skill demanded to run a household, thus removing the principal justification for insisting that "woman's place is in the home." World War II greatly accelerated the opening up of opportunities for women to demonstrate that there was little or nothing a man could do that they could not do at least as well. The indefensibility of the old barriers thus became more and more apparent. And so, one by one, they fell. Any that still remain are those of prejudice, not convention.

The range of choices opened up by the abrogation of conventions has been widened still further by the diminishing authority of institutions that used to be relied upon to foreclose whole areas of choice. Neither churches nor schools nor parents can count any longer on acquiescence in pronouncements asserting, "It's so because we say it's so." The Age of Reason began and the scientific method reinforced the propensity to inquire: Why? Is it really true? How do we know? While I would not have it otherwise—would resist, indeed, any attempt to restore the old order—the result is to require the individual to choose among options that did not previously exist. We select from a profusion of "lifestyles" a pattern that appeals to us the same way we select costumes and hairstyles. And who is to say that our new freedom to "make a statement," no matter how bizarre, leads us into more mistakes than we would previously have made? Indeed, some options—easier divorce, for instance—can simultaneously offer both escape from past mistakes and the opportunity to make new ones.

Some of the choices that conventions no longer make for us and that authoritative institutions no longer foreclose have imposed themselves on an already overburdened national agenda. One example is the emergence of "the right to life" versus "freedom of choice" as a national, rather than state or local, issue. Congress has had to decide not only that the federal government should not pay for abortions but also that picketing abortion clinics should be a federal crime. Similarly, the early weeks of the Clinton administration were plagued by the question of whether or not homosexuals should be allowed to serve in the armed forces. Already divisive at the local level, the issue of distributing condoms to teenagers may yet show up on Capitol Hill. And what about guns in schoolrooms? Sexual harassment? Child abuse? This trend will have reached its logical endpoint when some Republican—Bob Dole, perhaps—proposes a Department of Family Values to replace one of the departments that will by then have been abolished. It will be interesting when this happens to witness the contortions that purport to reconcile these new federal responsibilities with greater reliance on state and local governments.

And so we come to the end of my examination of the causes of our complaints. As we have seen, all of them can be accounted for by the cumulative strains overloading our governmental structure and political system. Some of the factors contributing to overload, notably growth and complexity, are inexorable. Others—the weakening of conventions, for example—are stimulating counterattacks if not countertrends.

The resulting situation invites political quackery. When the quack exploits disenchantment with the democratic process itself, as did Ross Perot in 1992, his influence is especially noxious. If you had taken Perot seriously, you would have concluded that most of what ails us is a result of congressional incompetence, lethargy, or venality. According to the opinion polls, this view is widely shared. By any objective standard, it is wrong. Person for person and pound for pound, Congress is as good or better today than ever before in my political lifetime. I base that opinion, moreover, not only on more than forty years of direct exposure to the workings of Congress but also on the concurring opinions of the two best-informed and most fair-minded observers I know—David Broder, the *Washington Post*'s senior political reporter, and Norman Ornstein, resident scholar at the American Enterprise Institute.

Try to imagine what it's like to be in Congress nowadays. Picture the politician sitting under a bright light in the center of a circle. A hundred people, every one of whom represents an interest seeking congressional support, are seated in the semidarkness around the edge of the circle. For any one of the hundred, the others barely exist. Each judges the politician solely on the basis of the latter's responsiveness to his or her special interest. None, therefore, can understand how the congressperson could in good faith support a position inconsistent with his or her own.

This picture is, of course, starkly simplified. I only wish it were also greatly exaggerated. Unable to get across to one group of constituents the legitimacy of a competing group's claims or the necessity for compromise between them, the politician is quite literally caught in the middle. Despite never getting credit for courage or independence, the best of the breed call things as they see them anyway and accept the abuse as all in the day's work. The worst turn into vacillating calibrators of fluctuating public opinion. But even the good ones feel themselves under increasing pressure to serve up the simplistic solutions we so insistently demand.

Yet politics is still the most difficult of the arts and the noblest of the professions.[1] When I tell people this, they look at me as if to say, "You must be kidding!" Far from it. As to the difficulty of the art, consider for a

---

[1] I got this line from a speech by John Fischer, then editor of *Harper's*, sometime in the seventies.

moment what we expect of our politicians. We expect them to know everything, empathize with everyone, and reconcile our every clashing value, interest, or point of view. We expect them, moreover, to be more honest and more honorable than ourselves and never, never to say anything they wouldn't otherwise say just because we insist on their saying it. If they fail to meet any of these expectations, we feel a special rush of self-righteousness in denouncing their perfidy.

As to the nobility of the profession, it should be sufficient to point out that its task is to resolve difficult, hard-fought public issues in a way that serves the best interests of the society as a whole. Of course, no politician (not even the president) can deal with all of these interests. But neither does any one doctor or lawyer deal with every kind of medical or legal problem. Those professions, nevertheless, embrace the whole of medicine or the whole of law. Just so must the profession of politics embrace every kind of public interest. The preamble to the U.S. Constitution says it all: "We the people, in order to form a more perfect Union, establish justice, insure domestic tranquillity, provide for the common defense, promote the general welfare, and secure the blessings of liberty to ourselves and our posterity," have entrusted leadership to politicians. What calling could be nobler?

History is a game of inches. In the course of two centuries the American system has pulled off a lot of big plays. During that time the political process has adjusted to pressures that its designers could not have imagined. But what's past is the prologue to change as well as continuity. The longer we indulge unrealistic expectations, the more concerned we should be lest at some point they overwhelm our most precious institutions.

But my purpose is to prod, not to prophesy. If we can agree that democracy in America is threatened, we can agree that something should be done about it. As Lincoln said in the opening sentence of his "house divided" speech, "If we could first know where we are, and *whither* we are tending, we could then better judge *what* to do, and *how* to do it." I am trying to make clear where I think we are and whither we are tending. The question of what to do and how to do it comes next. In my view, the essential first step is to let the politicians know that we're ready to give our wholehearted support to those among them who will define our genuinely serious problems and approach their solutions in a clear, balanced, and objective way. But how should the message be delivered?

This was a question I had been thinking about for quite a while when, on a memorable day in January 1992, I had a flash of inspiration. Why hadn't I thought of it before? I would start a new grass-roots national organization called the "Cut the Crap Club." The CCC's mission would be to create a new spirit of free, open, and honest communication between the citizen and the politician. Its motto would be addressed to the politicians but speak for its members: If you level with us, we promise to level with ourselves.

January 1992, the beginning of a presidential election year, was the perfect time to launch the Cut the Crap Club. Only half-seriously, I tried the idea out on a number of savvy people. Every one of them enthusiastically volunteered to be a charter member. None doubted that we could easily sign up enormous numbers of our fellow citizens. Just think! Having emancipated itself from simplistic slogans, the CCC could give a real boost to political leaders committed to shaping workable strategies and reducing excessive expectations.

You know, of course, that the project did not get off the ground. Had it done so, you would certainly have heard a lot about the CCC and would very likely be a member. But ever since 1992, whenever another slick substitute for a genuine remedy is taken seriously, I feel a new pang of regret that I did not drop everything else and devote my entire energies to launching the CCC. For me it's too late, but perhaps someone else will pick up the idea. Meanwhile, if enough of us make our own individual pledge to cut the crap, we can set in motion a realistic effort to reduce overload. The necessary means fall under five headings: setting priorities, simplification, devolution, termination, and privatization.

Logically enough, priorities come first. Two very different but mutually reinforcing considerations underlie the necessity for setting them. One is that the resources that could effectively be devoted to dealing with our most serious problems will not solve any problem if they are spread across the whole array. The other is that the essential participants in the democratic process can engage in a fruitful exchange only if they are able to stick to a manageable number of important subjects.

But priorities don't just lie around out there waiting to be discovered. The process of setting them has to take as its raw material the interconnected whole in which deficient education, racial tension, and a growing gap between rich and poor coexist with symphony orchestras, stock exchanges, and the Internet. This process must also reckon with people's hopes, fears, illusions, values, beliefs, and conflicts as they are. From this teeming, discordant, heterogeneous agglomeration there must be extracted those combinations of elements that constitute separate and significant "problems." The problems thus identified can then be assessed in terms of their relative urgency, the probable effectiveness of the potential means of dealing with them, the comparative benefit to society of successful solutions, and the availability of the necessary resources. From these assessments priorities will emerge. Among these priorities will be some that are so intractable or so costly to deal with as to be incapable of yielding a workable approach. These can be put aside. But the problems thus deferred will not go away, and the effort to find workable approaches must not be abandoned.

And how can all this be done? That's a question we'll come to soon. Meanwhile, let's assume that it has been possible to achieve consensus on seven or eight top priorities. These can then be the subject of a focused public dialogue. True, the continuity of broad participation in the dialogue will often be interrupted by fast-breaking developments in the news: an international crisis, a bombing, a scandal, an assassination, or a natural disaster. But even in the intervals when public attention is distracted, the most concerned groups, both governmental and nongovernmental, can continue their essential though unnoticed work. As to the many serious problems that did not make the priority list, the best way of keeping them from elbowing their way into the national dialogue would be to reduce their claims for attention. Simplification, decentralization, termination, and privatization are all means to this end.

In the case of simplification, much can be done by clarifying objectives, condensing regulations, and scrapping excessive reporting requirements. Many of Vice President Gore's recommendations are relevant here. So too even now is the approach taken in 1972 to the radical simplification of HEW programs. Put forward in a two-hundred-page paper entitled "Comprehensive HEW Simplification and Reform" but aptly renamed "the Mega Proposal," it would have reduced the total number of HEW programs from over three hundred to about ninety and divided the ninety into three broadly defined groups (financial assistance to individuals, financial assistance to state and local governments, and building the capacity of human services agencies). One of its components would have replaced all other forms of federal aid to presecondary education with federal support for student assistance; another would have cut the number of service-development agencies from forty-seven to five. The plan would thus both have reduced the number of decisions that had to be submitted to successive layers of government and made the decision-making process more accessible to interested citizens. My keenest regret on going from HEW to Defense was having to leave the Mega Proposal on the launching pad.

Devolution enables the federal government to shorten its agenda by turning over (or turning back) to the states functions which in any case only support activities for which the states have primary responsibility. This is not a new idea. The Eisenhower administration mounted an ambitious effort to do just this under the auspices of a high-level group called the Federal-State Action Committee. By comparison with today, of course, the federal government had only a handful of comparatively few functions eligible for return to the states. Congress, moreover, still eager to show the folks back home what it had done for them lately, was unenthusiastic.

One of the Federal-State Action Committee's first concrete proposals sought to induce the states to take over the federal waste-treatment construction program in return for a share of the excise tax on telephone calls. The Senate Public Works Committee held a hearing on this proposal chaired by Senator Robert Kerr of Oklahoma. I was the administration witness. At the close of my testimony the chairman said, "Mr. Secretary, you sound to me like a young lawyer sent by his firm to plead a hopeless cause. I suggest you go back to the other end of Pennsylvania Avenue and remind those who sent you here of the inscription on the monument to the Greek soldiers slain at Thermopylae: 'Stranger who passeth by, go ye and tell the Athenians that we lie here obedient to their command.' "

There is no reason in principle why reliance on the federal tax base to equalize the capability of state and local governments should carry with it a requirement of strict accountability for exactly how the money is used. As long ago as 1967, in fact, I gave a lecture on federal-state relations at the University of Chicago making this argument in support of general revenue sharing. Equalization is also part of the justification for block grants targeted toward a particular national concern that might not otherwise be adequately addressed. It is, however, impossible to make sure that a block grant will be effectively applied. In the case, for example, of Job Training Partnership Act block grants, half of the money has often been absorbed by state and local administrative costs while the other half has gone into marginal projects. Hence, the greater the national interest in stimulating state and local action, the more compelling the need for specific conditions on the manner in which federal funds are applied. It thus seems anomalous that, at a time of fiscal stringency, "conservatives" should be so eager to get rid of federal oversight of state and local performance that we taxpayers will be left with no way of knowing whether or not our money has in fact advanced a national interest.

More radical than devolution, terminating federal programs, like pulling up weeds, clears space for more valuable growth. As the most clear-cut way of shrinking the federal agenda, it has the advantage of making it unnecessary to ask somebody else to pick up the pieces. Since, however, it leaves the "unmet need," whatever it was, still unmet, it is important to distinguish among several different ways of justifying or carrying out the termination of a federal program. It can be done (over the dead bodies of the program's votaries) for the simple reason that the program is not effective. It can be done through the impersonal application of a "sunset law" (an automatic cutoff that takes effect after a given number of years) when the evidence that the program continues to serve a significant purpose is no longer persuasive. And sometimes it is done for the simple reason that we're no longer willing to pay the program's cost. Skillfully employed, budget cutting can, like the pruning of a tree, eliminate the weakest programs. It's too bad, though, that, having neglected for a decade and a half to keep the deficit under control, we have now resorted to hacking away at it with a clumsy assortment of blunt tools.

And then there is privatization—turning over to for-profit entities functions heretofore in the hands of government. For countries like Russia or China, which, under the spell of socialist dogma, relied on government-owned entities to produce goods and services, this is an important—indeed, as Deng and Gorbachev discovered, essential—means of escaping economic stagnation. But for the United States, which has always preferred to protect the public interest by regulation rather than by public ownership, there aren't many significant opportunities to reduce government's role through the divestiture of government functions. The few worth considering—air-traffic control, perhaps, or tax collection—are so much imbued with the public interest (they would not otherwise have remained so long in government hands) that the turnover would inevitably be accompanied by an overlay of regulatory oversight so thick as to accomplish little by way of reducing the burden on government.

On a less significant scale there are, of course, any number of opportunities to do by contract what is now being done by a government agency. In order to stay within employment ceilings, a great many functions that used to be performed by government have already been farmed out to "Beltway bandits." While this can sometimes save money because most of the work is done by temporary employees with lower pay and benefits than civil servants, the quality of the work may also be lower. It's not at all apparent, therefore, that the public interest is better served by this kind of "privatization." It is, in any case, the government agency that selects the contract or remains accountable to the public for the contractor's performance. For example, in the case of the "privatization" of prisons, the aim of saving money conflicts with the aim of reducing recidivism. It is essential, moreover, not only that there be enough qualified providers to assure serious competition but also that the government panel have adequate capacity to monitor the contractor's performance.

The remedies for overload I've just finished summarizing are the best I know of. Indeed, they're the only ones. But it's one thing to prescribe and quite another to get the prescription followed. And where carrying out the indicated regime requires the concurrence and support of an entire nation, it is impossible to be confident that anything will really change. I have thus reluctantly been forced to the conclusion that there is only one way of making it happen. It is through strong and effective leadership.

Whenever in the past this nation has urgently needed such leadership, it has somehow materialized. In the cause of independence, we had Washington (surely one of the greatest natural leaders who ever lived); in holding the Union together, Lincoln; in combating the Great Depression, Roosevelt; in containing communism, Truman. But these highly visible demonstrations of leadership came in times of crisis. Throughout most of our history an unobtrusive approach has sufficed. The model is Eisenhower, a strong and decisive leader whose "hidden hand" presidency was exactly suited to the needs of the time.[8] For all the reasons I've been describing, however, we are now at the point where continuous out-front leadership has become all but indispensable to the workability of the system. And not even this will be adequate unless overload has been reduced to the maximum feasible extent.

That we have reached this degree of dependency on leadership is not for me a welcome thought. Two things about it bother me. One is that there is no conceivable way of making sure that our way of selecting presidents and vice presidents will come up with outstanding leaders. The other is that to be obliged to lean so heavily on one person goes against the grain of our democratic tradition. I'm somewhat reassured, nevertheless, by some offsetting considerations. For one thing, the kind of leadership that is now most needed doesn't demand extraordinary gifts. An individual endowed with the energy, commitment, and intelligence it takes to get to the White House is likely to be able to give this kind of leadership provided that he—how soon she?—clearly understands its requirements. It is also reassuring to bear in mind that in a democracy successful leadership does not rest on authority but on the ability to enlist public support. Rather, therefore, than being a threat to democracy, leadership can be a builder of it.

What, then, are the requirements I'm talking about? My views on this question began to take form in 1980 when I was President Carter's special representative for the United Nations Conference on the Law of the Sea. Like most people at that time I saw Jimmy Carter as a conscientious, highly intelligent man with a deep commitment to the welfare and security of his fellow citizens. Why, then, had he not been more successful? Carter's problem, I concluded, was that he had immersed himself so deeply in the details of a host of worthy causes that he found it impossible to establish clear priorities among them. But of course you can't set priorities without making choices, and you can't fulfill priorities without formulating workable strategies. And none of the above is possible without establishing and communicating goals. If, on the other hand, you get the sequence right, you can set in motion a self-reinforcing cycle that will create consensus and build support.

---

[8] Fred I. Greenstein, *The Hidden-Hand Presidency: Eisenhower As Leader* (New York: Basic Books, 1982).

Describing this self-reinforcing cycle to a friend, I put it in graphic form on the back of an envelope like so:

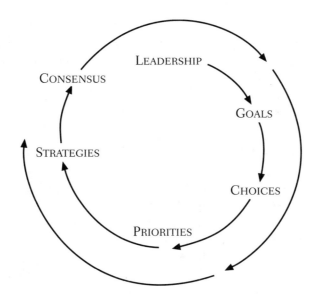

Here, plainly displayed, are the requirements of democratic leadership. It is, I hope, apparent why goals come first. As Casey Stengel—or was it Yogi Berra?—is supposed to have said, "If you don't know where you're going, you might end up somewhere else."

Since I first came up with that chart it has struck me that I should perhaps have put VISION before GOALS. Vision, after all, is essential to the projection of goals. In this connection I will never forget a meeting in 1987 with Deng Xiaoping. Then eighty-three, he was still in full control of China's policies. He described a vision for the future of China that embraced a decentralized, market-driven economy, a continually improving standard of living, and progressively more democratic political institutions, all moving forward together step by step. Although greatly impressed by the clarity of this vision, I was struck even more by the intensity of his determination to make it so tangible and so indelible that the Chinese people would continue to be inspired by it long after he was gone.

It would be hard to think of a sharper contrast than George Bush's disparaging reference to "the vision thing." As it happened, an invitation to speak to the Rotary Club of Lexington, Kentucky, gave me quite convincing evidence of President Bush's disinclination to form and communicate his own vision for the future. My assigned topic was an assessment of the new president's first seventy days in office. I gave high marks to his performance to date. Then, drawing on some of the same thoughts restated here, I went on to say that by early summer he would need to begin to project his goals and priorities.

When I got back to Washington, I decided that I should try to make sure that the White House was thinking along the same lines. With this in mind, I sent a copy of my Lexington speech outline to John Sununu, then the president's chief of staff. A covering note called attention to the relevant paragraphs and suggested that it might be worthwhile for us to discuss the subject. I met instead with an assistant to Sununu. A few days later I ran into a senior presidential adviser and told him what had happened. He said, "Never mind, Elliot. It wouldn't have made any difference even if you'd seen the president himself. He just doesn't think that way."

Right there, I think, is a sufficient explanation of why George Bush did not win a second term. But even a leader who does have vision and who has translated this vision into goals may still be predisposed to avoid a rigorous examination of their costs or their compatibility. The longer he can defer choosing among his goals those that are the most important and attainable, the longer he can delay having to disappoint any interested group. But choice is necessary to setting priorities, and priorities are necessary both to a manageable dialogue and to the rational allocation of resources. As to how a coherent set of priorities can be arrived at—the question I said we'd be coming to soon—the answer is: only through a White House–directed process drawing on all the resources of the executive branch. But if the final product is to be fully convincing, the impress of presidential leadership is crucial.

A president who has the realism and courage to choose priorities can count on having to face another difficult task—that of shaping cost-effective strategies for carrying them out. In the national context, a strategy has a twofold purpose. In addition to being a plan by which to get there from here, it should also be perceived and used as a framework for a second stage in the national dialogue. (The first addresses priorities.)

For the president, expounding his strategy provides opportunities both to explain the things he seeks to accomplish and to obtain constructive ideas as to how to make his plans more acceptable or more workable. But flexibility of method presupposes consistency of purpose. The leader who keeps altering course with every change of public mood or who will not persist in the pursuit of his goals is not a leader at all.

Throughout the sequence from goals through choices to priorities and strategies, the president must be the orchestrator as well as the conductor of a process of political give and take that will, if successful, lead to consensus. Drawing on that consensus, he gains augmented strength. And while it is impossible for even the most successful leader to sustain this momentum throughout an entire political agenda, the chances of his doing so get better at every stage so long as integrity of purpose and honesty in facing the facts are consistently and tenaciously maintained. This is the most important contribution to the viability of the democratic process that effective leadership can make.

Judged by these standards, Bill Clinton's presidency has been a disappointment. While he has from time to time articulated goals that could have been translated into clear priorities and made the subject of coherent strategies, the goals themselves have all too visibly been the product of constant recalculation and modification in response to day-by-day and week-by-week political developments. In these respects the contrast between Clinton and Reagan could hardly be sharper.

At first I thought that Clinton's performance might be accounted for by his lack of previous exposure to the scale, complexity, and pressure of the White House. Indeed, the one Ross Perot utterance in the 1992 campaign that rang a bell with me was his remark that governing a small state was no better preparation for leading the nation than running a small store would be for managing Wal-Mart. By the end of his third year in office it was clear that there had to be a deeper-lying explanation. I now think that what we have been seeing is a consequence of Clinton's immersion in the competitive, tactical side of politics for virtually his entire adult life. By the time he entered the White House he had become a compulsive politician in that sense, and no matter how objectively demonstrable is the need for the kind of leadership described above, he simply has not been able to break himself of this compulsive behavior. If he wins a second term, the combination of the Twenty-second Amendment's two-term limit and an eye toward the verdict of history may yet break him of this habit. He has the heart and mind to be an outstanding president. All he needs is the perspective.

But there can be no leadership without followership; to give birth to any good result there must be a coupling between the two. And here we come back to our point of departure. We the people are not now doing our part, and we are not likely to do so until we stop rewarding politicians for promising us whatever we think we want rather than for telling it like it is. Instead of letting it appear that we would prefer not to have to face unwanted facts, we must let it be known that we're ready for them; instead of making irreconcilable demands without recognizing their inconsistency, we must accept the impossibility of having it both ways.

We can fulfill the responsibilities of citizenship. No supreme sacrifices are called for; no transformation of humans into angels. Our obligations to ourselves, to our families, and to our communities are compatible with these responsibilities. It is to be expected that we will, as necessary, pursue our and their interests. All that is required to make the system workable is a mere change of attitude. The cynics are always wrong. Why not, then, try realism?

Public Service

We Americans regard everyone on a public payroll, from the president on down, as working for us. We're right to do so because those of our fellow citizens who perform governmental functions do so by virtue of powers we have entrusted to them. They must accordingly be responsive as well as accountable to us, and their actions must be open to our scrutiny. If they don't measure up, we terminate their employment. This, in fact, is a way of describing our version of democracy.

The character of public service in the United States owes much to these attitudes. Fortunately, they show no signs of weakening. We do, however, push too far our tendency to think of a public servant as a servant. Even a person who is above looking down on servants seldom looks up to them. Indeed, we're inclined to feel that they should be grateful for the privilege of working for us. And it goes without saying that I'm hard to convince that anyone who works for me should be paid more than I am.

For the American people, as for any employer, the most desirable attributes in a servant are competence and loyalty. Competence is achieved through experience and grows with time on the job. Loyalty attaches to a leader, a party, or a principle. When these are changed with a change of administration, a certain tension between competence and loyalty is inevitable. Just as a professional who stays on from one administration to the next cannot be expected to become a true believer in both, so the loyalist newly brought on board cannot be expected to possess the savvy of an old hand. After each election the permanent government needs time to adjust to changes in the will of the people. The newcomers need time to find out how the system works. The greater the emphasis on democratic values, the greater the pressure to bring in new people. The greater the emphasis on competence, the greater the resistance to that pressure.

All this was demonstrated in the campaign that elected Andrew Jackson in 1828. It was the first to involve a grass-roots party organization. It was also the first in which ordinary people had a stronger voice than the men of property who until then had dominated the electoral process. The principal builders of the then new Democratic Party were a group of New York politicians known as the Albany Regency. Led by Martin Van Buren, they were strong believers in democracy. They saw the redistribution of federal offices as a way of breaking the hold of old ideas and established interests. Bringing in new people, they argued, would help to restore the people's faith in government while at the same time creating an incentive to work for the party. Senator William L. Marcy, one of the leaders of the Albany Regency, defended this policy against an attack by Senator Henry Clay. The politicians of New York, Marcy declared, "see nothing wrong in the rule that to the victor belong the spoils of the enemy."

That remark gave a name to a practice already well established at the state level when Jackson took office. He was the first president, however, to apply the "spoils system" to federal appointments. Why not, after all? As he pointed out in a message to Congress, "the duties of all public offices are . . . so plain and simple that men of intelligence may readily qualify themselves for their performance. . . ." In fact, many of the officeholders evicted by the spoils system were able and honest; some of those it brought in were incompetent or corrupt. Abuse of the spoils system would in time give the term a venal connotation. In *The Age of Jackson,* Arthur M. Schlesinger, Jr., delivered a more balanced assessment:

There can be small doubt today that, whatever evils it brought into American life, its historical function was to narrow the gap between the people and the government—to expand popular participation in the workings of democracy.

The Jacksonians emphasized the link between political loyalty and responsiveness to democracy while minimizing the need for competence. At least tacitly, however, they recognized that experience did in fact have value. Of the 612 presidential appointees on the federal payroll when he took office, Jackson removed only 252. Still, as the country grew and with it the size of the government, coping with the spoils system became a chore. Abraham Lincoln could not have been feeling greatly indebted to Jackson when, a little more than thirty years later, he complained that the government was in danger of "falling a prey to the rapacity of the office-seeking class." For every job he gave out he created ten enemies and one ingrate.

As the nation grew and prospered, the number of public jobs rose less rapidly than the proportion of those jobs for which basic intelligence was not a sufficient qualification. The government had an increasing need for doctors, naval architects, chemists, statisticians, lawyers, and other specialists. In 1883 Congress finally yielded to the demand for civil service reform and passed a law "classifying" certain government positions and reserving them for the winners of competitive examinations administered by the Civil Service Commission. Although in the beginning only about 10 percent of federal jobs were classified, now all but a tiny fraction of federal employees are covered by some form of merit system.

But the spirit of the Jacksonian era still lives. We see it now in the determination of modern presidents to impose their philosophies, their policies, and their promises on the permanent government. They do so through putting their own people in key positions. Not counting ambassadors, U.S. attorneys, or U.S. marshals, upward of three thousand jobs change hands when a new president takes office. (More accurately, three thousand people leave; it can take months—over a year sometimes—to put their successors in place.) Although recent turnovers have been twelve times larger than Jackson's, no one mentions the spoils system anymore. This, no doubt, is primarily because the job changes involve such a small percentage of today's nearly three million federal employees, but it may also owe something to general awareness that appointees to senior positions go through an inquisition considerably tougher in its own way than a civil service test.

These periodic purges are a clear example of the shaping of public service in the United States by the American experience. In the other leading industrial democracies fewer than one hundred jobs change hands as the result of a change of government. This is the case, moreover, notwithstanding that a parliamentary election can bring about much more radical redirection of policy than occurs when control of the White House shifts from one broad-based coalition to the other. The British election of 1979, for example, replaced a Labour-dominated socialist government with a right-wing Conservative government. Margaret Thatcher, nevertheless, kept on as her cabinet secretary the same man, Robert Armstrong, who held the position under her predecessor, Jim Callaghan. Altogether, Mrs. Thatcher brought to No. 10 Downing Street only about half a dozen of her own people. When Bill Clinton took office, he replaced George Bush's entire White House staff of 461 with 419 new people of his own.

In the United States, a new presidential administration has discretion over three thousand federal government jobs; nearly half of these are the most interesting, rewarding, and challenging positions the federal government has to offer. As of January 1, 1996, these included 547 filled by the president with the advice and consent of the Senate ("PAS positions"), 110 filled by the president but not subject to Senate confirmation, and 670 noncareer senior executive service positions filled by agency heads. The remaining 1,647 are holders of "Schedule C" policy-related jobs. In a U.S. cabinet department a change of government sweeps out everyone in the top three echelons—the secretary and deputy secretary, several under secretaries, and all the assistant secretaries. A large number of deputy assistant secretaries are also replaced.

The submergence of this country's civil servants beneath several politically appointive layers is one reason why they have never been accorded the prestige enjoyed by their counterparts in the United Kingdom, Germany, France, and Japan. In a British cabinet-level department a new government replaces only the minister and three to six junior ministers, all MPs. The newcomers find in place a solid pyramid of civil servants headed by the permanent under secretary. No career position in the United States possesses comparable power and prestige.

Known collectively as "the mandarins" after the survivors of imperial China's even more Darwinian civil service system, Great Britain's permanent under secretaries meet frequently to coordinate policy, resolve turf battles, and devise means of preventing their political masters from making other than deliberate mistakes. When at the age of sixty they are obliged to retire, they can count on a good job—master of a college, nonexecutive chairman of a corporate board, or head of a large public charity. Many are knighted and some go to the House of Lords as life peers. Robert Armstrong is now Lord Armstrong of Ilminster.

The Japanese counterparts of the British mandarins retire at fifty-five and routinely go on to a well-paid position in a business or trade association under the purview of the ministry in which they served. Known as "the descent from heaven," this practice so often leads to a post with a big company that it was considered newsworthy last year when a retired vice minister of posts and telecommunications became the CEO of a relatively small telephone company instead of a senior officer in one of Japan's telecommunications giants.

The other leading democracies are societies in which the powers of government derive from the sovereign rather than the people. In those societies loyal service to the crown was a ladder to a level of power and prestige not otherwise attainable by a person, however talented and energetic, who had no prospect of inheriting wealth or status. The traditions thereby developed are still very much alive. Oxford and Cambridge remain the most important incubators of Great Britain's career services. Although not established until soon after World War II, the École Nationale d'Administration has from the outset attracted many of the most brilliant graduates of French postsecondary institutions. In Japan, where competition for entrance to any of the top universities is feverish, admission to the University of Tokyo is the *ascent* to heaven. Of the twenty-five top-ranking students graduating each year from the University of Tokyo, the Ministry of Finance and the Ministry of Trade and Industry still manage to skim off eighteen or twenty.

From our standpoint, the ability of these and other countries to attract talented young people into public service year after year is both admirable and enviable. The downside, however, is that some of the best and brightest, conscious of being a true elite, acquire a condescending attitude toward mere politicians. They can even on occasion display impatience with the democratic process itself. The BBC's witty TV series *Yes,*

Minister, devastatingly satirized this tendency. Featuring Nigel Hawthorne in the role of a conniving cabinet secretary who shamelessly manipulates his well-meaning political chief, the program had a devoted following.

Japan has its own real-life version of *Yes, Minister.* When, in October 1993, Prime Minister Morihiro Hosokawa's coalition government floated a proposal to transfer a modest share of decisionmaking power from the bureaucracy to politicians, the ministerial bureaucrats did not take it lying down. The *Nikkei Weekly,* which is published in the United States by Japan's leading business journal, reported that they held a secret strategy session to discuss ways of counteracting the government's plan. The *Weekly* quoted a senior official as asking, "'How can inexperienced politicians make practical policies? . . . If politicians begin interfering with our policymaking processes, they'll soon start meddling in our personnel management affairs.'"[1] Given much more of this, how long will it be before a Japanese prime minister takes his cue from Senator Marcy?

But Japan's need to deflate the status of its bureaucracy cannot be more urgent than our need to inflate the status of our own. We badly require better-motivated, better-trained, and better-qualified public servants, and this requirement will continue to grow as far ahead as we can see. Our political system is already confronted by excessive demands. Serious new problems that only the government can deal with continue to multiply. Government's attempt to do this while handling its existing responsibilities adds to its top-heaviness and distances it from popular understanding and control. How successfully these tendencies are combated will depend crucially on the knowledge, skill, and ingenuity of the civil servants who shape and administer the necessary remedial actions.

The urgency of recruiting and retaining outstanding people for the American government's career services is clear. The evidence as to how we're doing is less conclusive. Yet such indications as we have are not encouraging. One disturbing sign is the contrast between the attractiveness of career public service to young people in our sister democracies and its lack of appeal to their contemporaries in this country.

In 1987 the National Commission on the Public Service, chaired by Paul Volcker, asked Harvard president Derek Bok to head a task force on education and training for the public service. The task force compiled

---

[1] *Nikkei Weekly,* January 10, 1994, pp. 1, 5.

the results of half a dozen surveys pointing to declines in student interest in public service and in the academic records of students recently recruited by federal agencies. The commission's own survey of top graduates found that they did not perceive public service as an occupation in which talented people could get ahead. Eighty-six percent thought that a federal job would not allow them to use their abilities to the fullest. Even Harvard's Kennedy School of Government, whose mission is to educate for public service, found that only 20 percent of its master of public policy graduates had jobs in any part of the federal government, including the legislative branch.

Disturbing though these findings are, two considerations suggest that the situation may be at least partially remediable. For one thing, the same surveys showed that the respondents attached high importance to making money. This could mean that their profession of distaste for public service may be a rationalization for reluctance to accept its financial limitations. For another thing, the surveys expose a remarkable lack of awareness that the challenges of public service can more than fully engage the highest level of ability. It follows that an effectively targeted campaign should be able to highlight the nonpecuniary rewards of public service and create greater awareness of its challenging character and content.

At that time, according to the survey, the government's weak gestures toward recruitment were not even coming close to these targets. On the task force's recommendation the Volcker Commission urged the government to launch an aggressive and imaginative assault on the deficiencies of its recruitment and hiring practices. The commission also proposed a Presidential Public Service Scholarship Program aimed at a thousand students each year, the strengthening of programs for attracting college graduates into public careers, and expansion of the Presidential Management Internship Program from four hundred to a thousand positions per year.

But there's more to public service than an intellectual challenge. In talking with students, I always tell them that what government people at any given level do matters more and has more social impact than what business people at a comparable level do. What business people do is good for the management and the stockholders, and sometimes, if they're lucky, for all the customers as well. A public servant's day-to-day role can affect the well-being, the survival even, of millions of people. Other factors, however, have weakened the force of this appeal. Public service is losing its attraction even for the most senior ranks of the civil service. The Volcker Commission reported that between 1979, when the Senior Executive Service was created, and 1985, 52 percent of its original members had left. Since then the number of senior executives who choose to leave government service before normal retirement age has become even more disturbing. In 1994, nearly 10 percent of them resigned or retired.

While there are, of course, many contributors to these trends, I'm convinced that one of the most important has been the shrinkage of opportunities at the top. FDR's administration in 1933 had only seventy-one Senate-confirmed presidential appointees; by 1960 Eisenhower's had around two hundred. The president had the benefit of direct advice from professionals in the Bureau of the Budget as well as his political advisers. In those administrations, moreover, it was easy to involve senior civil servants in high-level policy discussions. Most political appointees had functional rather than program-related roles. As one of ten PAS appointees at HEW in the late fifties, I had across-the-board responsibility for legislation. This assignment gave me both the need and the opportunity to stay in close touch with senior career people throughout the department.

In 1980 HEW was split into two departments (the Department of Education and the Department of Health and Human Services) which between them now have forty-one assistant secretaries or the equivalent, each of whom is surrounded by a cluster of Schedule-C political appointees. Similar increases have occurred throughout the government. The numbers and the layering get in the way of the departmental leadership's access to the expertise, institutional memory, and candid advice of their career colleagues. A parallel consequence has been to restrict the permanent staff's opportunities to broaden their perspective on policy issues. As Hugh Heclo has well said:

> When careerists are denied access to an understanding of the political rationales for top-level decision-making, they inevitably become divorced from the "big picture" and incapable of communicating it to subordinates.[2]

---

[2] Hugh Heclo, "The In-and-Outer System: A Critical Assessment," in *The In-and-Outers*, ed. G. Calvin Mackenzie (Baltimore: Johns Hopkins University Press, 1987), p. 202.

The result of these developments has been to diminish both the job satisfaction of a public-service career and the career services' value to the political appointees to whom they report.

An additional factor reducing the appeal of a career in government has been political encroachment on the fourth-echelon positions previously reserved for career people. Carrying the title of deputy assistant secretary or the equivalent, these positions may not look impressive from the outside. In fact, almost any job at that level can have a wider impact on the national interest than all but a few senior corporate positions. In the State Department a deputy assistant secretary was until recently responsible for all of Southeast Asia. In the Commerce Department, a deputy assistant secretary was in charge of export controls. A deputy assistant attorney general headed the war against organized crime. Comparable responsibilities belonged to every similar position throughout the federal government.

Since the mid-80s these and other comparable roles have been converted into new PAS positions, thereby placing them out of the reach of career people. And though each such position has its own quota of deputies, the number of those slots to which a career person can aspire has been contracting, diminished by their diversion to deserving Reaganites, true-blue Bush supporters, or friends of Bill. Worse, the political appointees chosen to fill the preempted positions have often been minimally qualified. Since these are concededly fourth-echelon slots, a White House personnel assistant sees them as ideal rewards for fourth-echelon political types—a campaign advance man, for instance, or a regional political organizer. For a senior civil servant who has spent twenty or thirty years preparing for a high-level position that has always been held by a career person, it can't help but be irksome to see it given to an outsider. It becomes especially so when the outsider doesn't know the difference between an audit exception and an authorizing bill.

But, you may say, to complain about this is to emphasize competence at the expense of loyalty. The president and his department heads need key subordinates who can be counted upon to pursue the administration's goals and priorities. Moreover, there has been a steady and inexorable increase in the number, difficulty, and complexity of programs for which political leadership is needed. These are both valid points. It does not follow, however, that interposing additional layers of political appointees will meet these needs. On the contrary, the result can be to promote delay, confuse lines of communication, augment the likelihood of mixed signals, and exacerbate turf battles. People are much more disturbed nowadays by what they think of as a lack of performance than by a lack of responsiveness to political leadership. In any case, the number of cabinet and subcabinet appointees has escalated far more rapidly than the expansion of government programs. It went from 73 to 152 between 1933 and 1965 during a period of rapid expansion in governmental responsibilities. Between 1965 and 1989, while federal civilian employment held steady, it shot up to 573, almost four times the 1965 level.

As early as 1978 Fred Malek, who worked with me at HEW and later became director of the Office of Presidential Personnel in the Nixon White House, foresaw the negative consequences of this trend:

> Layering the civil service with even more political appointees would only serve to widen the gulf between the chiefs and the Indians, robbing the career executives of an opportunity to carry out many of the more demanding jobs in the government, weakening the attraction of civil service, and reducing the incentive of the best career people to remain in government.

He concluded that the optimum balance between the number of career and noncareer appointments "should be struck in favor of fewer political appointees, not more."[3]

In 1989 the Volcker Commission's task force on the relations between political appointees and career executives came to the same conclusion. Fred Malek was a member of this group and I was its chairman.[4] The Volcker Commission endorsed our recommendation for a reduction in the number of presidential appointees from three thousand to no more than two thousand. The proposal caused a mild stir at the time but went nowhere—hardly surprising, perhaps, considering that it came out just when George Bush got his first chance to reward his own loyalists.

---

[3] Frederic V. Malek, *Washington's Hidden Tragedy* (New York: The Free Press, 1987), pp. 102–3.

[4] The other members were Robert McFarlane, Walter Mondale, Benjamin Read, Anne Wexler, and Alan Wolff. The project director was Professor James P. Pfiffner of George Mason University.

For a new president's principal appointments, the interval between inauguration and confirmation has risen from 2.4 months under Kennedy to 8.5 months under Clinton. Think how much better Bill Clinton's recruitment record might have been if he'd had only two-thirds as many jobs to fill!

In addition to diminishing the attractiveness of government service, the ballooning of political appointments has magnified the suspicion that career people are not to be trusted to give full and loyal support to their political superiors. When I became Secretary of Health, Education, and Welfare in 1970, the *Washington Post* ran a cartoon by Oliphant depicting a cluster of slimy-looking males beckoning me to my new desk. Their spokesman is saying, "Come in, sir! We represent the thousands on your staff. You'll find us petty, uncooperative, devious, unreliable, and thoroughly bureaucratic. Welcome!" It was a funny cartoon, and the assumption it reflected has, regrettably, been shared by all too many political appointees entering government service for the first time. Republicans in particular are prone to believe that senior civil servants lie awake at night scheming about how to sabotage the president's agenda in order to advance their own.

Having worked with most of the career services under five administrations, I can emphatically attest that this is not true. To the contrary, while many civil servants have ideas they are glad to put forward and would like to see adopted, they do not see themselves as performing a policymaking role. Indeed, they are just as often criticized for being too reluctant to stick their necks out or hurl themselves in the path of administration policy. They limit themselves instead to doing their jobs from day to day competently but unobtrusively while counting on periodic promotions. Why heroic gestures should be expected in circumstances where there is every reason to believe they will be futile has never been clear to me. When approached with distrust, they respond with reservation and sometimes with hostility, and the loser is the public interest. A successful relationship between political appointees and career public servants depends upon effective cooperation between political managers who know what they want to accomplish and experienced bureaucrats who know how to get things done.

Of course, not all civil servants are models of efficiency. As Alice Rivlin, then deputy director of the Office of Management and Budget, observed in 1994, "The federal government doesn't have a satisfactory way of reducing the number of poor performers." That is certainly true. It's also true that performance appraisals tend to be virtually meaningless. But then, the whole purpose of making it difficult to get rid of civil servants was to curb the spoils system, assure high standards of merit, and to reduce their vulnerability to improper influence. Here again the problem—so often the case—is one of balance. The critics, however, need to be reminded that much of what they most dislike about government—the complicated regulations, the red tape, and the costly layers of supervisors—is the direct consequence of distrust of government. In fact, the single greatest progenitor of these bureaucratic excrescences is the belief that government agencies are rife with "waste, fraud, and abuse."

And let us not forget the legions of conscientious public servants in unglamorous roles who do their jobs well year after year. "Perhaps it is time," observed James MacGregor Burns in a *Washington Post* column a couple of years ago, "we looked on federal workers as just that—not punching bags, but fellow citizens working with us and for us in a national community." It should not have taken the Oklahoma City tragedy to remind their fellow citizens that Professor Burns is right—that civil servants are decent, hardworking, family-loving people like themselves.

This was the feeling about government employees I brought with me to the State Department in 1969 from my earlier experience at HEW. Although prepared to meet my foreign service colleagues more than halfway, I was somewhat put off by their reserve. Perhaps, I thought, it's just a product of skepticism toward a politician with scant background in foreign policy. I soon learned, however, that a lifted eyebrow, a suppressed smile, or a quick glance toward a colleague should be taken as my cue to ask a question. When I did, I invariably got an answer that supplied useful information, shed light on a relevant policy consideration, or brought to bear relevant experience. But why did I have to ask? Why wasn't the information volunteered as soon as its pertinence became apparent? The explanation, I concluded, had to be that these reticent professionals had too often encountered political appointees who did not think they had anything to learn from "the striped-pants set."

That first exposure to the foreign service and three subsequent State Department assignments have made me realize that the American people are fortunate in the high caliber of this country's career diplomats. Selected from a large pool of applicants, promoted pursuant to a rigorous review process, and subject in the later stages of their careers to a draconian up-or-out system, they are at least as good as any in the world. I've never known a time, though, when the foreign service was not in the throes of a morale crisis. At one time its focus was McCarthyism, at another an overhaul of the career structure, at still another a glut of senior officers. One factor, however, remains constant. This is the foreign service's perception—in my view too often justified—that its members are not adequately appreciated by the top brass.

Given this chronic state of affairs, why has the quality of the foreign service remained so high? Because, I think, it offers extraordinarily interesting careers. Where else can you get foreign-language training, travel widely, be exposed to other cultures, help to define and promote U.S. interests abroad, and have a role in coping with crises threatening peace and security? All that with a good shot as well at achieving the multifaceted role of ambassador. The responsibilities of U.S. leadership in an increasingly interdependent world are making the task of chief of mission more challenging than ever. Meanwhile, the false impression that modern telecommunications have turned ambassadors into glorified errand boys continues to produce nominees whose principal qualification is the generosity of their campaign contributions.

It's interesting, by the way, that tensions between political appointees and the career services are less acute in the Pentagon than in the State Department. One reason may be that laymen are more confident of their opinions on foreign policy than of their competence in military affairs. Complementing the Pentagon appointees' readiness to defer to military professionalism is the deeply ingrained military tradition of support for civilian leadership. When, as not infrequently happens, the secretary of a service department is a well-meaning front man without much grasp of substance, the service chief and his staff still do their considerable best to prop him up and make him look good.

Civil servants generally have had a tougher time of it lately than the foreign and military services. In addition to the other factors already mentioned, there is the discouraging reality that the buoyant days are gone when government was optimistically pressing ahead on many fronts. Our problems have turned out to be more deep-rooted and intractable than we used to think they were. Fiscal constraints are more restrictive. I'll never forget a remark made spontaneously by President-elect George Bush in the receiving line of a Christmas party at the vice president's house in 1988. The moment we shook hands he said, "This deficit is a bitch!" I thought I understood what he meant: with a brutal fiscal squeeze holding down existing programs, there would be little room for new initiatives.

Granted that throwing money at problems doesn't make them go away, it's not much fun to have to say no when money could make a difference. The plight of the homeless is a poignant example. The best of the career people at the Department of Housing and Urban Development know all too well how much more could be done to help the homeless if only the necessary funding could be found. They chose government service because for them helping people is more rewarding than making money. Not being able to meet more than a fraction of the needs they see is bound to be painful and frustrating. It is bound also to diminish the satisfaction of their jobs.

How different it was in the years of the Great Depression! For most people the thirties were the worst of times. With 25 percent of the workforce unemployed, the scale of human suffering then endured is almost unimaginable now. Yet for those engaged in administering relief measures, shaping social legislation, or carrying out regulatory reforms those were the best of times. The New Deal not only showed government as a positive force but also accomplished dramatic results. Some of its initiatives—the dole, debt relief, and the job programs—were intended only to be emergency measures, but they helped millions of people. Other innovations—Social Security, the minimum wage, unemployment compensation, the Securities and Exchange Commission, National Labor Relations Board, Tennessee Valley Authority, agricultural price supports, utilities regulations, and much more—have long been as integral to the national scene as the Capitol dome and the Washington Monument. Few people remember how bitterly these programs were resisted. For those in public service it was challenging, exciting, and deeply gratifying to have a role in those landmark achievements.

The combination at that time of highly rewarding opportunities in government and a scarcity of jobs in the private sector brought into public service an extraordinary influx of bright, able, and energetic young people. And hardly had the New Deal reforms been put in place when World War II thrust an entire generation into some form of public service. This conjunction of events assured that the two decades after the war would be great years for the U.S. career services. Those were years in which most of the senior positions were held by people who had gone to work for the government in the thirties or joined it soon after World War II.

Our own time, nevertheless, offers challenges to the career services that are as exciting in their own very different way as those of the Great Depression. Surmounting these challenges could be equally rewarding. They derive from demands on government that had already reached crisis proportions when the Clinton-Gore team took office. But to take full advantage of the career services' potential the president and his key advisers must first do their parts. They must set attainable goals, establish sound priorities, and shape workable strategies. How much can then be accomplished depends on the intelligent and imaginative use of limited political, managerial, and fiscal resources. And since these are exceedingly demanding tasks in which career people can and should be full partners, they offer the prospect of satisfaction no less rewarding than those of government's expansionary era.

To make the most of their opportunities civil servants must be able to grasp the full dimensions of the problems they are called upon to address and to assess the comparative advantages of various ways of dealing with them. They must also be able to cooperate with other federal agencies, create a synergistic relationship with state and local governments, work with nonprofit as well as for-profit entities in the private sector, maintain vigorous cost controls, motivate and inspire subordinates, and evaluate outcomes. These are the kinds of tasks that belong in the hands of career people. The wisdom, experience, talent, and skill that they can bring to bear will in large part determine how well those tasks are carried out.

In the can-do climate of the New Deal policymakers and program designers didn't worry about the risk that government intervention would have undesired side effects. More recent experience has taught (or should have taught) government managers that they must be alert to this possibility. To minimize it they need sophisticated understanding of the systemic relations affected by government action. Given a variety of tools ranging from tax incentives and regulatory mechanisms to matching grants and administrative sanctions, they must be able to select those best adapted to the task at hand. Our society can no longer afford the clumsiness, ignorance, or insensitivity that has so often in the past led to further intervention in order to correct the mistakes caused by the initial intervention.

There remain those, nevertheless, who still insist that the government has no need for career employees with abilities more than barely sufficient to meet its minimum and routine requirements. This view was expressed in a *Wall Street Journal* article several years ago by a former associate director of the Office of Personnel Management in the Reagan administration. "The government should be content," he wrote, "to hire competent people, not the best and most talented people." Indeed, the "best and brightest" should not work in government at all, but should instead be channeled into the private sector, where national wealth is created.[5] I'm reminded of the justification offered by Senator Roman Hruska, a Nebraska Republican, for the G. Harrold Carswell nomination in 1970: there are a lot of mediocre people in this country, and they're entitled to be represented on the Supreme Court by a mediocre justice.

This view, I hope, is not widely shared. In fact, the federal government urgently needs a new generation of gifted public servants like those who held key positions at HEW when I came there in 1957. They were all products of the New Deal–World War II era. Rufus Miles, who joined the government in 1936 as an assistant to the director of recruitment for the Civilian Conservation Corps, was the assistant secretary for administration. Robert Ball, who in 1939 joined the Bureau of Old Age and Survivors Insurance, was the deputy commissioner of Social Security. Mary Switzer, the director of vocational rehabilitation, began her public service as an assistant secretary for the Minimum Wage Board in 1921. My closest associate was the assistant general counsel for legislation, Reginald Conley, who joined the Federal Security Agency, the precedessor of HEW, as a young lawyer in 1937 and remained at HEW, except for a wartime stint with the War Manpower Commission, until his retirement in 1968.

Each of these individuals was a superb public servant. All of them would have been outstanding in a private-sector capacity. They also exemplified what it means to be a good bureaucrat. An oxymoron? No. A

---

[5] Terry W. Culler, *Wall Street Journal*, May 21, 1986, p. 32.

good bureaucrat is a manager who knows how to define and meet clear objectives within a large organizational framework—public or private—that is resistant to change and staffed by people who are not easy to remove. Lacking strong line authority, a good bureaucrat must be able to promote consensus and build cooperation. In carrying out the administration's policies, the good bureaucrat must be sensitive to the ideas and attitudes of Capitol Hill, the general public, the press, and the affected interest groups.

The notion that private-sector bureaucracies are invariably well run and efficient while government bureaucracies are invariably incompetent deserves to be knocked firmly on the head. In fact, two decades of the myopia and constipation of Big Steel and the Big Three automakers probably cost the United States more in jobs, exports, and GNP growth than all the failures of the federal bureaucracy in that period put together. Government agencies, on the other hand, can be and often are highly efficient. One of the best was the human resources division of the Office of Management and Budget during the time I was secretary of HEW. The division was headed by Paul O'Neill, a career public servant who later became deputy director of OMB under President Ford. On leaving government early in the Carter administration, he went to work for the International Paper Company as its vice president for corporate planning.

About five or six weeks after Paul O'Neill joined International Paper I had lunch with him in New York. I asked him about his new job. "It's interesting, and I like the people," he said, "but you can't believe the top-heaviness, the delays, the overlap, and the waste they have around there. We wouldn't stand for it in the government!" Now, this didn't come from an ex–civil servant who found himself ill suited to the world of business. On the contrary. Within a few years Paul O'Neill had become the president of International Paper and, two years after that, the CEO of ALCOA.

For thirty-five years more or less I've kept in my head a continually updated roster of All-Time All-American Bureaucrats. All of the above-mentioned HEW colleagues are on that roster. Mary Switzer and Bob Ball have always been tied for number one. Like other outstanding government managers, they were tenacious and resourceful champions of their programs. Their persuasiveness was reinforced by unfailing charm and good humor. As true believers in democratic accountability, they never forgot that in the executive branch the last word lies with the president and the secretary. (They also knew they would be around to fight another day.)

Some critics of the bureaucracy seem to believe that civil servants shouldn't fight for their programs; they should merely manage them. This is a silly idea. Anyone who has spent most of his or her life running maternal- and child-health programs and isn't ready to fight for them must be either an opportunist or a time-server. But the fighting I'm talking about is not squabbling. It's like the fighting a lawyer does for a client. Another word for it is advocacy. The president or the department head is to the bureaucrat what the judge is to the lawyer. The bureaucrat's program and the lawyer's client both have a right to be heard and a claim to due process.

Rufus Miles, one of the wisest as well as most skilled public servants with whom I've ever been associated, is famous for Miles's Law: "Where you stand depends on where you sit." Where you sit determines what responsibilities you have, and those responsibilities determine where you stand. If you're a program manager, you owe the people served by your program an all-out effort to obtain the funding, staff, and administrative support it needs. If you don't make that effort, who will?

Having so often changed jobs, I have good reason to be conscious of Miles's Law. I recall, for example, a conversation with Congressman F. Edward Hébert of Louisiana, chairman of the House Committee on Armed Services, shortly before I became secretary of defense. Mr. Hébert was the principal sponsor of legislation to establish an Armed Services Medical Academy. HEW had opposed the bill on the ground that military medicine was not so different from civilian medicine as to justify setting up a special school. Mr. Hébert asked about my position on his bill. "Well, Mr. Chairman," I said, "as secretary of HEW I opposed it, but as secretary of defense I'll be glad to take another look at it." Meanwhile, Caspar Weinberger, the director of OMB, had been chosen to succeed me at HEW. By way of a backhanded compliment to his budget-cutting zeal, he had become known as "Cap the Knife." "Not to worry," I said to my apprehensive HEW colleagues, "when Cap gets here you're going to see the greatest demonstration of Miles's Law in history." And so they did.

Acknowledgment of the force of Miles's Law would go a long way toward facilitating mutual understanding between career and noncareer public servants. So also would a clear fix on the distinction between administering a program, providing a service, or analyzing a problem and tasks such as choosing a policy, formulating a strategy, or adopting a solution. The former properly belong within the sphere of career people, the latter within that of political people.

I saw a clear demonstration of this distinction in the summer of 1959. The Democrats had proposed health insurance for the elderly under the Social Security system. My boss, Arthur S. Flemming, and I believed that there should be a Republican-sponsored alternative to this proposal. I accordingly convened a small group of career people to help me turn this broadly defined objective into a concrete plan. We met several times in the next two weeks but seemed to be going nowhere. Then it dawned on me what the problem might be: I was asking career colleagues to make assumptions about policy choices that should have been made at the political level *before* they were called upon for their technical expertise. I promptly got to work on a short memorandum spelling out the elements of a recognizably Republican approach: the program would be financed via the Social Security payroll tax, beneficiaries would have a choice among benefit packages of equal value offered by private carriers, and beneficiaries would receive vouchers with which to pay the premiums. (The latter device, incidentally, was recently hailed by the columnist James K. Glassman as a "very interesting idea" that "congressional leaders are quietly considering.") The civil servants now had all they needed to develop the program's detailed specifications.

The final report of the Personnel Management Project of 1977 whose director, Dwight Ink, is perhaps the most broadly experienced of modern American bureaucrats, made a number of recommendations addressed to this division of roles. The report recommended, for example, identifying all positions that should be administered on a nonpartisan basis and all positions concerned with managing ongoing programs, but without a major policy-formulating requirement. These would be reserved for career employees. The remainder would be filled by career or noncareer managers at the discretion of the agency head.

A key recommendation by my Volcker Commission task force was that the orientation of new presidential appointees should have a high priority in any new administration. The orientation should be conducted under the auspices of the White House itself, and attendance should be mandatory. The briefings would, of course, cover such basics as personnel rules, budget procedures, dealing with the press, relations with Congress, and legal and ethical guidelines. There should also be full discussion of the relationship between political appointees and career executives with emphasis on the practical considerations touched on here.

The value of preparing political appointees for a constructive relationship with their career colleagues was highlighted by a series of surveys conducted annually between 1964 and 1984. Sponsored by the National Academy of Public Administration, these surveys asked the appointees of the five presidents who served in that period to assess the competence and responsibility of the career executives in their agencies. The favorable percentage declined year by year from 92 percent of the Johnson appointees to 77 percent of the Reagan appointees. The surveys don't tell us how these former officials regarded the career services when they were first appointed. It's possible, even likely, that the Johnson appointees started out with a more favorable attitude toward "the bureaucracy" than the Reagan appointees. It seems probable, however, that whatever suspicions toward career people the appointees may initially have had were diminished by the experience of working together. Early and adequate orientation could shorten the accommodation process.

Meanwhile, the attractiveness of public service to prospective political appointees has been undermined by an absurdly protracted clearance process. Background investigations, I'm told, now routinely include a question about whether or not a prospective appointee has ever been known to make a joke that might be regarded as disparaging the other gender or an ethnic group. The list of things that have to be checked is now so long that in 1989 it took five months to clear me for an appointment by President Bush to a part-time job as his representative to the multilateral aid program in the Philippines. This was more time than the aggregate consumed by the clearances for all of my nine preceding presidential appointments put together.

The clearance process has taken on of late the self-righteous, finger-pointing character of a witch-hunt, obliterating the distinction between appearance and reality. The embarrassment to the White House arising from such disclosures as Judge Douglas H. Ginsburg's pot smoking and Zoë Baird's unregistered nanny turned every subsequent background investigation into an agonizing exercise. The employment of an unregistered immigrant is a clear violation of the law: how serious a violation depends on differences in degree. Were Social Security taxes paid? Was an effort made to get the employee a green card? Was the situation corrected before or only after it became publicly known? The relationship of the violation to the nature of the proposed public trust may also be important. Does it matter that Judge Ginsburg was proposed for the nation's highest court or Ms. Baird its highest law enforcement position? Of course, the distinctions between infractions of the law or instances of unethical conduct that should be disqualifying (or disqualifying for particular positions) and those that should not can be close. But then, a hard call is always a hard call.

The ethics of public service and the rewards of public service are inseparable. Both the ethics and the rewards are implicit in the two words "public" and "service." When the public servant goes to work in the morning, her paramount ethical obligation is to try to discern the public interest and serve it as best she can. The satisfaction of helping others, doing good, and doing the right thing is very real. The private sector, to be sure, also serves essential public interests, but the primary incentive, and hence the principal reward, of private enterprise is personal gain. The primary incentive, and hence the principal reward, of public service is service itself. For example, a civil engineer who works for the Bureau of Reclamation has credentials and experience that would translate readily into a higher-paying position in the private sector. In his own eyes, however, he's not just a civil engineer who's paid less than his private-sector counterparts because he had the bad luck to work for the federal government. He chooses to work for the government because for him there can be no greater reward than the satisfaction of applying his professional knowledge to the benefit of his fellow citizens.

For the true public servant the going can from time to time be tough. The more visible the role—and this applies particularly to political appointees—the more likely you are to be shot at. But that need not diminish the satisfaction of the job. It can add to it. In World War II, I was a litter-bearer platoon leader with the Fourth Infantry Division. The task of getting to the wounded and bringing them back to a place where they could be treated was immensely rewarding. What could be more unambiguously good than saving lives, alleviating pain, and helping to prevent permanent disability? It was a dangerous job, but there were times in those days when I felt a sense of exhilaration I had never felt before and have never felt since.

Though less intense, the sense of satisfaction I've had in public service is of the same kind. And I am not alone. I have many friends who once held responsible but not necessarily prominent roles in government and who now occupy prestigious and well-paid positions in the private sector—some of them very prestigious and very well paid. Not one finds his present occupation as rewarding as his government service. Could this be the reason why business executives are paid so much more than their government counterparts? It can hardly be an accident that people whom society regards as rewarded by a high level of psychic income— teachers, ministers, nurses, and public servants—are so consistently to be found at the low end of the pay scale.

We presume too much, however, on the dedication of our public servants. Psychic income doesn't pay the bills. In a book written after his retirement from the Harvard presidency, *The Cost of Talent*,[6] Derek Bok addresses the extreme differences in the earnings growth of business executives and other professionals between the early seventies and 1990. In that period the base salaries of CEOs doubled while their bonuses soared. The real earnings of federal officials were meanwhile falling steadily. When, in 1990, at the urging of the Volcker Commission, Congress voted a partial catchup, federal salaries had dropped 30 percent below comparable private-sector positions. The Senior Executive Association found that even after the 1990 changes and more recent extension to Senior Executive Service officials of eligibility for locality pay, their total cash compensation would have to increase 35 to 114 percent to become comparable with salaries in the private sector.

The civil service does, it is true, have partially offsetting advantages in security of tenure and retirement benefits. Still, the disparity with the private sector has been so wide for so long that the attractiveness of a government career is bound to have suffered badly. But as indicated by the data cited above, the attractiveness of career public service has suf-

---

[6] (New York: The Free Press, 1993).

fered since the publication of the Volcker Commission Report even more seriously in respects other than compensation.

Admittedly, the indicators are not definitive. We need a systematic means of comparing the ability of public service to attract good people with that of other occupations. Its development was to be a function of the National Commission on the Public Service created by Congress on the recommendation of the Volcker Commission. Intended to ensure that the state of the public service remains high on the national agenda, this statutory commission was given scant attention by President Bush and denied funding by President Clinton. This is a serious setback. By building on and refining the Volcker Commission's findings, the National Commission could have become a comprehensive source of continually updated information about the state of the public service. As it is, no entity, public or private, has either the mandate or the resources necessary for this purpose. I know that because, in the course of writing this essay, I made a considerable effort to find objective indicators of current trends in the public service and came up with very little. I did learn, however, that, contrary to the urging of the Volcker Commission, the federal government's training and education programs are being badly neglected. At a time of downsizing and restructuring, such programs are more than an enhancement of the attractiveness of a government career. They're a necessary means of developing the competence demanded by increasing workloads. Only the government-bashers can take satisfaction in the lack of such competence.

One thing is clear. Whatever restores esteem for public service will augment the rewards of public service. It would help if the president and the vice president talked about service and not just about performance. It would help if the media saw their way making clear to either—and preferably both—of two course corrections: one, the recognition that a fixation on waste, fraud, and abuse (or cheating, lying, and greed) is misleading and two, the acceptance of an affirmative responsibility for fairness toward the public service. Let's reduce the number of political appointees, increase opportunities for career people, strengthen the relationship between political appointees and the career services, and make sure that the compensation of public servants remains adequate to attract and retain people of outstanding quality.

One final thought. Whatever augments the rewards of public service renews the pact we made with ourselves over two hundred years ago—the pact between us the people and those to whom we entrusted responsibility for things we cannot do for ourselves but that concern us in common. This mutual undertaking was, has always been, is now, and shall, I trust, long continue to be the foundation of our unique and precious form of government.

Misplaced Concreteness

I'm not convinced that this is the "information age." It's true, of course, that we have more information about more things than ever before. It's true, too, that dramatic new technologies enable us instantly to locate, summon up, and disseminate any item in this vast store. Ditto the capacity to crunch a huge number of huge numbers. I'm also aware that the "stone age," the "bronze age," and the "iron age" were named for their eras' dominant technologies.

If I'm reluctant to join in proclaiming a new age, it's not because I do not appreciate information technology's phenomenal feats. On the contrary, I delight in knowing that a gigaflop is a billion calculations per second, and I hold in awe the capacity of parallel-processors to operate at a multigigaflop rate. It strikes me, however, as rushing things a bit to name an age for a set of technologies no more than a few decades old. Besides, instant access to a limitless store of information will mainly benefit the comparatively few with a high degree of professional or avocational interest in a particular subject. For them the Internet is already a great resource. For the rest of us the new technologies are more likely to be transmitters of entertainment than of information. We do well if on a given day we are able to skim the morning newspaper, listen to *All*

Things Considered on the way home, and watch the evening news. The only advance in information technology that would help us much—an increase in the capacity of our brains to absorb and process the information they already receive—is not likely to come soon.

There will be others, meanwhile, less well anchored to reality, whom the information highway will draw into another world. The *Washington Post* recently ran a disturbing story indicative of just this tendency. It was about an eighteen-year-old who became so immersed in computer role-playing games that he all but gave up on sleeping and got killed by an oncoming truck when he nodded off at the wheel of the family car. Wanting to understand what had happened, the young man's father made contact with his son's electronic pen pals. He learned, as the *Post* put it, that "some people have found something so compelling in this on-line computer world that they have all but pulled up stakes and moved into cyberspace. . . ." That would be a frightening prospect if "some people" became "many people."

Almost fifty years ago Norbert Wiener, the father of cybernetics, foresaw our present situation. He then wrote, "The world of the future will be an ever more demanding struggle against the limitations of our intelligence, not a comfortable hammock in which we can lie down to be waited upon by our robot slaves."

While we have no choice but to accept the limitations *of* our intelligence, that is not true of self-inflicted limitations *on* our intelligence. Although names, concepts, classifications, measurements, and hypotheses are indispensable to our ability to grasp and communicate information, we tend to let these tools get in the way of reality. In the pages that follow I hope to make clear why, in this increasingly complex and ever more closely interconnected world, it is essential that we recognize and learn to discipline this deluding tendency.

Two experiences widely separated in time but closely related in content alerted me to the tricks that our habits of mind can play on us. At the time of the first of these experiences I was in the seventh grade at a boys' day school in Brookline, Massachusetts, where our art and nature studies teacher was a young man named Roger Tory Peterson. A superb ornithologist and a gifted artist, he was working in his spare time on a field guide to birds.

Just before spring vacation Mr. Peterson invited all interested seventh-graders to enter a contest to see how many birds we could identify between Easter and the end of the school year. My father gave me a pair of binoculars, and I threw myself into this contest with great enthusiasm. Soon after daybreak every morning I would prowl the neighborhood looking for birds. Immediately upon getting back to the house I would search through the incomparable color plates in Edward H. Forbush's *Birds of Massachusetts and Other New England States* for the new birds I had just seen. Some were so distinctive they were easy to identify. Others looked so much alike I couldn't be sure which one I'd spotted. In those cases I would compare the pictures very carefully and pick out for each bird some distinguishing mark—a white eye-ring, a buffy breast, or a long tail—so that the next time I saw one of these look-alikes I could tell which one it was. Day by day I added to the list of birds I could name. Although recognizing a bird taught me nothing about it that I had not already observed, naming it somehow made me feel that I knew it well. It had become part of my world.

Sixty-some years later I encountered the role of names from the opposite side. This time my assignment was to explore the opportunities for greater harmonization of the rules and customs that govern trading in the leading stock exchanges. Although qualified to deal with the policy issues, I knew little either about the trading process or about the securities being traded. To make up for this shortcoming, I assembled dozens of articles from seven or eight different publications. From these articles I excerpted seemingly relevant passages varying in length from one to several sentences. Although the excerpts were loaded with unfamiliar words and phrases, I eventually succeeded in arranging these bits and pieces in a sequence that read quite smoothly. Only the lead sentences and connective phrases were in my own words.

As this exercise went forward, I developed an increasingly secure sense of what the strange words and phrases must mean. By the time I finished the memorandum, I could almost visualize an arcane financial world I hardly knew at all. This was the exact reverse of my bird-naming experience. There, though I had actually seen the birds, I felt that I knew them only when I learned their names. Here I had the names from the beginning; using them made me think I knew what they meant.

The second of these experiences reminded me of the first, and both led me to wonder whether they might be accounted for by an era when naming things made our ancestors feel more secure in a world they had no hope of understanding. We attach a name to everything we need to be able to talk about. All existence has a name: the universe. Lesser material things have categories of names extending from general to particular: cars, Fords, Tauruses, station wagons, the Taurus station wagon with Virginia license plate ALTO TWO, my wife's voice part. At the opposite end of the scale, abstract concepts have names: truth, falsehood, justice, evil. Once attached, a name is a more or less permanent handle on the subject. Although, as my birding and financial examples suggest, we can sometimes mistake the knowledge of names for the knowledge of things, it is not until we get to concepts that we encounter a tendency to let names get in the way of reality.

A concept is a name twice removed from reality. You cannot match it up with an object. It stands for some unique attribute or aspect of reality from which everything else has been cut away. Put the other way around, a concept has been cut out of, or abstracted from, the rest of reality. The very loftiness of concepts endows them with the power to conjure up a world of their own. "Truth is beauty, beauty truth" is so evocative it sounds as if it must mean something. Abstractions, however, are not real, and it is a mistake to think of them as real. The great English philosopher Alfred North Whitehead called the attribution of reality to concepts "the fallacy of misplaced concreteness." As he also pointed out, "All truths are half-truths. It is trying to treat them as whole truths that plays the devil."

The misplacement of concreteness occurs in many contexts. Take the concept of "sovereignty." Considered as real, it implies exclusivity. This was the premise of the maxim *Imperium in imperio non potest*—two governments cannot exert power in the same territory. When in 1787 the framers of the U.S. Constitution came together in Philadelphia, this maxim had never been questioned. Unfazed by learned authority, the framers stood the maxim on its ear simply by postulating a federal structure allocating powers between the national government and the states in such a way that some powers are exclusively national, some are concurrent, and the rest reserved to the states.

The attribution of concreteness to concepts can also result in obliviousness toward relevant similarities. I call this form of concreteness the "Mount Washington fallacy" after an episode in my 1964 campaign for lieutenant governor of Massachusetts. In those days a campaign had to have a "field organization." Such an organization had a few key people at the top, a few in each county, and a large number of local "coordinators."

My campaign manager gave high priority to recruiting a coordinator for every one of the Commonwealth's 351 cities and towns. He informed me one day that he had recruited a coordinator for Mount Washington, a town with only thirty-eight voters. The roster was now complete. I thanked him warmly but couldn't resist asking whether he intended to recruit a coordinator for every apartment house with thirty-eight voters or more. Of course not. Why not? Because coordinators are for voters who live in *cities and towns*. You don't have coordinators for voters who live in *apartment houses*!

I recalled this conversation in 1970 after a year and a half of working with Yitzhak Rabin, then Israel's ambassador to the United States, and Obdul Hamid Sharaf, the Jordanian ambassador, in a vain effort to encourage negotiations among the parties to the Arab-Israeli conflict. I had by then realized that it was the Palestinians, as the people aggrieved by the creation of the state of Israel, who were mainly responsible for keeping the conflict alive. Until their grievances were addressed, their continuing agitation and violence would frustrate progress toward peace. Yet for more than twenty years they had been treated not as a nation but as "the refugee problem." Refugees don't rate a seat at the United Nations and have no ambassadors in foreign capitals.

Once I came to understand the inappropriateness in the context of the Arab-Israeli conflict of a rigid distinction between a nation and a people, I began to look for responsible Palestinians who might take leading roles in negotiations with Israel for the autonomy of the West Bank and the Gaza Strip. This effort was cut off by my transfer to HEW in May of 1970. Before I left the State Department, however, I wrote a memorandum warning that there would never be an Arab-Israeli peace agreement until and unless the Palestinians were brought into the negotiations on the same footing as the front-line Arab states.

Like concepts, classifications have to correspond with reality—the better the fit, the better both serve their functions. But just as it is a fallacy to endow concepts with concreteness, it is equally fallacious to think of classifications as real. Yet it goes without saying that classifications have many uses. By highlighting the similarities and differences among the members of a class, a taxonomic system calls attention to their distinctive features. Take mushrooms, for instance. If you know how to distinguish their families and species, you can tell which ones are poisonous and which are safe to eat. Traced backward in time, taxonomies also map the evolution of life-forms; we can see, for example, the stages at which birds became separated from reptiles.

Although the usefulness of a classification depends on its congruence with reality, it is, nevertheless, a product of our own design. The size and shape of its boxes, how they're arranged, and what goes into each box are choices influenced not only by observable distinctions but also by considerations of utility. The excellence of the design, however, is not an excuse for treating reality as if it came in a taxonomic package. Yet this is what happens whenever a scholar comes to believe that the universe is organized like a course catalog. Although an ordinarily harmless delusion, it allows barriers and gaps to develop between one field of study and those surrounding it, and this can lead to hostility toward integrative ideas. That's why, when I'm introduced to a distinguished economist, I have to restrain myself from saying, "I'm so pleased to meet you. I've always felt that yours is such an important branch of psychology!"

The artificial boundaries separating academic disciplines have their counterparts in bureaucracy and the professions. As I've seen all too many times, this has pernicious consequences where human services are concerned. To many administrators of these services, categorical programs belong to the real world; their clients are only statistics. There is no one in the system whose job it is to respond to the needs of a whole person or a whole family. The needs of a welfare mother struggling to free herself from dependency may include anything or everything from counseling, medical care, rehabilitation, homemaker services, and day care for her children so that she can get into a job-training program. But there is no one place to which she can go for help. She will be shuttled from one agency to another, required to fill out endless forms, given incomplete information, and—almost surely—emerge believing that "the system" has not only failed but abused her. Not surprisingly, many taxpayers have come to feel the same way.

The so-called helping professions divide people into pieces without bureaucratic prompting. I've lost more than one battle to get social workers, public health people, and rehabilitation counselors to integrate their services. At other times I tried in vain to encourage the training of family counselors who would serve both as the first point of contact for a family in need of help and as a knowledgeable source of information about the capabilities of the more specialized occupations and agencies. The Allied Services Act of 1972 was aimed at overcoming bureaucratic and professional compartmentalization, and one of my great regrets on leaving HEW was having to abandon my championship of this legislation which, after that, never got beyond the hearings stage.

Classifications can also get in the way of reality through obscuring differences in degree. An orderly arrangement of labels seems on its face to denote things as separate as different kinds of owls. Very often, however, the labels merely mark off segments of a continuum, like red, purple, or blue or like the points on a compass. All kinds of practical situations—for example, the need to pick a winner, award a contract, or assess effectiveness—make it necessary to draw such lines. That's why we have scoring systems, winning bids, and performance evaluations.

We should never forget, though we often do, that in any close call the decisive margin can be minuscule. This is obvious in the case of athletic contests where a single point or run or stroke, or a hundredth of a second or pound or inch, can separate the gold medalist from the runner-up. But it's easy to lose sight of the complexity of the factors that determine such margins. Take football. The setting is elaborately prescribed: a playing field of a certain length and width marked off with lines where two eleven-member teams are allowed sixty minutes in which to execute a series of ingeniously contrived and carefully timed collisions. To administer and enforce the rules, seven zebra-striped bureaucrats are required to be on the field at all times. In a close game the final score is the product of countless interacting variables: strength, intelligence, surehandedness, quickness, timing, a lucky bounce, and countless other things. Make the slightest change in any one of these variables, and the game might go the other way.

We're all familiar with many other kinds of situations whose outcomes turn on the cumulative impact of differences of degree. A prime example is a political campaign, which is like a football game with fewer rules, self-appointed umpires, and a victory margin determined by crowd noise. It's surprising in the circumstances that we are not more alert to differences of degree in other, less conventional settings. The failure to recognize such differences generates a lot of unnecessary conflict and confusion. A case in point was the assumption by many intelligent liberals, most of whom had opposed the Vietnam War, that the successful use of military force to roll back Iraq's conquest of Kuwait set a precedent for using it against the Serbs in the totally different circumstances of the Bosnian civil war.

The disregard of differences in degree is particularly conspicuous in the case of fundamental doctrines of the kind commonly known as "principles." The true believer in a principle thinks of it as completely free of competing considerations: the principle is deemed to be real in the same way that the fallacy of misplaced concreteness treats a concept as real.

At the core of any such simplistic position is an emotional attitude so deeply embedded as to be inaccessible to reasoned argument. To the liberals shocked by the Serbs' "ethnic cleansing" of Muslims, the commitment of American ground forces was justified notwithstanding that no vital American interest was at stake. Other liberals are so committed to the separation of church and state that they would like to see "In God We Trust" removed from our coins. To the conservative diehards who provide the National Rifle Association's hard-core support, any restriction on the sale of handguns is an encroachment on a nonexistent "right to bear arms." And to the right-to-life fanatics who picket abortion clinics, an embryo is protected by the Bill of Rights.

"Extremism in the defense of liberty is no vice," proclaimed Barry Goldwater. In wartime, perhaps. But no political system can be democratic that allows itself to be dominated by a dogma that cannot tolerate dissent. Nor can a judicial system be fair that is unable to balance competing interests. These, surely, were the thoughts that my greatest teacher, Judge Learned Hand, had in mind when he warned, as I heard him do on several occasions, "Beware the man of principle!" They also explain why he was so fond of Oliver Cromwell's appeal to the General Assembly of the Church of Scotland, his version of which was, "I beseech ye in the bowels of Christ, think that ye may be mistaken." He would like, he said, to have these words inscribed above the portals of every church, school, courthouse, and legislative body in the United States.

Thomas Reed Powell, one of the most incisive members of Harvard's brilliant Law School faculty in the days when I was a student there, taught a course in constitutional law built around the proposition that all hard questions are questions of degree. This is not hard to see when the issue is whether or not the unreasonableness of a law or regulation is extreme enough to amount to a denial of "due process of law." The point is less obvious but equally demonstrable where freedom of speech or freedom of the press is at stake. These freedoms are commonly spoken of as if they were absolutes that admitted of no qualification or curtailment—as if, in other words, they enjoyed an irrevocable preference over any competing public interest. It is still true, however, as it was in Professor Powell's day, that free expression, like any other constitutionally protected right, can on occasion be subordinated to a clear and compelling national interest. Whether or not in a given case that interest is sufficient to tip the scales is quintessentially a matter of degree.

The scales thereby tipped are, of course, a measuring device. The metaphor thus supplies an appropriate transition to measurement's other uses. As a means of defining reality, measurement is a tool no less essential than names, concepts, hypotheses, and taxonomies in terms of their indispensability to our grasp of reality. Given the pace at which complexity has been increasing in the past fifty years, it's fortunate that the same period has seen remarkable improvement both in our ability to measure things and in the reliability of the measurements. Their depth, range, and precision are integral to our sense of place and identity. They tell us where we've been, where we're headed, and what to expect.

Symbolic of the distance that the art of measurement has come is the contrast between an old-time sailing ship's and a modern vessel's means of ascertaining their positions and forecasting the weather. To determine his approximate longitude and latitude the sailing ship captain had only a chronometer showing the difference between Greenwich time and ship's time and a sextant to measure the altitude of the sun above the horizon at noon. For a guess at the weather he could check the barometer, look at the clouds, and put a finger in the wind. On a modern vessel, signals from a satellite, sound waves bounced back from the sea bottom to a depth finder, and radio waves from shore stations can come within one hundred feet of pinpointing its precise position. Buoys placed at intervals throughout the world's oceans beam barometric pressures, wind velocities, and temperatures to satellites which relay these readings, together with the satellite's own cloud-formation pictures, to ground-based supercomputers whose constantly updated weather maps and forecasts are televised to the ship.

Statistical counterparts of modern navigational equipment enable us to track social and economic developments. Without them we could not even identify our problems. We would not know the crime rate, the incidence of poverty, the prevalence of drug abuse, or the extent of functional illiteracy. Sophisticated sampling techniques notify us of the decline in manufacturing employment, the loss of topsoil, the depletion of energy resources, and the increase in single-parent families. They enable us to gauge the effectiveness of efforts to cope with homelessness, hunger, environmental degradation, and the escalation of health-care costs. We argue interminably about the best way to cope with these issues, and sometimes, as in the calculation of the consumer price index, for example, we challenge the statistical methods that generate the numbers. On the whole, however, we have learned to trust the integrity with which our statistical systems are administered.

And a good thing, too. Without reliable statistical data, the political process would long since have been overwhelmed. Can you imagine what a presidential campaign would be like if nobody believed the inflation, unemployment, or economic-growth figures? This struck me forcibly during the Ford-Carter campaign in 1976 when Jack Anderson charged in one of his columns that someone in the Commerce Department had been manipulating economic data to make the administration look good. As secretary of commerce at the time, I ordered an immediate investigation. As it turned out, Anderson had been given inaccurate information, and I called a press conference to set the record straight.

It should go without saying, but doesn't, that we need to be careful about how we use numbers. You've no doubt heard a statistician defined as someone with one foot in a bucket of ice and the other on a bed of hot coals who, when asked how he feels, replies, "On the average, I'm fine." That's the kind of answer we get when we fail to think through what we need to know.

In the same category is the inappropriate use of the information we have because it's too much trouble to get the information we want. Another old joke illustrates this anomaly. A man is looking for his car keys under a street lamp. A passerby offers to help. Finding nothing, he asks the man where he lost the keys. "Over there," says the man, pointing into the darkness. "Why then have we been looking for them under the street lamp?" "Because this is where the light is."

The use of national economic accounts to measure and compare national performance is a conspicuous example of looking where the light is. Although much has been done of late to develop such social indicators as infant mortality, literacy, average school-leaving age, longevity, and crime rates, we do not yet have indices capable of comparing one nation's ability to achieve well-being with that of another nation. Until we do, the national economic accounts, especially per capita income, are at least indicative of the standard of living. To use them, however, to rank national performance with respect to the qualitative aspects of well-being can be misleading. Japan's economic performance is certainly better than Great Britain's. Where the enjoyment of a pleasant existence is concerned, however, the call might go the other way. Ask anyone who has lived in both Tokyo and London!

Keeping score in the "competitiveness" game on the basis of economic accounts is bound to have an unhealthy influence on the way in which national priorities are established and national resources allocated. It puts money ahead of morality, long hours ahead of leisure. It induces countries that have done well in creating the conditions of a decent life for their citizens to undervalue their achievements and to compare themselves unfavorably with rivals whose economic growth, productivity, and favorable trade balances are rising faster. Lacking data that would show the superiority of their performance in the things that matter most to people, these enlightened countries get drawn into competing on the basis of the comparisons for which data exist. These data supply such light as there is.

To neutralize this distorting effect, we should continue to improve the existing social indicators, but a true "national well-being account" will also need to reflect values not yet reducible to statistical propositions. It will have to give appropriate weight, for example, to such key elements of the quality of life as respect for human rights, an independent judiciary, free elections, and the availability of rewarding work. Such a well-being account must seek to encompass what matters most: if not happiness, at least contentment; if not achievement, at least comfort; if not creativity, at least widespread participation in creative pursuits.

If we decide that it's important to measure national well-being, we shall have to make up our minds to search in the darkness. Economists and statisticians did just that many years ago when they were developing the economic accounts we now have. That was a prolonged, demanding, and ultimately successful effort. Indeed, were the indices it fashioned less widely accepted, they would not have been put to inappropriate use.

On two occasions in 1976 I invited to the Department of Commerce a number of leading economists from inside and outside the government for a discussion of essentially the same points I'm making now.

Though varying in language and emphasis, their responses came down to this: It's too hard to measure the things you're talking about. Each time they said this I would reply, "I know it's hard, but that doesn't mean it's impossible. If it's also important, why don't we get started?" We didn't get started then, and the task is even more important now. So why don't we get started now?

Let's turn now to hypotheses, which enable us to account for how and why things have happened, are happening, and are likely to happen the way they do. We have come to this point by way of a route that has taken us from the particularity of names to the remoteness of abstractions, and from the neatness of taxonomies to the parametric role of measurements. Hypotheses do for explanations what names do for recognition, concepts do for thought, taxonomies do for order, and measurements do for comparisons. Like their companions, however, hypotheses can get in the way of reality, and it is this propensity, once again, that I want to highlight.

A satisfactory hypothesis should account for no more and no less than the facts you know. Suppose that to you the land stretching away from your village looks flat on every side. When you leave the village, it makes no apparent difference how far you go or in what direction: the land continues to look flat. Every day you see the sun rise in the east and travel across the sky until it sets in the west. You conclude that, just as the sun moves across the earth from east to west during the day, it must go back to the east underneath the earth during the night. This for you is a satisfactory hypothesis.

Now let's suppose that your great-grandchildren have learned both that one day each year is longer than any other and that one day each year is shorter than any other. They have also noticed that midway between those two days are another two days when day and night have the same duration. One comes in a season when day by day the sun has been rising earlier, climbing higher in the sky, and setting later. The other comes in a season when day by day the sun has been rising later, losing height at noon, and setting earlier. The first heralds warm weather; that's when the crops begin to grow. The second portends cold weather; soon nothing will grow.

The original hypothesis cannot account for these additional facts. The great-grandchildren conclude that the best explanation of these annual changes in the behavior of the sun is that they are under the control of a sun god. But it follows that what the sun god can do, the sun god can stop doing. They prudently decide, therefore, to make appropriate sacrifices in order to keep the sun god in a benign mood.

After a thousand years or so along comes an iconoclast who questions this more elaborate but less rational hypothesis. He purports to explain the sun's behavior on the basis that the earth is round, not flat, rotates once a day, and journeys around the sun once a year. To account for the varying lengths of the day he adds the simple assumption that the earth is tipped on its axis. Beautiful! It all fits. Best of all, this new hypothesis is corroborated by the nightly alterations in the apparent position of the stars.

Your remote descendants, however, do not hail the iconoclast as a benefactor. In eliminating any need to propitiate the sun god he has also diminished his people's significance in their own eyes: they have been reduced from communicants with a deity to passive subjects of impersonal laws. Rather than reorder their perception of reality, the people denounce the iconoclast as a blasphemer, and he is duly executed.

Only in the last three centuries could a clear-eyed hypothesizer like that courageous pioneer be confident of escaping a similar fate. Decade by decade the cool impersonality of mathematics has gradually enlarged the domain of science and thereby made its victories easier. As Galileo observed, the "Book of Nature is . . . written in mathematical characters." Radical new formulations, nevertheless—Darwin's theory of evolution, Einstein's equation of mass and energy, Freud's exploration of the subconscious—have provoked reactions ranging from resistance through hostility to ridicule. Had Darwin come along two centuries earlier, he, like Galileo himself, might well have been forced by an ecclesiastical court to admit his "errors."

Most educated people now applaud science's continuous modification of old hypotheses and occasional substitution of new ones. Its explorations embrace subatomic particles so infinitesimal and distances so vast that few of us can even conceive of their dimensions. Although further diminishing humanity in the scale of things, these extensions of our universe have at the same time augmented our sense of awe. The more we learn about the Big Bang, black holes, and the origin of life, the more miraculous seems the cosmological order.

The tests that apply to the validity of hypotheses explaining the universe—coherence, consistency, economy, and adequacy—apply equally to the hypotheses we work with every day. A reasonable person does not purposely act on a hypothesis that does not hang together, contains built-in contradictions, is more complicated than it needs to be, or does not fully account for all the facts it purports to explain. If you show such a person that her hypothesis is flawed in one of these ways, she will revise or abandon it. Hypotheses, nevertheless, in common with our other means of getting an intelligent grip on the world, have a kind of service-ability that all too easily induces us to substitute them for reality. That this should be the case is not, when you think about it, hard to understand. We inhabit our hypothetical constructs the way we live in a house. They give us security and comfort. There are people, therefore, who persist in ignoring pertinent facts because they might disturb a familiar hypothesis or who base an otherwise insupportable hypothesis on selected facts that may also be wrong. When you run into someone like that, you know that you're dealing with an ideologue, a bigot, a fundamentalist, or a fanatic. Some of the "principles" touched on above rest on hypotheses like that. So too do history's most hateful doctrines—anti-Semitism, for instance, and white supremacy.

The way to keep a hypothesis abreast of reality is to stay in contact with the facts it purports to explain. This also applies to managing a situation, solving a problem, or dealing with a dispute. The more firmly we pin down the relevant facts, the easier it is to figure out what to do next. In many cases, the facts themselves will point to a solution. It makes sense that similar problems involving similar facts should be resolved in similar ways. Long before history was written, communities were developing rules of thumb for dealing with many kinds of disputes, and which rule applied depended on the facts of the case.

The education of lawyers has always drawn on their societies' store of experience with this fact-based approach to problem solving. In this country law students start with the facts set forth in judicial opinions deciding actual cases. Drawing on these facts, they learn how to formulate general rules and test their applicability to varying sets of facts. Later on in practice they will apply the same methodology to their clients' problems.

For many purposes this approach to problem solving works well. The facts in a "case," however, are fixed in a frozen cross-section of time. This horizontal slice may embrace plans, hopes, and hatreds side by side with the weather, economic forces, and creative ideas, but these and all the other data it contains have been artificially immobilized. Time's dimension is linear, and in this dimension everything reacts to and interacts with everything else. Treating facts as if they were static can be a serious mistake in situations—commercial, political, or international—where achieving a desired outcome depends on influencing an array of dynamically interacting relationships.

Dealing with the horizontal dimension calls for tactical skills. Dealing with the linear dimension calls for strategic planning. A lawyer's training is better suited to the former than the latter. When I was at the State Department in 1969–70, my boss was William P. Rogers, a former deputy attorney general and attorney general of the United States and a highly successful practicing lawyer. Although possessed of superior judgment in dealing with critical situations, he was impatient to the point of indifference with long-range geostrategic analysis. Indeed, he told me once that he regarded it as a waste of time. Richard Nixon, on the other hand, reveled in it and excelled at it. He needed someone to test his ideas on, and Henry Kissinger's scholarly background and intellectual acuity made him the perfect foil for the president's thinking. He was also close at hand. It did not take long for Kissinger to insert himself between the secretary and the president. Although widely believed to possess Machiavellian skills, Henry had no need to employ them for this purpose. All he had to do was fill a vacuum.

While this went on I was learning that our ability to influence the forces shaping events around the world depended on understanding their components, anticipating their likely course, and reckoning with their interactions. As I was soon to find out, the same is true of the forces shaping domestic affairs. For these purposes, an approach that starts with freezing the facts in a cross-section of time can go badly wrong. Ever since learning this I have always made a point of reminding my colleagues that every action we take is an intervention into a flow. In deciding how to intervene, therefore, we should not be looking just at the point of intervention but trying to calculate its downstream consequences.

After delivering this message several dozen times it occurred to me that I might be able to encourage my teammates to think in dynamic and longitudinal terms if I could get them to use metaphors drawn from the field of fluid dynamics instead of the battlefield or the sports arena. Phrases such as "frontal attack," "hit them where they ain't," "pull a squeeze play," and "full court press" smack of tactical ploys rather than strategic plans. Recalling that my former Defense Department colleague Bob Seamans had recently become head of the National Academy of Engineering, I asked him to recommend a textbook on fluid dynamics in which I might be able to find formulations that could be turned into useful figures of speech. I should have known better. The textbook was loaded with mathematical equations I couldn't even read, much less translate into metaphorical language.

Still, a course in fluid dynamics might have helped the Bush administration people who fought the "War on Drugs." To them the flow of illegal substances was a static pattern on a map with shaded patches for crop-growing areas, dotted lines connecting shipment routes, boxes for depots, retorts for processing centers, and so on. If you look at drug trafficking that way, you can convince yourself that eradicating crops, pinching off supply routes, and arresting distributors will radically reduce its volume. You're surprised and disappointed when new areas are cultivated, shipment routes are switched, and arrests are offset by stepped-up recruitment, and new, more efficient cartel leaderships replace the old.

If, on the other hand, you had visualized drug trafficking as a process driven by powerful economic forces, you would have been under no such illusion. You would have seen that the price paid to growers could be raised indefinitely, thus assuring that the supply would be maintained. You would also have seen that, without widely available and effective drug abuse education, treatment, and rehabilitation, the demand would continue to be both stable and inelastic. Being aware that the annual tax-free rate of return on a drug lord's investment is at least 200 percent, you would expect him to regard the cost of repairing damage to sources, supply routes, and marketing systems as cheap at the price. And so indeed it has been: The total amount of cocaine consumed in the United States has been stuck at its mid-1980s peak for almost a decade.

Through my wife's chairmanship of the advisory board of Second Genesis, Inc., which operates five residential therapeutic communities in the Washington, D.C., area, I've seen what a really good rehabilitation program can accomplish. Three-fourths of the severely addicted drug users treated by Second Genesis have been referred by the courts; the remainder are volunteers. A federally funded study completed in 1994 followed up a random sample of graduates from Second Genesis's twelve-month course of treatment. The study found that 85 percent of this group were wholly free of both drug use and criminal behavior and that most were employed. While few such programs achieve that rate of success, a recent Rand analysis showed that treatment is seven times more cost-effective in reducing cocaine consumption than supply control.

A similar underestimation of dynamic forces is a defect of most prescriptions for the containment of health-care costs. These prescriptions rely heavily on ferreting out nonessential procedures and then making sure that they do not get paid for. This approach, however, belies the word "containment." Whatever makes health-care costs go up faster than the cost-of-living index has to be the resultant of psychological, epidemiological, and demographic forces. Withholding payment for nonessential procedures will save money, but it won't diminish the strength of these forces.

Some examples of plausible managed-care mechanisms will make clear why the most that can be expected of them is a combination of one-time savings with safeguards against new forms of waste. The examples might include a computerized system that cuts out 90 percent of the paperwork that now goes into processing health-insurance claims, uniform standards that discourage unnecessary operations, and payment ceilings that maximize ambulatory and outpatient services, minimize hospitalization, and squeeze out redundant laboratory tests. When at the end of five years these controls are fully in place, total health-care spending will have dropped by the aggregate amount of the savings thus achieved. It's apparent, however, that the forces pushing up the cost of the procedures still being performed will not have been touched. The cost will continue to rise at the same rate, though from a lower base.

The only measures capable of reining in the forces that make health-care costs go up faster than the basic rate of inflation are not likely to command broad support. We could, for instance, slow down the development of high-cost means of prolonging the lives of sufferers from AIDS or Alzheimer's disease. We could prevent the use of organ transplants and joint replacements from continuing to expand. Or we could cut back on the treatment of the very old by an amount proportional to their increasing fraction of the total population. Meanwhile, additional upward pressure on the nation's health-care bill results from the priority we give to preventing premature death and disability and to pursuing breakthroughs in basic biomedical research. Reducing the death toll from fatal heart attacks and automobile accidents adds to the number of terminal illnesses that will eventually have to be treated. New discoveries in molecular biology lead to improved methods of diagnosis and treatment that will for a long time be very expensive. Are you any longer surprised that you hear more about managed care than cost containment?

Although I have long conceived of the linear dimension as a stream whose velocity, turbulence, and direction needed to be gauged, it occurred to me recently that this conception should also reckon with the fact that the stream is swelling in volume and gaining in speed. Year by year its laden waters carry more, and everything it carries more quickly disappears from sight.

One consequence of this increase in velocity and volume is the diminishing half-life of a newsworthy "event." The acceleration of its descent into oblivion could be demonstrated by comparing the coverage of similar stories at ten-year intervals. The first step would be to define a "Class 1 news story" in, say, 1925 as one that appeared on the front pages of most of the nation's major dailies when it first broke and got follow-up stories somewhere in those papers on at least two of the next three days. A particularly bad train wreck might qualify as such a story. You would then locate and list by subject all the stories which, in that year, met the Class 1 definition. In addition to doing the same thing for 1935, 1945, and so on up to 1995, you would also ascertain for each year what coverage, if any, was given to stories that would have been given Class 1 treatment in previous decades. Finally, you would determine for all of the dailies surveyed the average size of their news slots in each decade.

Whether or not anyone has actually done this I don't know. I'm certain, though, that such a survey would show that each decade's Class 1 stories received progressively less prominence in the next and subsequent decades. It would also show that for that entire period the column inches available for news stories remained roughly the same. It would be clear that decade by decade the number of events reported had gone up while the depth and duration of each event's coverage had gone down. You would see, moreover, that over the same period the standard of "newsworthiness" that a nonregional story had to meet in order to make the front page got tougher and tougher. A similar survey of radio and television news programs would undoubtedly reveal parallel trends. The explanation of these developments could only be that a steady increase in competition for a fixed amount of space and time had resulted from exponential growth in the number and scale of significant events in an ever more closely interconnected world.

The constant acceleration of the rate at which today's events recede from sight is having a number of significant consequences. One is that a business, an athletic team, or a politician is judged by a progressively shorter record of past performance. George Bush found that out when the recession of 1991–92 totally eclipsed his triumph in the Gulf War. Another consequence is that most of what happens in the next three months will have been forgotten three months later. Bill Clinton, I thought, was acting on this awareness when, soon after taking office, he called for ending the ban on gays in the military. Although at the time many Washington insiders regarded this as a beginner's mistake, it could, in fact, have been a smart move: Clinton had made a firm commitment to the gays, and if he put off acting on it, they would surely keep agitating the issue until he did something about it. Sure enough, by the end of Clinton's first year in office the subject had indeed all but disappeared, though not so completely as to prevent the 1994 congressional campaigns from giving it another burst of attention.

News has to be new. No matter how interesting, important, sensational, or dramatic a happening may have been, its coverage ends when new developments, revelations, interpretations, and comments have been exhausted. The earlier the facts are exposed, the sooner the story dies. If indeed Bill Clinton acted on that assumption when he gave early prominence to the gays issue, why didn't he, as soon as the Whitewater story began to break, immediately unload every scrap of information that might bear on it? The only answer I can come up with is that he underestimated the media's ability to make the affair look bigger than it was.

Ever since Watergate demonstrated the power of investigative reporting, the media have been casting at every rise in the hope of landing another trophy-sized scandal. It looked for a while as if the Iran-Contra affair might measure up, but it got away in the end. Recent catches—Nannygate, for instance—have been small. But sizes are relative, after all: a huge trout is a small salmon, and a huge salmon is a small tuna. Given the dearth of major malfeasance, it should not have been surprising that so much would have been made of Whitewater's long-ago, small-town improprieties. In fact, its treatment was all too reminiscent of the way a fisherman will try to make his modest catch look bigger by holding it out at arm's length toward the camera. But the most striking indicator of how poor the scandal season has been of late was the inflated play given to the briefing by Treasury officials of White House staff members which precipitated the resignation of White House counsel. In Japan, where for a decade or more its media have been reeling in hefty specimens of large-scale corruption—bribery, kickbacks, mob connections, and the like—a story like that would have been thrown back.

A second side effect of the rapidity with which the past recedes is that our society no longer has leading citizens. When I was in school the views of broadly experienced people of secure reputation like Henry L. Stimson, Alfred P. Sloan, Albert Einstein, and John Dewey were widely reported. Nowadays, if you aren't a celebrity, you don't exist. The media no longer have time or space to maintain the visibility of individuals who are merely wise. Not even Benjamin Franklin, were he now alive and in his eighties, would have anything like the influence he enjoyed in the late years of his actual lifetime. As a society we are the poorer for being denied the balance and perspective of our sagest citizens.

A third and still more serious consequence is the weakening of our sense of history. In my view, the true value of history lies not in the "lessons" it teaches but in the awareness it creates of the ways in which large forces interact with each other and are acted upon by individuals and ideas in the linear dimension. "Great man" theories of history and socioeconomic theories of history are both incomplete. Rulers, peasants, saints, scholars, writers, market forces, famines, plagues, inventions, discoveries, conquests, and migrations have all played parts in making things happen the way they did. The circumstance that Harry Truman was a history buff goes a long way, I believe, toward explaining why he, although otherwise apparently unprepared for the presidency, was able to meet the threat of unprecedented dangers and make decisions that set our geostrategic course for the next forty years. It's my guess also that a lack of historic sense was a factor in the drifting we saw when Jimmy Carter, trained as an engineer, was in the White House. Indeed, we might have recognized a clue to this deficiency in the regularity with which he hailed every new departure as a "historic first."

We live in the midst of yesterday's outcomes. Yesterday gave us today's interests, attitudes, and aspirations, and these will influence tomorrow's actions. Today uses yesterday to predict tomorrow. The 8-to-1 odds against Sweet William's winning the Kentucky Derby cannot be affected by the possibility that Sweet William will have a particularly fast workout an hour from now. The odds will shorten, however, as soon as the horse does in fact have such a workout. But few people study the *Daily Telegraph*. Most of us would rather bet on a hunch.

The linear dimension is an endless stream of changing probabilities. The odds in favor of some propositions (e.g., that the sun will rise tomorrow morning) are indescribably short; against others (e.g., that the sun will explode tomorrow morning), inconceivably long. In a horse race 100-to-1 odds against a long shot are as long as we can easily encompass. The differences in order of magnitude between a million, 100 million, and a billion are exceedingly difficult to grasp. We all know that $1 billion is a huge amount of money. Most of us, however, would be astonished to learn that to spend $1 billion at the rate of $1,000 a day starting in A.D. 1 would take until A.D. 2740!

Small wonder, then, that it's so hard for us to deal realistically with comparative-risk assessments. The odds against getting killed are one million to one while traveling a thousand miles by automobile, five million to one against while traveling by train, and, on a scheduled flight, ten million to one against. Not many people, I would guess, let these odds influence their mode of travel.

Some people would stop eating broccoli if they knew it contained natural carcinogens in a number of parts per billion sufficient, if they were pesticide residues, to force the Food and Drug Administration to ban its sale. Others would give up a trip to Barbados because of a crisis in Pakistan. When I run into a person like that, I feel like saying, "Look, if that's the way you want to live, you should shut yourself up in a one-story padded house, put a lid on the bathtub, and never go out of doors."

Statistics, nevertheless, are the key to foresight capability. The ability to project statistical trends will not make us wise in our choice of goals. It will not tell us how to weigh competing claims. If we have no heed for the morrow, it will not force prudence upon us. The foresight capability that statistical projections make possible can, however, alert us to the potential consequences of our present choices. It can also give us a precious chance to adjust our course, our goal, or both.

One ambitious effort to foresee the future was the subject of a report published in 1980 near the end of the Carter administration by the Council on Environmental Quality. Called *The Global 2000 Report,* it projected trends in population growth, agricultural production, deforestation, nonrenewable-resource depletion, greenhouse-gas accumulation, environmental degradation, and the like. Early in the following year Russell Train, then head of the World Wildlife Fund, assembled a group called "The Year 2000 Committee." I was one of its members. *The Global 2000 Report* itself pointed out that the data on which its projections were based were inconsistent and incomplete and that the computer models it used were inadequate. The committee accordingly decided that its first priority should be to persuade the executive branch to take immediate steps toward overcoming these deficiencies. To this end several of us paid calls on key people in the executive branch. One of my prospects was David Stockman, the director of the Office of Management and Budget. I made an earnest appeal for our cause, but it made no dent on Stockman. "We do well around here," he said, "if we can foresee anything more than two months ahead!"

Could the explanation of this dismissive response, I wondered, be that the Reagan White House was suspicious of foresight capability? Foresight stimulates planning, and planning aims at changing the course that events would otherwise take. This can lead to government intervention into the private sector. Private enterprise is good. Government intervention is bad. Foresight, therefore, is to be avoided.

A less ideological attitude would have led to the opposite conclusion. Most of the planning made possible by improved foresight capability would be that undertaken by the private sector. Better private-sector planning would tend to reduce the need for government intervention, not to increase it. Recent U.S. history overflows with examples of botched regulation whose unintended and undesirable side effects were correctable only by additional regulation. Better foresight capability would have resulted in more surgical, and ultimately less intrusive, intervention. Ironically, business has come a long way toward reducing its own myopia while an even more shortsighted government has been insisting that it could see well enough.

In some areas even a marginal gain in the improvement of foresight capability would be worth far more than the expense of achieving it. A particularly dramatic example is the threat of climate change. The devastation that could result from substantial global warming would far exceed the harm caused by any previous human impact on the globe (except the population explosion). Averting it, however, might bring worldwide economic growth to a virtual halt. The very possibility of achieving consensus on effective remedial action thus depends on narrowing the range of statistical uncertainty.

What most impresses me as I look back over the ways in which we have allowed our means of grasping reality to impair our ability to deal with it is that there is no good reason why any of us should let this happen. Giving concreteness to concepts, freezing categories, clinging to hypotheses, ignoring the dynamic dimension, and all the rest can be avoided simply by reminding ourselves that they are habits of mind, nothing more. When we let them get in the way of reality, it's because we have been unable simultaneously to use them and see beyond them. They're like those theater curtains that look opaque in one kind of light but under different lighting let you see the stage set behind them.

Some people seem to have a natural ability to structure facts without letting the structure impair their vision. To have this capacity is to have what I call "a clear head." It accounts, I'm sure, for Warren Buffett's extraordinary ability to identify undervalued companies. It accounts also for the fair but undeceived character of David Broder's observation of the political scene.

Another individual whose possession of a clear head stands out in my mind is Thomas C. Schelling, now teaching at the University of Maryland. I first encountered Professor Schelling's clarity of vision when, as U.S. attorney for Massachusetts, I was trying to assemble a comprehensive picture of Mafia operations in New England. Someone gave me a paper of his on the economics of organized crime arguing that law enforcement is essential to the very existence of organized crime. My first reaction was incredulous. At the end I said to myself, "Of course! Why didn't I think of that?"

Tom Schelling's thesis was basically this: A business supplying an illegal product or service wouldn't be profitable enough to be worthwhile if anyone could easily enter it. The criminal business must therefore be able to get and keep a near monopoly. Few of those who might otherwise become competitors are willing to pay off the police, bribe judges, execute stoolies, and risk going to jail. These requirements are consequences of substantial law enforcement pressure. Such pressure is therefore necessary to the acquisition and protection of the monopoly. Aren't you now wondering why you didn't think of that?

But not even a head as clear as that of the boy who saw that the emperor had no clothes is sufficient by itself to assure a rounded perception of reality. For that, imagination is also necessary. Although the word "imagination" in common usage is most frequently applied to a world of fantasy, it also embraces the real but unseen; its role, says the dictionary, is the "formation of mental images of objects not present to the senses." Since the fraction of reality actually present to the senses at any given time is insignificant, imagination has a lot to do. Drawing on whatever it can summon up of remembered experience, actual or vicarious, the imagination supplies the missing pieces, the interpretations, and the empathy needed to give vividness and vitality to an unseen world.

A good historian can give us the feeling that we know what some corner of the past was really like. For me an unforgettable example is the picture in Garrett Mattingly's *The Armada* of Philip II, alone in his cell-like cabinet in the Escorial, writing in the margin of an optimistic report from his ambassador in Paris, "Nothing of this is true."

I was similarly struck by a CBS radio program simulating a news report from the scene of the burning of Joan of Arc. A CBS correspondent is in the main square of Rouen, where a throng of spectators is waiting for the condemned girl to be brought to the stake. He notices a man whose neat beard, black suit, and lace collar make him stand out from the crowd. Using snatches of rudimentary French, the correspondent makes his way to the stranger. After eliciting the observation that the British are about to make the mistake of creating a martyr, the correspondent asks the stranger how he happens to be in Rouen. The latter replies in Italian-accented English, "I am collecting books for Lorenzo de' Medici."

What history can do for the past, good reporting can at least partially do for the present. But it is the imagination we bring to a news report that makes the difference between merely taking in what it says and really *getting* it. That's why print and radio are often more successful than television in communicating reality. Fixing its eye on the most dramatic, sensational, or heart-rending features of any situation, the TV camera preempts the role of the imagination. The result can be less true to reality than a word picture.

When the camera zooms in on a bombed-out building, it creates the impression that the entire surrounding area must be equally devastated. You are not told that this is the only badly damaged building in the area. When I went to Baghdad in June of 1991, three months after the end of the Gulf War, televised news reports had led me to expect widespread devastation. So precise, in fact, had been the air strikes against the city that almost all its seriously damaged structures were government buildings, power plants, airfields, and military installations.

Our imaginations can help us to anticipate the future in the same way that they can make the past come alive or enlarge our comprehension of the present. How close imagination can come to grasping actuality, past, present, or future, depends on the adequacy of the available information as well as the understanding with which this information has been interpreted. We have more information about the past than about the present, and more about the present than about the future. This makes a difference, however, with respect only to the completeness of the picture that the imagination is able to create. A well-trained imagination works with the information it has. When this is scanty, it can build on the facts at hand the same way a paleontologist can turn a handful of bone fragments into a skeleton.

I said "well-trained imagination." But is it actually possible to train the imagination? I got into a discussion of that question with a couple of skeptical friends not long ago. I argued that the imagination's capacity to grasp reality can be trained by use. A worthwhile training program might employ exercises in which the trainee would be given a set of facts and a time limit within which to imagine their real-world significance. The subjects of these exercises could be drawn from any field—business, politics, the Civil War, modern technology—that supplied a factual base from which the imagination could take off. After the allotted time had expired, the trainee's imagined construct would be compared with its actual counterpart.

To illustrate what I mean, take the practical problems that have had to be solved in order to recover oil and gas from sedimentary layers half a mile beneath the muck underlying eight hundred feet of salt water. I once had a chance to learn something about these problems during a visit to an offshore drilling rig in the North Sea, and it was an eye-opening experience. Trial and error had taught the operators the answers to all kinds of questions I would not even have thought of asking. A participant in an imagination-training session would do well to identify such questions as: How would the drilling platform be supported? Would it float, or rest on stilts? Would stilts eight hundred feet long be practical? If not, how could a floating platform be kept level despite differently placed loads of steel pipe varying in weight from day to day? How would the rig be enabled to ride out North Sea gales? Would you need to worry about blowouts? And so on. It occurred to me then that being asked merely to identify questions such as these would be the perfect imagination-training exercise, assuming, of course, that the trainee had no prior knowledge of the relevant methodology.

But the most important corrective—even more important than the imagination—of the weaknesses to which our means of dealing with reality are prone is awareness of them. Once alerted to these tendencies, reasonable people do not have to be exhorted to combat them. They are not called upon either to embrace a new set of beliefs or to modify old ones. Their situation, rather, is like that of a man who has been told that his fly is open or of a woman who learns that her slip is showing. In both cases to be made aware of the situation is to be prompted to take corrective action. It's only the extremists who cannot be reached by polite reminders. But then, neither can they be reached by exhortation.

Information age or not, it's certain that we'll be hard put to keep our footing in the midst of information's onrush. As time goes on, therefore, we shall be less and less well able to afford misuse of our means of grasping reality. The achievement of discipline in avoiding these tendencies should be seen as essential to our intellectual development. There is no subject in any curriculum that could not be made the vehicle for teaching the proper use of the intellectual tools I have been discussing here. And come to think of it, journalists, politicians, lawyers, and diplomats would all do well to reassess the realism of their own thought processes. Just think what a difference that could make!

Bureaucratics

I remember well what first made me think that I might be a "manager." It was reading the press notices on my nomination as secretary of health, education, and welfare. They said that HEW had become an "unmanageable conglomerate" and that I had been chosen for the job because I had demonstrated "management skills" as number two in the Department of State, the job I then held. What, *me* a manager? I felt like the character in Molière's *Le Bourgeois gentilhomme* who exclaimed, "Good heavens! For more than forty years I have been speaking prose without knowing it."

Whatever I'd been doing right was not learned from any textbook. It reflected, rather, a set of quite simple assumptions about people and public service. Several years later I chanced upon an article in the *Radcliffe Quarterly* by Mary Howell, M.D., Ph.D., describing the skills applied by women to the management of their families.[1] I read the article with a shock of recognition. There, described with great succinctness, were glimpses into nearly everything I had learned about how to manage

---

[1] *Radcliffe Quarterly* 63, no. 4 (1977): 5.

a government department. Take, for example, the manner in which a tearful child is put to bed, which illustrates the importance of "regarding process as highly as product." Encouraging children to take an increasing part in household affairs calls for "task assignments that . . . offer opportunities for progressive and creative assumption of responsibility." The addition of an adult to a household of teenagers requires "setting rules, goals, and procedures, meant to vary according to the collective makeup of persons working together." The model housewife also practices "ongoing self-evaluation and self-correction," is aware that "job descriptions can be altered more easily than personalities or work styles," and perceives the need for the "evaluation of outcomes."

From time to time since running across that article I've thought about teaching a course on managing government agencies. I'd call it "Advanced Bureaucratics" and draw heavily on Dr. Howell's observations. The first part of the course would examine the ways in which our system of government depends on the competent practice of bureaucratics to assure openness and due process, the presentation of alternative courses of action, the matching of means to ends, and the achievement of cost-effectiveness. The course would also touch on the role of conceptual frameworks, the significance of systemic interrelationships, and the identification of opportunities for synergy among programs. And if I decided to talk about "learning organizations," the management gurus' current enthusiasm, I'd credit not them, but Dr. Howell.

Most of what any bureaucracy does is, of course, routine, repetitive, and unglamorous. It's essential, nonetheless, that it be done right. A story told to me by a friend who had recently taken over the chairmanship of a badly neglected municipal hospital makes this point all too well. Upon learning that the hospital's infection rate was shockingly high, my friend promptly got in touch with Dr. Carl Walter, a Harvard Medical School professor renowned for his expertise in surgical asepsis, and persuaded him to visit the hospital. On the appointed day Dr. Walter inspected the operating rooms in the company of the hospital administrator, the chief of surgery, and the head surgical nurse. Appalled by what he found, Dr. Walter prescribed what had to be done to bring the operating rooms up to scratch. Upon taking his departure he said he'd come back before long to check up on the progress being made.

Over the next several weeks, whenever the head surgical nurse ran into the hospital administrator, she would ask when Dr. Walter was coming back. The administrator would respond, "I don't know. I haven't yet heard from him." After this had happened several times, the administrator, with some exasperation, asked, "Why are you so anxious to know?" "Because," she snapped, "I'm getting damn sick of keeping the operating rooms so clean!"

Fortunately, the people who direct planes into airports, scrutinize stock offerings, inspect poultry, collect intelligence, and track hurricanes don't get sick of doing those tasks well. When the rare lapse occurs, two kinds of harm result: the direct harm caused by that particular failure and the indirect harm to public confidence in government. My least favorite cliché—"close enough for government work"—is a product of the latter.

Backing up the performance of routine operations is a second area of bureaucratic activity. Though engaging fewer people, it is central to government's role. This is the area of planning, program development, and evaluation. Such tools are indispensable to finding cost-effective ways of attacking serious issues. Without them we have little realistic hope of overcoming such chronic ills as welfare dependency, substance abuse, urban decay, or the self-perpetuating cycle of discrimination, functional illiteracy, lack of job training, and poverty.

Bureaucracy's third normal function is dealing with troublesome situations. Mediating a strike, reacting to a coup attempt, and distributing disaster relief are governmental equivalents of stopping a leak, putting out a brushfire, or staving off repossession of the car. They call for a high order of skill, judgment, and determination.

Activities falling within each of bureaucracy's provinces can be found in all government organizations. Their scale and status, however, differ widely from one organization to another. Departments like Health and Human Services or Housing and Urban Development manage a large number of repetitive functions (Social Security payments, review of new drug applications, housing loans, rent subsidies, and the like). Those and other domestic agencies are seldom called upon to handle an emergency. Their most interesting and challenging tasks belong to the second area— the development of better ways of coping with difficult problems.

In my time at HEW, the predecessor of HHS, the department's ongoing functions were by and large well managed. The Social Security Administration's overhead costs, for instance, were only 2 percent of benefit payments as against 6 percent for the insurance industry. Turning over smoothly, ongoing activities seldom gave rise to a problem requiring front-office attention. The department had even less occasion to cope with crises. The only one I can recall, apart from a few troublesome school desegregation cases, was the ten-week takeover by Sioux activists of the village of Wounded Knee, South Dakota, in commemoration of the massacre inflicted there in 1890. Our highest priorities, and hence most prestigious assignments, were devoted to welfare reform, the development of a many-faceted health-care program, and the integration of human services.

At the State Department, from which I had just come, the allocation of resources and priorities could not have been more different. At State the only significant routine function was the processing of passport and visa applications. Unlike HEW, State grappled continually with dozens of critical situations. Every day in every country of the world embassy officers collected, sifted, and reported on developments calling for supportive, preventive, or corrective action. In important situations, the secretary of state, the National Security Council, and even the president would draw on these and other sources for policy decisions that would then get fed into instructions to the embassies on how to proceed. In lesser cases the geographical bureaus would write the instructions on their own. Having performed as directed, the embassies communicated the outcome back to Washington for the formulation of follow-up instructions. To handle the "traffic" thereby generated, the Executive Secretariat had a staff of about four hundred which processed an average of eight thousand incoming and five thousand outgoing telegrams a day. HEW's equivalent office had only about forty people and a correspondingly small paper flow.

The lifeblood of the State Department still circulates in the same way. Supplying and tending this system are the department's all-absorbing, high-prestige preoccupations. So pressing are these immediate functions that little time remains for conceptual thinking, strategic planning, or the ordering of priorities. That's why the Policy Planning Staff has almost always been a stepchild at State—not much listened to and seldom at the center of things. This fact, indeed, goes a long way toward explaining many of the shortcomings in the conduct of U.S. foreign policy.

When I went to the Defense Department early in 1973, I found another markedly different pattern. At DOD all three functions—day-to-day routines, planning and analysis, maintaining a high state of readiness, and dealing with situations ranging from troublesome to dangerous—embody roughly equal requirements. As military officers go up the ladder in rank and responsibility, their successive tours of duty ordinarily embrace assignments in each of these three areas.

You could do worse than define a bureaucracy as an organization that performs these three functions. Since all three can be found in all large organizations, it should follow that all large organizations are bureaucracies. For some odd reason, however, the notion persists that "bureaucracy" is an affliction peculiar to government. A comparison with business should be instructive.

Let's take a look, then, at what business organizations and government organizations have in common. Both are hierarchical in structure. Both are headed by chief executives to whom a variety of second-echelon line and staff officials report. A big corporation's financial controller and personnel manager perform roles much like those of the controller and personnel director in a government agency. Nonprofit organizations—foundations, universities, hospitals, and youth-service agencies, for instance—have similar features and behave in similar ways.

All bureaucracies are subject to some kind of accountability: in the case of businesses, to their owners, employers, and customers; in the case of philanthropies, to their donors and beneficiaries; in the case of government agencies, to the general public. Watching over the private sector are the IRS, the SEC, the Antitrust Division of the Department of Justice, outside accountants, and a host of state and local bodies. Watching over government are Congress, the General Accounting Office, the media, and countless interest groups. To satisfy the watchdogs, both private and public, bureaucracies are required to be prodigious generators of red tape.

All bureaucracies also compete: businesses, for profits; philanthropies, for donations; government agencies, for public support. Business people and public servants alike strive to win or, failing that, at least to be identified with a winner. Dedication to the public interest does not exorcise competitiveness. On the contrary, public-sector bureaucrats, like their private-sector counterparts, want their units to excel. If the unit can't be bigger than the rest, let it be better; if it can't be more successful, let it get more public attention. Win, lose, or draw, it's theirs.

One of the many things I regret about Gerald Ford's defeat in 1976 is that the ending of my service as secretary of commerce averted a turf battle that, for the sake of preserving Republican unity, I had reluctantly deferred until after the election. The Commerce Department provocation was Treasury's usurpation of primacy in matters of international economic policy, notwithstanding that most of the data collection, economic analysis, and professional talent relied upon by Treasury belonged to Commerce. In short, Treasury was getting credit for Commerce's work. Although I was convinced, of course, that the public interest would be better served if the whole area were consolidated under us, I can't deny that competitiveness had something to do with my eagerness for the fray.

Within an organization, too much competition can promote fragmentation and frustrate cooperation. A good way, therefore, of giving the competitors an organizational perspective is to expose them to the merits of one anothers' claims. When I came to HEW in 1970, I found a markedly sour atmosphere. My predecessor had restricted the policy-making process to a small inside group. Decisions emerged without any clear explanation of how they had been reached. To remedy the situation I asked the bureau chiefs to bring with them to any meeting at which an important policy issue was to be discussed all the people, no matter how junior, who had worked on it. This made for a pretty crowded conference room, but it assured that the staffers who had participated in preparing their boss's case would get direct exposure to the opposing arguments. The staffers would also gather from the tenor of my questions that I was genuinely trying to understand the problem. No matter what the eventual outcome, none of those who had attended the meeting could reasonably believe that their side had been robbed. A secondary benefit was preventing leaks of the sort that commonly come from sore losers.

I have cited similarities between business and government bureaucracies. There are also important differences. Though both are hierarchical, the upper echelons of the former are less diffuse and possess considerably more authority than those of the latter. Business bosses are more or less free to hire and fire, promote and demote, reward and penalize. In these respects politically appointed government managers are hardly bosses at all: the tenure of most of their subordinates began before they came, cannot easily be terminated, and is likely to last long after they have left.

Top managers in business commonly come up through the ranks. When they are recruited from outside it is almost always on the basis of relevant prior experience. When they get to the top and perform well, they can count on staying for a while, even for decades. Presidential appointees at the level of assistant secretary and above, on the other hand, often come to government with limited substantive background and little experience in dealing with the political process. And as their numbers have grown from 441 at the beginning of the Nixon administration to 581 at the beginning of the Clinton administration, their average tenure, only 2.6 years then, continues to be shorter.

Where accountability is concerned, the principal similarity between the publics with which a business is involved and the general public to which government is answerable is that both demand performance. The differences are glaring, however, in the makeup of these publics as well as in their ability to judge performance. The constituents of a business share a common interest in its long-term profitability, though they may not agree as to how the pie should be divided. Shareholders look at the bottom line; employees look at wages, benefits, and working conditions; customers look at quality, price, and service. In each case the results are communicable in relatively clear and objective terms. Although any given business has some chance of becoming the subject of intense public scrutiny, few ever receive it. Indeed, given the decades of inertia before American business recently began to reinvent itself, the public might have been better off if business had had more such scrutiny.

In assessing government performance, on the other hand, the general public brings to bear manifold interests and a host of criteria, many of them contradictory. Each of the types of government functions touched on above is subject to a different set of standards. Any random list makes the point—for example, the efficient administration of Social Security benefits, the shaping of a workable approach to reducing violent crime, and the deterrence of nuclear proliferation. Moreover, to a degree unknown in business, government is constantly being forced to change its direction and priorities in response to the outcomes of intense political struggles. And though performance standards for government need to be made clearer and more objective than they are now, it is obvious that they can never be reduced to a "bottom line." Meanwhile, the scale and impact of government programs assures that public managers will continue to operate under the floodlights beamed at them by Congress, the media, and legions of special-interest groups. The watchdogs, I should add, are not looking for opportunities to hand out bouquets.

Being aware both of the number and the force of the claims

imposed on government and of the improbability that more than a few can be fully satisfied, public servants take it for granted that they will hear more criticism than praise. The need for a self-protective paper trail is a major reason why government red tape has always been voluminous. The erosion of trust that began with Watergate has led to the proliferation of more and more elaborate defensive devices. Meanwhile, deficit-cutting measures have generated delays by holding down the number of civil servants available to administer the resulting increase in the red-tape burden.

Three comparatively recent phenomena illustrate the degenerative process stemming from distrust. One is an emphasis on appearing to be ethical which rests on the assumption that no one is ethical. Another is the presumption that any possessor of discretionary authority will easily yield to pressure: hence the reams of regulations aimed at foreclosing the possibility of some outside connection that might influence an official action. The third is the concern that a potential appointee's past conduct might cause future embarrassment.

Clearance procedures for nominees to top posts that used to take three or four weeks now take months, even years. On top of all this, every oversight body and interest group has its own demands for the elimination of remote risks or the bestowal of marginal benefits. Congressman James C. Greenwood, a Republican congressman from Pennsylvania, has said that when he was a social worker trying to protect children, he had to spend at least a day and a half each week filling out federal forms. Worse, the suspicion that "waste, fraud, and abuse" are everywhere rampant has set in motion a vicious circle that starts with congressional micromanagement, leads to more paperwork, and ends up with cost increases imposed by private-sector contractors resentful of being distrusted. Former secretary of defense James R. Schlesinger estimates that this vicious circle has doubled the cost of defense procurement in constant dollars over the past twenty-five years.

As already noted, business executives have considerably more authority than government managers. This difference between business and government bureaucracies brings to mind a conversation I had in 1970 with the executive vice president of a large high-tech manufacturing company, to whom I had offered the job of assistant secretary of HEW for administration and management. Having taken some time to think about the offer and discuss it with his wife, he was back in Washington for a second meeting. "I'm here to tell you," he said, "that I would like to help you with your decisionmaking." I couldn't help laughing. "That's wonderful news," I replied, "but I hope you realize that making decisions is the easiest thing I do. The hard part is persuading other people—my HEW colleagues, the Office of Management and Budget, the White House, outside groups, the press, the Congress, and people in general— to go along with what I've decided."

Many of the business people brought into government never fully adjust to the need to shift their priorities from decisionmaking to building consensus and generating support. This explains why success as a corporate executive is no guarantee of success in government. On the other hand, two of my most effective fellow bureaucrats at HEW, to their own surprise as much as mine, were professors of medicine. Could that have been because their skills were closer than a business person's to those of a woman who manages a family?

It is certainly true, in any case, that in a government bureaucracy, as in a household, an important managerial function is that of casting director. It makes more sense to make the most of the people you find on board than to try to get them transferred or removed. People do well what they're good at and not so well what they're less good at. In the capacity of casting director, the manager's job is to select roles for colleagues that take advantage of the former and to find someone else who would be better suited for the latter. At times it's necessary to tailor a job description to fit the actual capabilities of the incumbent, handing out where necessary both increased responsibility and an advancement in rank, or—less often—reducing responsibility and lowering rank.

These are things I began to learn in the army. Not long after reporting for duty as a platoon leader in Company B of the Fourth Medical Battalion, I had to decide what to do about two privates who were constantly causing trouble. They were, let's face it, what the army used to call "fuckups." Someone else might have made it tough on them, but I concluded that the reason they caused so much trouble was that they had natural but misdirected leadership capacities. I accordingly promoted them both to corporal and made them squad leaders. From then on they performed outstandingly well, especially in combat. One received the Silver Star and the other the Bronze Star for Heroic Service.

Years later, when I was lieutenant governor of Massachusetts, I had on my staff a young woman who seemed unmotivated, prone to complain, and barely adequate in her performance. The obvious thing would have been to replace her. She was, however, very bright and showed flashes of energy when given a genuinely challenging task. Remembering my army experience, I gave her more work and more responsibility. She thrived on it, and at the peak of her subsequent career she served as the chief of staff for the president of a large university.

I think back on those people with some pride, as I also do toward my relationship with two government colleagues whom I felt compelled to demote. Both held very senior positions, but it had become apparent that they were not up to their jobs. In each case, a quiet, unhurried conversation led to a decision to step down to a less demanding assignment. Both men were not only relieved but grateful, and they remain to this day two of my most loyal friends.

Once the players have been appropriately cast, they need to be given the feeling that they are part of a common undertaking to which their individual efforts are making a valuable contribution. The key to creating this feeling is engaging them in a common commitment to a worthwhile purpose—something larger than themselves. They also need to believe both that the effort to fulfill this purpose is being carried out on the merits and that no other consideration will derail it.

Throughout my government service, I invariably made a point of dealing with people in the bureaucracy, the White House, and on the Hill as though they had no other concern than the best achievable solution of the problem at hand. I might suspect—indeed, have good reason to believe—that this was not wholly true, that they did in fact have less worthy motives. But I found that if, despite this suspicion, I went ahead as if no such unacknowledged interest existed, it became increasingly difficult for any of them to bring it up.

This approach worked remarkably well on the Hill. That, I concluded, was because most American politicians want to sound like statesmen—at least to a presidential appointee. Counting on this, I would encourage a member of Congress to expand on all the high-minded reasons why he would like to support, if he could, the position I was urging upon him. It was rather like drawing an animal away from its bolt-hole: at some point you get it far enough from the hole so that you can cut off its line of retreat. By the time the congressman had sufficiently expatiated on his broad-gauged and sympathetic understanding of the subject at issue, it was too late for him to fall back on some small-

minded justification for backing away from what he'd just said. This approach, by the way, was less apt to work with British politicians. I remember once making an earnest pitch to a British M.P. who simply laughed and said, "Come now, Mr. Ambassador, I couldn't do that. If I did, my constituents would 'ave my 'ide!'"

Of course, you can't hope to keep a discussion focused on the merits of an issue unless you're on top of it yourself. You must have a solid grasp of the relevant facts, a clear understanding of the competing arguments, and a fair assessment of the interests at stake. In my own case, by the time I reached that stage I had also made up my mind as to just how much ground I was willing to give. Where a lot was at stake I was prepared to resign if I could not hold that line. By the time the showdown came, I felt secure. Again and again, in situations like that, the opposition dissolved. I may have been deluding myself, but I sometimes had the feeling that the force of my convictions had somehow gotten across in advance.

The importance of dealing with the merits deserves a few more words. If your only interest is in finding the solution to the problem at hand, you're ready to accept any useful suggestion. And since you will have made it clear from the outset that a better idea is welcome from whatever source it comes, taking advantage of the suggestion is easy. Indeed, a lack of eagerness to welcome a better idea can only mean either that you think you're always right or that you think other people are always wrong.

My own tendency as a bureaucrat to think that I was right—and I could be pretty dogmatic about it—was tempered by the knowledge that I was easily capable of overlooking or not properly evaluating some important factor. That's why one of the qualities I most valued in Jonathan Moore, my chief of staff at State, HEW, Defense, and Justice, was his readiness to take me on. He would sometimes have a hard time getting his point across, and the argument could become quite heated. When he finally got through—and this happened more than half the time—I would say, *"Of course! Why didn't I see that?"* I was always glad to have such outcomes witnessed by colleagues who didn't know me well. They would be encouraged, I hoped, to follow Jonathan's example.

The combination of consistent emphasis on the merits and studied disregard of ulterior motives worked so well for me in all my years in Washington that until the first stage of my last full-time assignment I had no occasion to give any thought to the process of negotiation. I might, in fact, have lived out the rest of my life without becoming aware of this gap in my education had I not in 1977 become head of the U.S. delegation to the United Nations Conference on the Law of the Sea, then and perhaps even now the largest and most ambitious assembly of its kind.

A clue to my ignorance surfaced in the third week of my job when I gave a talk about the conference at a luncheon on Capitol Hill. "I do not approach this assignment," I said, "in the spirit of a haggler in a rug bazaar. I see myself, rather, as a contributor to rational accommodations among valid competing interests." Though rather pleased with this remark at the time, I soon came to realize that it was one of the most fatuous statements I had ever made. Within weeks I had been introduced to real negotiation: it's a matter, I discovered, of convincing the other guy that what you have to offer is worth more than he realized and that he doesn't have much time to get it, while simultaneously convincing him that what he's offering is worth less to you than he thought and that you have all the time in the world. I was in a rug bazaar, all right!

All bureaucracies, both public and private, tend to become rigid, top-heavy, and overweight. They do not adjust well to complexity, changes of circumstance, or new systemic interconnections. The resulting inertial tendencies, leading as they do to the loss of flexibility, innovative capacity, and adaptiveness, become increasingly hard to overcome. In the case of business, Big Steel, the Big Three automakers, and IBM not long ago supplied conspicuous examples of these tendencies. In varying degrees and combinations, they sat too long on established markets, delayed technological innovation, tolerated top-heaviness, and neglected quality controls. Big Steel ignored the possibility that its loyal customers might choose to buy foreign-made steel merely because it was cheaper. The Big Three conveyed the impression that car buyers shouldn't want to pay for safety instead of recognizing that this was a choice that belonged to the buyers. IBM took it for granted that what worked well yesterday—its corporate structure, management systems, and reliance on mainframe computers—would work equally well tomorrow. Shortsightedness, indeed, was endemic to American businesses. We saw that in their fixation on the stock market's reaction to their next quarterly reports. We saw it also in their inclination to seek shelter behind import quotas and restrictions rather than pursue export opportunities.

On the government side, it's not hard to line up an equally damning litany of errors and omissions. One example is the federal bureaucracy's fixation on input as opposed to output measures of performance, a fallacy that I've inveighed against as long as I can remember. In the same category belong the neglect of information technology, the avoidance of evaluation, and constipated regulatory procedures. Vice President Gore's National Performance Review Report zeroes in on these deficiencies and upon every federal program and agency to get on with planning and performance measurement. To push this process, an Office of Government Performance would be charged with formulating measurable outcomes.

The National Performance Review Report also resurrects an approach that used to be called "management by objectives." It's one I relied on in all the departments where I served. To make it work, you have to understand the difference between goals and objectives. Goals are ends that we want to achieve—things like reducing crime, improving education, and achieving sustainable economic growth. But a goal is too broad and abstract to be the target of a concrete plan of action. An objective, on the other hand, marks a specific stage of progress toward a goal. In the case of reducing crime, an objective might be to increase the visible presence of police officers in crime-infested neighborhoods. In the case of education, it might be to use natural history as a bridge to teaching biology, or in the case of sustainable growth, to adjust national economic accounts to reflect the depletion of nonrenewable resources. Each of these aims is specific enough to be made the objective of a concrete plan embodying quantifiable measures of progress.

The ability to measure progress, I should add, is critical. Without it the utilization of objectives is reduced from a disciplined process to a subjective exercise. Discovering this taught me never to choose for management purposes an objective toward which progress is not measurable. From this two things followed: first, that the target should be refocused whenever sharper definition will improve the measurement of progress toward it; second, that where the existing means of measurement are inadequate, developing better methods should get high priority. That's probably why, throughout my years in government, I was always looking for ways of quantifying the unquantifiable.

At HEW, for example, we could have done a much better job in evaluating our programs if inputs of time, skill, and money had been reducible to a single quantum. This quantum, called a "hew," would have enabled us to make definitive comparisons of the results achieved by varying combinations of these inputs. A highly useful tool, wouldn't you agree?

Other departments have similar needs to quantify the unquantifiable. At State, for example, whether or not, and if so how, to respond to a critical situation depends on the magnitude of the interests at stake, the probable extent to which each possible response will advance or set back those interests, and, for each response, the costs likely to be incurred. If you could in fact quantify each of these variables, you'd have a pretty good idea of what action, if any, to take. Elsewhere in this book are equally useful suggestions for measuring the rate of increase in complexity, a system of national well-being accounts, and a standard of newsworthiness.

But even if you don't share my enthusiasm for quantifying the unquantifiable, you will, I'm sure, agree that the effective performance of bureaucratic tasks demands more than a periodic fix on the rate of progress toward their objectives. It demands as well the continuous adaptation of present practices to foreseeable requirements. Old structures must be made to give way to new combinations of people and resources that are geared to these requirements: a structure, after all, like the taxonomy to which it conforms, fulfills no function other than the convenient grouping of similar things. Thus, no matter how suitable the structure, there will still be a need for integration and synthesis.

At HEW programs, and therefore structures, were built around age groups, disease categories, types of disability, income status, forms of substance abuse, educational level, and so on. Individuals and families, on the other hand, are integral. It is essential, therefore, to try to overcome the fragmented, piecemeal, episodic treatment of people that results from the bureaucratic compartmentalization of human services. And what is true of human services is also true, of course, of other problem-directed government programs.

The usual response to fragmentation is "coordination." Coordination is all right as far as it goes, but it doesn't go very far. I found that out as lieutenant governor of Massachusetts many years ago. Since that office has very few duties, I agreed to run for it only after the gubernatorial candidate, John A. Volpe, promised that if we were both elected, he would delegate to me responsibility for coordinating all the state's human resources programs. Both of us won, albeit narrowly, and on inauguration day I had ready for the governor's signature a letter carrying out the promised delegation.

Thus it came about that from the beginning of the Volpe administration I met regularly with the heads of the public welfare, public health, mental health, vocational rehabilitation, education, corrections, and youth services agencies. And though we collectively identified problems of overlap, duplication, omission, and inconsistency, we seldom succeeded in solving them. From time to time, as a by-product of better communication, we were able to iron out some particular difficulty or take a unified position on a budgetary or administrative issue. In the course of our meetings, however, it became increasingly apparent that to reduce fragmentation it would be necessary to add to coordination at least two other ingredients: first, joint planning among service providers, and second, a means of assuring that the joint plan was carried out. Where the convener of the participating agencies does not have line authority over them, these two ingredients are essential to reducing fragmentation. But even where such authority does exist, the practical bureaucratic limitations I've already mentioned call for building consensus.

All of these considerations apply twice over to the presidency of the United States. The president is in principle not only the chief conductor for the executive branch but its principal composer and orchestrator as well. Although the "White House" is not often thought of as a bureaucracy, it is in principle the bureaucracies' bureaucracy, and the Office of Management and Budget is its control center. In fact, however, principle and practice are far apart. One reason for this is that OMB's management role has never had adequate attention or support. Dwight Ink, an expert on management who during thirty-seven years in government held an extraordinary number of high-level career positions, has put his finger on the problem:

> [T]he combining of budget and management staffs never achieves its intended goals. Budget pressures simply drive out sustained work on most management issues. Furthermore, agencies come to look at management initiatives as mere tools for OMB control and budget cutting.

Ink's solution, which makes sense to me, is a separation of functions with an Office of Federal Management that would serve as the management arm of the president.

Another reason for the presidency's bureaucratic weakness, though obvious, is seldom noticed. It is that the president has even less control over cabinet departments than those departments have over their own multiple bureaus and agencies. Calvin Coolidge's vice president, Charles G. Dawes, who had previously served as the first director of the Bureau of the Budget, OMB's predecessor, had it right: "Cabinet secretaries," he said, "are vice presidents in charge of spending, and as such are the natural enemies of the president."

Mr. Dawes was pointing, of course, to a manifestation of Miles's Law. No department head can be expected to judge impartially the merit or priority of his own programs over those of other departments. The secretary of health and human services is duty bound to make the best possible case for the claims of medical research. The secretary of transportation is equally obliged to assert those of civil aviation. Neither knows enough about the affairs of the other to be qualified to address them. No department head, therefore, wants to expose his or her special interests to the crossfire of fellow cabinet officers who may be battling for the same turf or resources. Jesse Jones, secretary of commerce under Franklin D. Roosevelt, put it this way: "There was no one at the table who could be of help to me except the president, and when I needed to consult him I did not choose a cabinet meeting to do so."

One giant step toward strengthening the president's leadership of the executive branch would be reform of the cabinet. For the reasons just mentioned, the cabinet as presently constituted is incapable of being the kind of deliberative body to which the president can usefully submit key issues. Among all the cabinet meetings I attended under three presidents, I can recall only one at which a difficult issue was then and there resolved.[2] The rest focused on bland common denominators like the economic outlook, displays of budgetary breakdowns, or the status of the administration's legislative proposals. In the Nixon cabinet, as a spe-

---

[2] This was early in 1959, and I was at the meeting because my boss, Arthur Flemming, had persuaded Eisenhower to put on the agenda an education bill that his staff did not support but that was my particular baby. I had made up my mind that if the president chose not to send the bill to the Hill, I would resign. At the end of a long and sometimes acrimonious discussion in which Vice President Nixon's timely interventions knocked down the key objections to the bill, Eisenhower decided to let it go forward. Nixon, it seems, was saving my resignation for himself.

cial treat, Vice President Spiro T. Agnew would from time to time be allowed to give us a travelogue.

For the same reasons that the cabinet is incapable of being a deliberative body, it is hardly better able to perform an integrative function. Cabinet committees chaired by a senior department head can, to be sure, be useful. Their value is limited, however, by the fact that no cabinet member will accept direction from any other cabinet member. Since all of them report directly to the president, each is deemed to have a right of appeal to the chief executive. On this account no president, so far as I know, has ever felt able to give the chairman or a majority of a cabinet committee the authority to make a decision that a dissenting member is obliged to accept.

For purposes of policy deliberation the president needs to be able to call upon a cabinet composed of people who can be counted on to share a broad perspective. The likeliest candidates for this role are presidential appointees whose responsibilities transcend departmental boundaries. They include the chief of staff, the director of OMB, the special assistant for national security affairs, the United States trade representative, and the principal presidential staff advisers on economics, domestic policy, the environment, and science. (To assure accountability to the Congress and the public, these appointments would need to be made subject to Senate confirmation.) There could then be added to this group the secretaries of state, defense, and treasury, each of whom has responsibilities that span broad areas of national policy.

A cabinet re-formed in this manner could perform an integrative role without having to leave open the opportunity for direct appeal to the president. Individual members of the reconstituted cabinet could be given the authority to resolve interdepartmental disagreements on matters not needing the president's personal attention. This new regime would also permit the ad hoc designation of assistant presidents who could help to share the presidential load, an impossibility so long as all department heads have cabinet rank. Meanwhile, department heads, and perhaps key agency heads as well, should continue to meet from time to time, but as members of a new body with a name like "The Executive Council."

It is, I take it, obvious that this proposal would not affect the mandate, structure, or political accountability of departments not represented in the cabinet. After all, the Veterans Administration, the U.S. Office of Education, and the Federal Energy Administration did not, merely as a consequence of being given new names and "elevated" to cabinet status, acquire any new role or responsibility. The Environmental Protection Administration would operate just as it does now if it were to be similarly favored. Conversely, nothing of great consequence turns on whether or not the collection of agencies now called the "Department of Commerce" continues to bear that label and report to a person with the title of "secretary" rather than "administrator."

Abolishing functions is something else again. It can matter quite a lot whether or not entities now in the Department of Commerce such as the National Oceanic and Atmospheric Administration (NOAA) or the National Institute of Standards and Technology, each of which fulfills a unique role, continues in existence. And if either or both of those entities were made part of some new umbrella organization, it would also make a difference whether or not the new combination constituted a whole greater than the sum of its parts.

There is, however, something to be said for consolidating departments. In the Nixon administration the Ash Commission recommended reducing their number from twelve to eight. State, Defense, Treasury, and Justice would have remained intact. The others would have been brought together under four substantively related headings—Human Resources, Community Development, Natural Resources, and Economic Development—thus inserting an integrative capacity between the White House and the major interest groups now directly tied to departments like Agriculture, Labor, and Commerce. If this didn't surprise those who assumed that Nixon's every move was calculated to enlarge his opportunity for secretive manipulation, it should have. For the net effect of these consolidations would have been to diminish substantially the number of interdepartmental issues that would previously have had to be handled by anonymous presidential assistants. It would have transferred these issues instead to superdepartment heads visible to the public, available to the media, and accountable to Congress. That, in my view, was the strongest argument for the Ash Commission proposals. Except, however, by reducing its size, these moves would not have helped to convert the cabinet into a deliberative or policymaking body.

But even if the wisdom of my views does not immediately win over the interest groups clustered around the existing and would-be cabinet departments, the president should continue to give a high priority to strengthening the federal government's planning capability. A first step would be to accelerate the repair of the data-collection processes whose deterioration seems to have been an almost deliberate aim of the Reagan administration. And when more comprehensive and more consistent data collection has been supplemented by computer-based modeling capacity, the components of foresight capability will at last have come together.

The relentless increase in complexity makes forward-looking planning both more necessary and more difficult. Bureaucrats, however, commonly react by focusing ever more narrowly on their own limited zones of responsibility. And since they cannot by themselves transcend those limitations, the precondition of their doing so is political leadership that defines goals, chooses priorities, and develops strategies for fulfilling those priorities. Only if this precondition has been met can the bureaucracy perform optimally. Just as a competent musician can play whatever notes have been written for her instrument, so a competent bureaucrat can meet whatever responsibilities are within the range of her skills. But neither good music nor good public service can be produced without a good score to play from. IRS agents don't write the tax laws they administer; other people enact them. To be regarded as successful the bureaucracy must not only perform well but be given the right tasks.

Vice President Gore's National Performance Review Report did not, in my view, sufficiently stress the inseparability between the appropriateness with which the tasks to be performed have been defined and the standards by which the performers are to be judged. To call once more on the orchestral analogy, we should have bureaucracy critics whose job would be to write "performance reviews." Like music critics, performance critics should be expected to appraise not only the performers' technique but the music they were given to play.

Where the orchestral analogy breaks down is in the matter of direction. On the stage of a symphony hall all the musicians can see and follow the conductor's beat—and they'd better follow, or else! A government department is a collection of orchestras each playing from a score differing, though in varying degrees, from the scores played by the others. The only good reason for assembling a given group of agencies under the roof of a single department is that the interrelationships among their programs are more significant than the divergences.

At HEW nothing on a random list of the department's most urgent concerns—poverty, drug abuse, alcoholism, juvenile delinquency, mental retardation, child development, the elderly, rehabilitation of the handicapped—fell within the exclusive province of any one operating agency. None was exclusively a "health" problem or an "education" problem or a "welfare problem." All involved aspects of each. I thought it was my job as department head to promote cooperative solutions, resolve jurisdictional disputes, and lead the development and execution of joint plans. My favorite word in those days was "synergy." Having sought synergy at HEW, I tried again to promote it at Defense, Justice, and Commerce. I was in each case at the first stage of an attempt to lead an orchestra playing more or less in unison, but I kept changing jobs too fast to find out how well I might have succeeded.

Government managers now have within reach a means of achieving functional integration that did not even exist in my day. The means is information technology. Top managers in a large corporation can now get instantaneous access to such indicators of unit performance as employment levels, hours worked, direct and overhead costs, inventory, backlog, sales, and profit margins. Any slippage or shortfall in meeting agreed-upon objectives shows up quickly. Mere inquiries and suggestions can thus take the place of control mechanisms administered through several supervisory layers. The result is a flatter structure, fewer mid-level managers, and greater reliance on the initiative of decentralized units.

If information technology can do all this for large corporations formerly dependent on top-down control, why shouldn't it be able to work in reverse for large government agencies? Why can't it, in other words, bring greater cohesion to a presently diffuse and fragmented coalition? In the front office of a government department, a central database continuously updated by information fed to it by constituent bureaus and agencies would quickly expose gaps, overlaps, duplications, and inefficiencies. Such a database would enormously facilitate the development of comprehensive plans involving participation by several agencies. Being continuously updated, it would also reveal immediately any failure by a participating agency to carry out its part in such a plan. Corrective action could then be stimulated merely by calling the problem to the attention of the responsible manager. Better yet, opportunities for synergy among programs administered by different agencies would be identified in such a way as to enhance the likelihood that the responsible officials would want to cooperate. Thus, the very same information-tracking resources that enable corporations to maintain cohesion with diminished control would enable government organizations to achieve cohesion without greater control.

The federal government, nevertheless, has been slow in introducing advanced information systems. Given the Reagan deficits, money to pay for them has, of course, been scarce. But that's not a good excuse. Once up and running, advanced information systems would soon pay for themselves through the savings thereby generated.

While the executive branch's slowness to take advantage of information technology may have resulted merely from a lack of imagination in grasping its potential, there could also be another explanation. This one rests on the coincidence between the period in which information technology was coming into its own in the corporate world and the period in which conservative Republicans controlled the White House. The same antigovernment bias that starved data collection, stood in the way of developing foresight capability, and questioned the need for abler civil servants may also have underlain the neglect of information technology.

If this conjecture does indeed account for the Reagan and Bush administrations' indifference toward high tech's capacity to upgrade governmental efficiency, I can only say that they underestimated this country's commitment to a creative balance between the necessary role of government and the freedom of the private sector. As to the indispensability of the latter, a visit to the Soviet Union in 1974 taught me a powerful lesson. It seemed to me obvious that so long as bureaucrats at the top and center persisted in trying to manage the civilian economy, the system could never be made responsive to regional, local, and individual preferences and choices. It was bound to lack sensitivity at the fingertips.

In all my meetings with senior Soviet officials I pressed them to tell me how an already overloaded central state planning system could be made to accommodate the even greater complexity that would be bound to result from their planned increases in consumer goods production. In every case I got the same reply: It would be done by adopting American management methods! It was hard to keep a straight face. No management methods known in America, I told them, would be capable of controlling a single sector of our own consumer economy, much less the whole of it. "If that's your best hope," I said, "you can't get there from here."

I left the Soviet Union with a new appreciation of the role of free markets. The laws of supply and demand let consumers make choices that central planners can only guess at. I was not surprised, therefore, when in due course Mikhail Gorbachev saw the necessity of opening the door to market forces. It was not, however, as a convert to capitalism but as a realistic bureaucrat that he did so.

Starting almost ten years earlier, awareness of the limitations of bureaucratic capacity had induced Deng Xiaoping to institute considerably more radical reforms. His first important action on taking power was to abolish state control of agricultural production. During the next several years, while market-oriented reforms were being introduced into other sectors of the economy, some 800 million Chinese peasants accumulated large amounts of savings. To tap those savings for capital investment in industry, the Chinese government could only offer savings accounts paying a fixed rate of interest. Why not, instead, find a way of funneling some of this money into shares in productive enterprises that would yield a return to the investor only if the enterprise made money?

Deng's response to that problem revealed remarkable flexibility. With his encouragement, the People's Bank of China in November of 1986 hosted in Beijing a four-day seminar on securities exchanges for two hundred bankers from all over China. The faculty for this seminar was assembled by the New York Stock Exchange. In addition to John Phelan, the Exchange's chairman, it included the chairmen of Merrill Lynch and First Boston, executives from Paine Webber and Shearson Lehman Brothers, former secretary of state William P. Rogers, and other Wall Street lawyers. As one of the organizers, I gave a talk on the roles of government and self-regulation in financial markets.

The day after the seminar ended, this conspicuous group of capitalists met with Deng Xiaoping in the Great Hall of the People. Turning first to John Phelan, Deng asked, "Do you know why you're here?" Phelan, responding in the vein usual to such occasions, alluded to friendship, cooperation, and learning from one another. When Phelan finished, Deng shook his head. "No," he said, "you're here so that we can exploit you!"[3]

---

[3] China now has two official stock exchanges. On a busy day in 1995, 38 million shares worth $2.7 billion were traded on the floor of the Shanghai Stock Exchange, the larger of the two.

Here at home, dedication to private-sector competition has in some ways made bureaucracy more pervasively intrusive and more substantively complex than it is in other industrial countries. We have always been unique in the degree to which we have relied on regulatory commissions to assure that private enterprises serve—or at least do not abuse—the public interest. As long ago as 1887 we created the Interstate Commerce Commission to protect shippers from rate discrimination and price gouging by the railroads. As in the course of time it became necessary to curb other quasimonopolistic abuses, new regulatory commissions were created. Their role was to regulate, and regulate they did. But the burden of proving that the public interest needs protection against some form of abuse has always rested with the protagonist of regulation. The existence of abuses, moreover, has never been an excuse for removing a category of business from private control.

The industrial countries of Europe came at the relationship between government and the private sector from the opposite side. When fearful that private industry might not be sufficiently dedicated to the public interest, their instinct was, if not to nationalize the industry, at least to create a state-owned corporation. And while this instinct undoubtedly sprang in part from socialist doctrine, Europe had kings long before it had socialists. Louis XIV, after all, was speaking no more than the truth when he said, "I am the state."

It did not occur to me then, but it strikes me now, that both influences were reflected in a conversation I had in 1975 with Lord Kearton, the chairman of the then newly formed British National Oil Corporation. He told me that BNOC would not be engaged in producing or marketing oil. Indeed, it would have no operational function whatever except to assure that Great Britain would be able to purchase the oil it needed. "If that's its only function," I asked, "why bother to create a state corporation?" "We need it," said the chairman, "so that the government will know what the North Sea oil companies are doing." The American answer, of course, would have been a law requiring them to furnish the needed information. BNOC, however, had come into existence under a socialist government, and Kearton was a member of the House of Lords.

Two other conversations in that same year pointed up this difference in bureaucratic style. One was with France's minister of industry, who informed me that virtually all France's industrial research was funded by the government through a peer-review system not unlike that used by our own National Institutes of Health for the support of bio-medical research. The other was with a lawyer for the British Iron and Steel Trades Union. Thinking that he must be a "labor lawyer" in the American sense, I asked him a question which elicited the fact that practically all he did was handle workmen's compensation cases. The U.K. had no labor lawyers because it had no labor law—no counterpart of the National Labor Relations Board and no legislation comparable to the Norris–La Guardia Act, the Wagner Act, the Taft-Hartley Act, or the Landrum-Griffin Act. In fact, Great Britain did not then regulate labor relations at all!

This country's determination to let free enterprise remain free has exacted a substantial bureaucratic price in the form of rules, regulations, reporting requirements, quasi-legislative administrative proceedings, and quasi-judicial administrative tribunals, all backed up by a panoply of potential civil and criminal penalties. The result is a wary, if not antago-nistic, relationship between business and government that also distin-guishes us from other industrial countries, particularly Japan. There, as a vice minister of trade and industry once pointed out to me, a harmonious and mutually supportive relationship grew out of the process from which Japanese industrialization evolved. After the Meiji Restoration in 1868 and the launching of Japan's effort to catch up with the Western world, the first nurturer of infant industry was the imperial household itself. It was soon realized that as the "infants" grew, this degree of intimacy might prove embarrassing, and the direct tie was severed. To this day, however, the filial relationship between government and industry, though considerably attenuated, is still strong.

It's not likely that we'll ever hear the slogan "State-owned corpora-tions of the world, cast off your bondage. Regulation will make you free!" Yet just such a liberating movement has been gathering momentum all over the world in recent years. In this respect, as in progress toward de-mocratization, the world has been paying a seldom acknowledged com-pliment to the American example. We ourselves, meanwhile, have come to a point where the cumulative effect of separately defensible regula-tions has been to create a serious drag on growth and productivity. You don't have to be a "conservative" to recognize the need to reduce this drag. In addition to streamlining and pruning existing regulations, future gov-ernment intervention, where it cannot be avoided, must be designed with an eye to fulfilling its purpose with maximum precision and minimum unwanted side effects. The institutional changes I've been discussing up to now are essential steps toward making this happen. But so are the people who will put them into effect—which is to say, the bureaucrats. What about them?

There are a lot of good things to be said about bureaucrats, and I've said many of them in my essay on public service. On the negative side, their worst sin is none of those commonly ascribed to them. It is resistance to change. This is true partly, no doubt, because it's always easier to keep on doing the same thing the same way than to learn a better way. Bureaucrats are no different from the tax lawyers I know who resisted reform of the Internal Revenue Code because they would have to learn a new set of section numbers. Bureaucrats also resist change because in the course of time they form alliances with the interest groups with which they regularly deal. Not surprisingly, therefore, old and ineffective programs are kept in place alongside the tried and true, new ideas are held back, and coherent strategies for change are slow to emerge and seldom get off the ground.

The competent political appointee knows that the career service's strengths—institutional memory and awareness of blind alleys and pitfalls, for example—were developed by the very same experience that also produced resistance to change. This resistance can be overcome only by raising the sights and challenging the imaginations of individual civil servants. That should be a primary task of the agency's top leadership, both career and noncareer.

Serious problems crying out for government action continue to multiply even as the government's capacity to deal with them progressively deteriorates. To check this slide it is urgent that we increase the premium on developing the knowledge, skill, and ingenuity brought to the design and administration of government policies and programs. To ensure that these programs do not unnecessarily restrict private-sector freedom, the means of intervention must be used with precision. When intervention is clumsy at the outset, it all too often compels further intervention. Hence, as our social and economic system grows in complexity, it has increasingly greater need for a new kind of bureaucrat. This new bureaucrat would have a deeper understanding of the systemic relationships affected by government action than was needed when precision was less essential. Such a bureaucrat would be equipped with the capacity to select from among a wide variety of tools—incentive devices, regulatory mechanisms, administrative procedures, and the like—the one best suited to the task at hand. To assist this choice and to assess its outcome, familiarity with sophisticated program evaluation, risk assessment, and hardheaded cost-benefit analysis would also be essential.

If our political leaders consistently faced up to the necessity of defining clear goals, making hard choices, and formulating coherent and comprehensible strategies; if our department and agency heads better understood what it takes to guide and motivate career public servants; if the process were addressed to better planning, better information, and clearer, better-administered performance standards, the federal bureaucracy would be humming as never before. This is not impossible. We do not need radical change. Incremental improvements will do, so long as they're across the board and consistently pursued.

It's going to take a while to get things up to scratch. And when we do, we mustn't let ourselves, like that head surgical nurse, get sick of keeping them that way.

Peace Enforcement

How many times in the history of human civilization has there occurred a major change that was at once sudden, transforming, and unnoticed? Not often, I would wager. And yet, as I propose to show, just such a change is occurring now.

The change I have in mind began in 1991. The events that marked it were visible enough. It was their significance that went unnoticed. These events were set in motion by a number of bloody conflicts each of which was internal to a single sovereign state and none of which engaged the vital interests of any major power. Yet each became the subject of a series of United Nations Security Council resolutions, which led to a variety of peace-enforcement efforts, including economic sanctions, air strikes, and the deployment of many thousands of troops.

As we all know, these actions have generated more than a little frustration and disillusionment. A surge of criticism has washed up against the United Nations, the United States, and NATO. This very criticism, nonetheless, is the best evidence that the significance of the developments being criticized has not been noticed. For the salient fact is that never before have major countries, least of all those remote from the scene, allowed themselves to become deeply involved in trying to suppress conflicts that did not engage their own vital interests.

Throughout history dozens of bloody conflicts have always been under way at any given time. Springing mainly from ancient tribal, ethnic, and religious enmities, they were easy for uninvolved countries to ignore. This was conspicuously true of the four decades of the Cold War. According to the United States Institute of Peace, there were 149 such wars in the course of those decades. During that period the international community bled with compassion for the victims of famines, floods, earthquakes, and tornadoes even while turning its back on the vastly greater death and destruction wreaked by those wars. Totalitarian rule, the systematic abuse of human rights, and wholesale brutality were endemic to many places, but it did not occur to the rest of the world that perhaps it should try to do something about them. Even the unspeakable atrocities committed by Idi Amin in Uganda evoked no stronger a reaction than outrage.

To account for my own fascination with this extraordinary shift in international behavior I need to go back to the end of World War II. On V-J Day I was at Camp Butner, North Carolina, where my division was being readied for the invasion of the island of Honshu. In common with all my fellow Americans, I felt an overwhelming surge of joy, relief, exhilaration, and hope. For me the strongest of these feelings was hope. The Charter of the United Nations had been signed in San Francisco only six weeks earlier. Now, for a second time in this century, there had come a chance to pursue the goal of preventing future wars.

I grew up in a family whose outlook was shaped by the expansive view of America's international role that first emerged in the era of Theodore Roosevelt. By the time I got to high school, I had come to regard the U.S. Senate's rejection of the League of Nations as a tragic mistake. In my eyes, Henry Cabot Lodge, the Massachusetts senator who masterminded the delaying tactics that led to this result, was a man without vision.

I still regard the task of devising better ways to prevent conflict and preserve peace as one that no setback should be allowed to discourage. Only an idealist could suppose that it will ever be fully successful. Only a cynic would dismiss it as a waste of time. Like all those whom H. L. Mencken called "the chronic hopers of the world," I'm convinced that the same tough-minded persistence that has gradually extended the reach of democracy and law will someday succeed in creating the capacity to keep the peace.

Hope has reached three high-water marks in this century, all in the aftermath of prolonged struggles against predatory regimes. It began to rise for the first time during the decade before the First World War and crested in Paris at its end. It rose again in the interval between the waning days of World War II and the onset of the Cold War. The new surge imparted by the end of the Cold War reached a peak with the United Nations victory in the Persian Gulf.

Justly called "the World War," the first of these struggles was more deadly, more destructive, and more engulfing than any previous armed conflict in all of human history. It was utterly appropriate that it should be followed by the creation of a League of Nations dedicated to maintaining peace. This new international organization's ability to carry out its mission was impaired, however, by its having been brought into being by the same flawed treaty that humiliated the losers in World War I. Plagued by the resentments thereby generated and weakened by the nonparticipation of the United States, the League was helpless against the acts of aggression that paved the way for another World War. Still, the League deserves to be remembered as a "noble experiment," for it served as the prototype for the next attempt to build on a past war the means of ending future wars.

Meeting at Yalta in February 1945, the leaders of the forces arrayed against the Axis powers agreed to call their alliance "The United Nations Organization." Thus was conceived the name bestowed in San Francisco on another new association of states committed to cooperation in the cause of peace. Article 1 of the United Nations Charter succinctly sets forth the purposes of their collective action: to prevent and remove threats to peace, to suppress acts of aggression or other breaches of the peace, and to adjust or settle international disputes or situations that might lead to a breach of the peace. For more than forty years the Cold War kept the United Nations not simply from developing but even from testing its full potential. It did, nevertheless, perform invaluable service in preventing new outbreaks of violence in Cyprus, the Middle East, and South Asia, and carrying out peace-enforcement actions in Korea and the Congo, while also leading humanitarian efforts on many fronts. Throughout the Cold War, moreover, it maintained a forum and a dialogue that proved conducive to the eventual thaw.

As of August 2, 1990, the day of Iraq's invasion of Kuwait, disappointment would have been a fairer verdict on the United Nations than disillusionment. Six months later, when Iraq surrendered, the world had proof that the United Nations was indeed capable of performing the role envisioned for it by the framers of its charter. But this achievement also confirmed what had long been obvious: that the United Nations, like the League of Nations before it, could fulfill its purposes only to the extent that its members were willing and able to work together. With the relaxation of tensions brought about by the end of the Cold War this had at last become possible. With the united support of the permanent members of the Security Council and under the leadership of the United States, twenty-eight nations played active parts in a counteroffensive against Iraq that destroyed the world's fourth-largest army. In hailing this mutual effort, President Bush pointed to "the long-held promise of a new world order—where brutality will go unrewarded and aggression will meet collective resistance." His next step, surely, would be to put aides to work on giving this concept substance and specificity. As I imagined his charge to them, it would go something like this: "Please, no pie in the sky. I don't want a blueprint for Utopia. But neither do I want objectives so limited that they might be achieved before I leave office." Astonishingly, Bush never attempted to explain what he meant by "the new world order." Was this because he thought it promised too much? Did he fear a conservative backlash? Or was it merely that he felt uncomfortable with its overtones of the "vision thing"? I wish I knew.

Others volunteered for the definitional role. Conferences, workshops, roundtables, task forces, and working groups sprang up like mushrooms. Their first task was to consider means of "peace enforcement" as distinguished from "peacekeeping." The latter, of course, has long been an established United Nations role. Employing lightly armed contingents of national troops, its function is to be a buffer between parties who, having agreed to a cease-fire, have also agreed to let the United Nations force perform this role. Casualties are rare, and the United Nations Security Council's decisions to deploy such units are seldom controversial.

"Peace enforcement," by contrast, has the very different function of stopping conflict between parties who have no thought of peace. Invoked only when all other approaches to halting violence have failed, peace enforcement necessarily entails coercion. The question of when and how to apply it involves agonizing decisions. As late, however, as the spring of

1994 the Clinton administration issued guidelines that compounded the confusion by treating peacekeeping and peace enforcement interchangeably and lumping them together under the catchall "multilateral peace operations."

In their discussions of peace enforcement, the "new world order" groups focused primarily on the threats to international peace and security created by cross-border aggression. The three I chaired assumed that the only wars the major powers needed to be concerned with were in the Gulf War category or bigger. As a result, the reports, recommendations, and agendas for action that emerged from these efforts broke little new ground. They dealt, rather, with the measures addressed by Chapter VII of the United Nations Charter—the designation of national forces for peace-enforcement roles, the need for joint training exercises, the activation of the Charter's Military Staff Committee, the feasibility of organizing a full-time rapid deployment force in United Nations uniforms, and the like.

By the time the study groups' recommendations began to appear, the Gulf War was already receding from view. Conflicts of a very different kind had come to the fore. The bloodshed in Bosnia, Somalia, Nagorno-Karabakh, Georgia, Rwanda, and Haiti engaged the concern and compassion of decent people all over the world. They looked to the United Nations for some sort of action that would stop the slaughter, alleviate the suffering, and end the brutalization of people whose only crime was belonging to a hated tribe or religion.

But all of these conflicts were taking place within the boundaries of a single sovereign state. Could they appropriately be dealt with as "threats to peace or breaches of the peace" under Chapter VII of the United Nations Charter? Or had they been declared off limits by the provision of Chapter I, which proscribes collective intervention "in matters which are essentially within the domestic jurisdiction of any state"? Undeterred by legal niceties and readier to displease local warlords than worldwide public opinion, the United Nations Security Council found no difficulty in classifying these internal conflicts as threats to peace. Straight they went to the top of its agenda. It soon appeared that the Security Council had opened, not Pandora's box, but a can of worms.

In place of the "new world order," the phrase now being heard was "new world disorder." In fact, the only thing that was new about the disorder in question was the attention it attracted. The conflicts now preoccupying the world community were no different in kind from the scores of similar conflicts so consistently ignored during the Cold War years. What had brought about this dramatic change of attitude? The new round of conflicts no more directly affected the vital interests of major powers than had the earlier ones. Despite a widespread impression to the contrary, neither did the change come about because small wars had suddenly become more numerous. A quantitative increase, in any case, could hardly be the reason for a qualitative change in attitude: countries unmoved by x number of small wars were not likely to be moved by $x + y$ small wars. Besides, the only new conflicts traceable to changes of circumstance were in the former Soviet Union and the former Yugoslavia, where long-smoldering hatreds burst into flame when they ceased to be contained by strong central governments.

But the most profound consequence of the end of the Cold War was the lifting of the menace of nuclear holocaust. So long as that menace loomed, it eclipsed lesser concerns. Throughout the Cold War people in every part of the globe were conscious that their survival might depend on the maintenance of a precarious superpower stalemate. For four dangerous decades the West's political leaders, diplomats, and strategic planners were unceasingly preoccupied by the unremitting demands of managing containment. The only small wars they and their counterparts in the Kremlin had time for were those between pro-Western and pro-Soviet antagonists. In the countries caught up in the East–West struggle—Vietnam, Laos, Cambodia, Afghanistan, Angola, Nicaragua, and El Salvador —this ruthless superpower game deepened the tragedy and multiplied the death toll of their domestic conflicts.

Most of the other 142 wars fought during those same four decades ran their course with little or no external interference. Then all at once, with the disappearance of danger, people were everywhere free to look at the world around them. And what did they see? Dozens of bloody wars still being waged, some of which, at least, could no longer be ignored. But the Iraqi invasion of Kuwait just then preempted world attention, and the lesser wars had to wait their turn yet a while longer.

But while the sudden awakening that came with the end of the Cold War can account for the difference between present-day attitudes and those of the recent past, it does not tell us why small wars now enlist a degree of concern never accorded to them in the more remote past. For this latter difference also, a survey of the world in the aftermath both of the Cold War and of victory in the Gulf suggests a persuasive explanation: for the first time in history the global strategic scene is dominated by one unchallenged superpower—the United States. For the first time, moreover, relations between or among important nations are almost completely free of serious politico-military rivalries or deep-seated enmities.

Although the need to keep a close eye on balance-of-power concerns has not gone away, neither is it acute. The question of how China will eventually choose to deploy its rapidly growing military and economic strength is clearly a matter calling for wise and restrained statesmanship, particularly on the part of the United States. It does not, however, arouse widespread concern at present. The political future of Russia is uncertain, and Russia still has tens of thousands of nuclear warheads. Scenarios in which that troubled nation might again assume a seriously destabilizing if not menacing role are not hard to imagine. Japan's international influence will in due course become more nearly commensurate with its economic strength, and it is obviously vital to our own national interest that Japan should remain a good friend and staunch ally. Meanwhile, the threat of nuclear proliferation demands constant vigilance and vigorous countermeasures.

We thus, at least for the moment, have a situation in which heads of state, foreign ministers, defense ministers, parliamentarians, and people everywhere have been liberated from anxieties about imminent military threats. Thus, like the fortunate people who, having no need to cope with big worries, make do with small ones, humanity's global concerns have been transferred to conflicts that would not previously have impinged on its consciousness.

But there can be no mistaking the genuineness of the compassion felt by countless millions of people all over the world for the suffering of civilians caught up in a senseless war or brutalized by an inhuman regime. Reinforcing our sense of common humanity is the capacity of modern telecommunications to bring us instantly to the scene of violence and destruction. And the media, no longer held captive by more portentous developments, have ample incentive to make sure that the world is made aware of the worst of the worst.

The nature of the sudden, transforming, and unnoticed change to which I referred at the outset should by now be clear. Needless to say, the factors that brought it about could yield before long to some massive new development, and I do not pretend to be a prophet. Meanwhile, we should urgently be trying to grasp the implications of what, for lack of a better term, I shall call the "new humanitarianism." Characterized by heightened readiness to call upon multilateral intervention and motivated by compassion, conscience, and civilized standards of behavior, the new humanitarianism is shared by the international community as a whole. Its newness, moreover, stems from the circumstance that it is evoked by conflicts that seldom directly concern any nations other than those in which they have erupted.

But consensus that there should be some kind of response to such conflicts raises some exceedingly difficult questions. What forms of intervention or coercion should be used? What should be their aims? Who should have ultimate strategic or tactical control? Most difficult of all, how much of what kind of aggregate commitment should the international community be prepared to make? From diplomatic pressure through economic sanctions to financial assessments and battlefield casualties the range is wide. So too is the size of the requisite military force. As to national shares in the total effort, the developed countries—and especially the United States—can hardly be expected to accept as their quotas of the blood risk a fraction determined by the United Nations formula for peacekeeping costs. But if not that, what? Population size?

In the case of civil wars, as contrasted with cross-border aggression, it will often be impossible to determine whether or not there is a "right side" on whose behalf to intervene. If a world organization like the United Nations had existed at the time of our own Civil War, would its equivalent of the Security Council have supported intervention? If yes, to what end? Would its aim have been simply to suppress the fighting? In that case, successful intervention would also have prevented the North from preserving the Union. Or would the United Nations have supported the antislavery side—the one clearly right by modern standards? Since, in either case, soldiers belonging to the United Nations force would be killed, there would be a net reduction of bloodshed only if, through shortening the war, intervention prevented more casualties than it cost.

Events in Bosnia, Somalia, Rwanda, and Haiti quickly dramatized these difficulties. It soon became apparent that the permanent members of the United Nations Security Council would have done well to take as their text these words from Abraham Lincoln's Second Annual Message to Congress: "As our case is new, so we must think anew and act anew. We must disenthrall ourselves. . . ." The permanent members' heads of state should have proclaimed loudly, clearly, and repeatedly that peace enforcement presents challenges and difficulties of a wholly new kind. Then, having made their publics fully aware of this fact, they should have systematically laid bare the problems they foresaw and emphasized that the resulting initiatives must necessarily be regarded as experimental.

Had world leaders done this in the aftermath of the Gulf War, not only would they have avoided being thrown on the defensive but they could also have afforded to be receptive to criticism. Instead, they assumed an air of confidence and cultivated the impression that everything was under control. When, as was inevitable, this proved not to be true, they came out looking much worse than needed to have been the case. In the process they made the United Nations itself look ineffectual, although, of course, the United Nations is not a true entity. Rather, in the words of Jonathan Moore, former ambassador of the United States to the Economic and Social Council, the United Nations "is only what its members allow it to be, and they regularly assign it missions impossible, shortfall on political and financial support, and then beat the hell out of it."[1]

Though no more than partly to blame for this state of affairs, the United States nonetheless became its principal victim. As the sole remaining superpower, we both accepted and affirmed responsibility for leadership. We were right to do so. We have a pervasive interest in global stability. Our economic weight, military power, and moral influence give us a large role in everything from the unobstructed flow of international trade and investment to the protection of human rights, the extension of the rule of law, and the spread of democracy. But capacity and desire are not enough. If the leader is to prepare his followers for the battle, the sound of the trumpet not only must be certain but also must reach receptive ears.

In the event, the new humanitarianism arrived with a swiftness that

---

[1] Jonathan Moore, *Morality and Interdependence* (Hanover, NH: The Nelson A. Rockefeller Center for the Social Sciences at Dartmouth College, 1994), p. 23. The reality might perhaps be made clearer if we spoke of the United Nations as "they" rather than "it."

overwhelmed the capacity of the United States government to readjust its goals and reeducate its followers. Neither task has yet been adequately addressed. Both will have to be accomplished, moreover, even while older concerns receive their appropriate shares of attention. Just as the need to keep an eye on the balance of power will not go away, neither will the requirement for readiness to deal with hard-to-foresee conflicts in the order of magnitude exemplified by the Gulf War. Such conflicts can be anticipated and planned for, but when or whether they will break out is inherently difficult to predict. It is understandable, therefore, that our military leaders are not eager to undertake commitments that, while individually small, are cumulatively capable of tying up substantial resources and thus reducing the nation's capacity to respond to a larger crisis.

Meanwhile, a handful of "rogue regimes" are still exerting a contingent claim on disposable coercive power. Their distinguishing features are dictatorship and repression of human rights coupled with some form of antisocial behavior toward the international community. The offensiveness of this combination can on occasion reach a stage that calls for disciplinary action. In the case of Iraq, it has been prompted by foot-dragging toward United Nations requirements for the dismantling of its facilities for the production of weapons of mass destruction. In the case of Libya, should disciplinary action again be called for, it would be because of some outrageous sequel to that country's long identification with international terrorism. And in the case of North Korea, it would be prompted by the resumed pursuit of nuclear weapons production in defiance of the nuclear nonproliferation treaty (1970) and the framework agreement of October 21, 1994, spelling out means of assuring that this did not occur.

All of these potential threats to world order would, if exacerbated, legitimately receive higher priority than internal conflicts. That being so, it has to be taken for granted that major-power involvement in the latter is bound to be cautious. While the torture, starvation, or massacre of another country's people can and should genuinely move outsiders, the feelings that reach out to distant suffering obviously cannot match in intensity those aroused by a threat to the security or well-being of one's own country. As we have seen in Somalia, Rwanda, and Bosnia, the response to the former is all too apt to be insufficient to impose a solution. The Bosnian example, indeed, suggested a simple equation: limited objectives times insufficient means equals prolonged agony. In Haiti, on the other hand, we saw what can be done where the intervening force is vastly stronger than the local opposition. Applying the principles enunciated in the Clinton administration's 1994 white paper on "peace operations," the Haiti formula is also simple: never use a sledgehammer except to hit nails.

Change has come. The new humanitarianism is a fact of life. In the light of experience with it to date, however, it is fair to ask whether the impulse to intervene in international conflicts should be curbed or suppressed. There can be no doubt, certainly, as to how the traditional real-politiker would answer this question.

As Henry Kissinger's recent book, *Diplomacy,* defines *realpolitik,* it is "foreign policy based on calculation of power and the national interest."[2] This definition leaves open, however, the really significant question: what is a national interest?" The only interests that *Diplomacy* seems to take seriously are hegemony, self-defense, stability, national pride, and the like. As for national pride, Kissinger takes it for granted that French *revanchisme* in the aftermath of the War of 1870 was the kind of reality that *realpolitik* can accept as ligitimate. It is quite clear, on the other hand, that he does not so regard Wilsonian idealism or contemporary multilateralism. Why not? Aren't these just as real and vastly more important than pride, not to mention such historic national motivators as imperial grandeur, a place in the sun, or the glory of God? Why not, then, the compassion that inspires the new humanitarianism?

A post-Kissingerian disciple of *realpolitik* might, of course, insist that the only valid concerns of *realpolitik* are national security and economic prosperity. Had such a hard-nosed regard for permanent national interests actually guided the conduct of foreign policy throughout the nation-state era, there would have been many fewer bloody conflicts. And while it may well be that the great practitioners of foreign policy—the Talleyrands, Metternichs, and Bismarcks—would have preferred to exclude nonrational values from their calculations, their indulgence of this preference would have been palpably unrealistic.

Ironically, a purist definition of realpolitik would have excluded as unrealistic the principal factors that led to the Cold War. Its driving forces were the compulsion to expand its geopolitical dominion and its

---

[2] Henry A. Kissinger, *Diplomacy* (New York: Simon & Schuster, 1994), p. 137.

zeal to add new adherents to the communist faith. The Western response was the resolve to preserve the free world's humane, democratic, and pluralistic system of values. Of course, once these forces were engaged, the moves and countermoves of each side gave a narrow version of *realpolitik* plenty to do.

Reflecting on this irony, I was reminded of the liberation of Paris on August 24, 1944. My company, a unit of the first American contingent to enter the city, was camped in the Bois de Vincennes. A few of the joyous Parisians who surrounded our tents discovered that I could speak passable French, and I was doing my best to be responsive. Then suddenly, from a middle-aged woman, came this question: "When Germany has been defeated, will you Americans keep on going until you destroy the Soviet armies?" Startled, I said, "That would be insane. The United States and the Soviet Union are allies. Both countries are rich in resources, and neither has a territorial claim against the other. After the war, each of us will have more than enough to do at home. Just because their ideas are wrong is no reason for going to war with them." Now, *that* was realism.

Although the values that united the West in the Cold War and that now inspire the new humanitarianism have ancient antecedents, their prominent linkage to the conduct of international relations dates only from the decade or two preceding World War I. This was when hard-headed statesmen in most of the Western industrial countries, perhaps in reaction against the narrowness of realpolitik, promoted the arbitration of conflicts as an international obligation. In this country William Howard Taft and Elihu Root, Theodore Roosevelt's secretary of war and secretary of state, were its leading proponents.

The emphasis on values identified with Woodrow Wilson has dominated American foreign policy even since World War I. Anthony Lake, President Clinton's national security adviser, gave it eloquent expression in a speech to the Council on Foreign Relations in September 1994:

> In defeating fascism, and prevailing over communism, we were defending an idea that comes under many names—democracy, liberty, civility, pluralism—but has a constant face. It is the face of the tolerant society, in which leaders and government exist not to use or abuse people, but to provide them with freedom and opportunity, to preserve individual human dignity.

Rather than brush aside such eloquence, an astute realpolitiker would affect a less confrontational attitude. He might, for example, though disparaging moral affirmations as poor guides to action, regard them as useful to the cultivation of patriotic fervor. He might even acknowledge that in appropriate circumstances there is a place for sympathetic noises and symbolic moves. He would insist, however, that the willingness to risk a significant fraction of national prestige, influence, or resources on a purely humanitarian venture is proof of naïveté.

Even from the standpoint of immediate national interest, this view is open to challenge. Poverty, repression, and misery are breeders of discontent, and its skillful exploitation by ambitious power-seekers may foster antagonisms among cultural and religious groups and lead to the formation of militant factions. Clashes among these factions can easily lead to violence, and where the factions have adherents in neighboring countries, the violence may spill over the borders. The belief that this kind of sequence is a genuinely dangerous prospect has been forcefully expressed of late, notably by United Nations Secretary-General Boutros Boutros-Ghali and Brian Atwood, administrator of the Agency for International Development. What they and others are saying is that it is a mistake to regard unchecked violence, repression, or the denial of human rights in any country as wholly insulated from the rest of the world. While such evils may not directly spill over into neighboring countries, they contribute in the aggregate to a spreading miasma of lawlessness. In this foul air may be nourished significant threats to the national security of other countries.

In my view, this is a realistic concern. It strengthens the case for acceptance of collective responsibility toward the protection and advancement of humane values. But if the new humanitarianism is a descriptive term, it has a more fundamental basis. A nation is more than an abstract entity, more than a territory, more than a government. It is a society of human beings. The members of one such society cannot help knowing that the members of other societies are also real. In common with most people everywhere, Americans want a safer, more stable, more orderly, and more humane world not simply because such a world is better for us but because it is better for others too.

Since, therefore, these are good reasons to continue to pursue the new humanitarianism—and since, in any case, the international community shows no disposition to abandon it—it would be worthwhile to ask what hindsight can teach us about how to get there from here. In my own rearview mirror three observations stand out. The first is that the United States is now experiencing a new version of an old dilemma: when and in what circumstances to take up arms in behalf of a moral cause. The second is that the Gulf War not only set precedents but also posted warnings. The third is that the world's unhappy dealings with Bosnia, Somalia, Rwanda, et al. have put it on notice as to the dilemmas that lie ahead. Each of these observations deserves discussion.

As to the first observation, it needs to be said at the outset that we Americans have every reason to feel proud of the justice of our nation's wars. Except for a brief flirtation with imperialism at the end of the last century, we have consistently acted in our national interest, but not for national advantage. In the century now about to end we have followed this course through five hot wars and one cold war. Two of the former were by-products of the latter. Each was unique in the duration of its several stages as well as in the evolution of our feelings toward it. All, however, embodied a recurring pattern of common elements. One such element was responsiveness to a powerful claim on our most fundamental values. Another was reluctance to put American lives at risk. A third was some threat or provocation which overcame that hesitancy and brought to bear our moral instincts. From that point onward we have always stayed the course if not until ultimate victory at least until the achievement of a defensible outcome.

Early in World War I Kaiser Wilhelm's ruthless imperialism aroused our antipathy, and our sympathy was aroused by the spectacle of Belgium's being trampled on by the boots of his spike-helmeted Prussians. These feelings, nevertheless, could not overcome our reluctance to get involved. It was, after all, the Europeans' war. When Germany finally goaded us into entering the war by resorting to unrestricted submarine warfare against our merchant shipping, our moral feelings surged to the fore, and overnight we became champions of a righteous cause. Had the safety of our ships been our real concern, however, keeping them out of the North Atlantic would have been a lot easier and a lot cheaper than going to war.

A new outbreak of war in Europe twenty years later found us sheltered behind the Neutrality Act of 1937. We had a minuscule army and looked at the rest of the world from an isolationist perspective hardened by the misery of the Great Depression. We disapproved of Hitler, but not until the evacuation of Dunkirk, the occupation of Paris, and the Battle of Britain did America's better nature begin to be deeply engaged. By then American public opinion was sharply divided. My college class became passionately caught up in that controversy, with fanatical America Firsters on one side and fervent advocates of Aid to the Allies on the other. Indeed, so central was this issue to our undergraduate experience that a detailed account of our involvement in it was made a special feature of our class yearbook.

Fortunately for the world, Hitler brought this often heated and sometimes bitter debate to an abrupt end by declaring war against the United States only a few days after Japan bombed Pearl Harbor. No one would have guessed, however, from the speeches I heard in England and Normandy at the ceremonies commemorating the fiftieth anniversary of the D-Day landings that we had been so irresolute for so long. One would have supposed, rather, that the United States had sprung to the cause of Hitler's destruction the day he invaded Poland.

The containment of Soviet expansionism presented a very different kind of challenge and received a very different kind of response. Harry Truman, Dean Acheson, George Marshall, and the other wise men who were "present at the creation" had the vision to understand that the prompt and effective erection of barriers to this expansionism might avert the necessity for far greater sacrifice at a later date. Thanks to them and their successors, this policy succeeded. Obedience to the logic of containment, however, did twice necessitate substantial American casualties, first in reaction to North Korea's Soviet-instigated invasion of South Korea and later when, alarmed by the prospect that Hanoi's takeover of South Vietnam might have a "domino effect," we allowed ourselves to slide into an all-out war.

If we had not already known that the policeman's lot is not a happy one, the latter experience would have convinced us of it. Recognizing this, Ronald Reagan artfully employed minimal uses of force to revive American self-esteem and to convince the rest of the world that we still stood tall. Rebounding from humiliation in Lebanon, he extracted major mileage from a hit-and-run strike against Muammar Qaddafi, the invasion of the tiny Caribbean island of Grenada, and the use against a Marxist regime in Nicaragua of proxies financed by the sale of arms to Iran. But none of these heroics prepared the United States for the leadership of multilateral responses to localized outbreaks of violence.

Iraq's invasion of Kuwait was no such localized event. It was a deliberate act of aggression in a geostrategically important area with no better excuse than a boundary dispute. Had there been no effective reaction, Iraq's next step would almost certainly have been to take over its weak but fabulously oil rich neighbor, Saudi Arabia. That would have given Saddam Hussein control over close to half of the entire world's known oil reserves. Heavily dependent on the region for fuel, Western Europe and Japan had a huge stake in seeing to it that this did not happen. Moreover, every country with a disputed boundary had something at risk. All this added up to a clear-cut case for collective action.

These are the facts that loom largest as I look back at the Gulf War in my rearview mirror. Some of its precedent-setting implications were touched on early in this essay. Chief among them were that cross-border aggression can evoke a widely shared international response and that, when the political stars are in the right configuration, the five permanent members of the United Nations Security Council are capable of supporting or at least not frustrating collective action. But my focus now is on what the Gulf War tells us both about the potency of this nation's capacity for global leadership and about the constraints on the exercise of that capacity.

The most striking—and overlooked—aspect of the potency in question is that we owed it all to Joseph Stalin and his successors. Two years after the end of World War II we were already well on the way toward dismantling our wartime forces. Absent the Soviet Union's predatory policies, it is not likely that we would have reversed this process and begun the military buildup that led to two essential preconditions for an effective response to Iraq's aggression. The first was our possession of the components of a powerful expeditionary force. The second was the part played by that same buildup in bringing about the disintegration that cleared the way for Russia's joining in a concerted reaction to Iraq's defiance of the United Nations Charter.

Taking advantage of the Cold War's contribution to American military might, a president other than George Bush might also have sent troops to the Gulf in numbers comparable to those initially deployed in Operation Desert Shield. It is by no means certain, however, that another president would have followed a course leading to the commitment of ground forces. Indeed, the boldness of this decision was highlighted on November 30, 1990, when at a meeting in Birmingham, Alabama, of ex-secretaries of defense convened by the Southern Center for International Studies it emerged that we unanimously opposed the use of ground forces before we knew what economic sanctions could accomplish. Caspar Weinberger, one of the two ex-secretaries not in Birmingham, wrote an op-ed piece to the same effect, which appeared two days later. The other absentee—Clark Clifford—made a similar statement soon after that. Only Don Rumsfeld was prepared to support the early use of airpower.

As it happened, however, our views had already been overtaken by President Bush's decision to increase greatly the number of ground forces in the Gulf. Once this increase had been carried out, the combat units still available to the United States would be so few that the rotation home of those already in the Gulf would not be feasible. This decision precluded keeping the troops in place and awaiting further developments. A ground attack would have to be launched no later than the early spring of 1991 and completed no later than the middle of May because from then until October the desert heat would preclude sustained combat. Should the operation encounter serious resistance the combination of combat losses and deteriorating morale would by the end of the year make replacements essential. This could well have made it necessary to seek a renewal of the draft, and the overhang of Vietnam would have been likely to doom this effort. And if our forces proved unable in a depleted state to do what they had not accomplished at full strength, the United States would then have had no choice but to swallow its humiliation and bring them home.

The die was thus cast on November 8, 1990, when the president announced the augmented deployment. Nine weeks later he sought and obtained by narrow margins congressional support for the use of military force and on February 24, 1991, he ordered the ground attack to go forward. The American people again united behind what they believed to be a just cause. In the end, however, other countries were the principal beneficiaries of our initiative. Although we had at most a 25 percent stake in the outcome, 75 percent of the ground troops in the Gulf, 74 percent of the planes, and nearly all of the naval firepower were American. It was inevitable that a roughly similar proportion of the casualties would also be American. And though we succeeded in persuading other countries to assume the current costs of Operation Desert Storm, passing the hat could not diminish our share of the blood risk. Nor was it ever suggested that we should ask anyone else to help us amortize the far larger investment we had already made in training, arming, and equipping our Persian Gulf forces.

When it was all over I wrote the president a letter. In it I saluted the courage, vision, and steadfastness with which he had guided the nation's response to Iraq's aggression. I also observed that I had been unable to think of any previous example of a presidential course of action whose only foreseeable outcomes were triumph or disaster, with nothing in between.

In this retrospective review of the salient features of the Gulf War, the warning signs are all too plainly visible. The first is that the unilateral commitment of American units in retaliation against some similar act of aggression is not an option for any future president. Although the United States possessed the military strength to conduct an all-out unilateral assault on Iraq, there was never the slightest chance that we would do so. Had President Bush not been able both to obtain the United Nations Security Council's endorsement of the use of force and to assemble a broad-based military coalition, he could not conceivably have obtained congressional acquiescence in a large-scale attack by American ground forces.

Second, it is not likely that there will be many future crises of comparable size that will so clearly call for a large-scale collective response. The odds are even more heavily against there being another such crisis in which the economic stakes will be so high, the terrain so favorable, or the casualties so light. Hence, although the Defense Department's current planning calls for force levels capable of winning two simultaneous Gulf War–size conflicts, known in Pentagonese as "Major Regional Conflicts" or "MRCs," it might be wiser to plan bigger and be ready to act smaller.

Third, the Gulf War posted a clear warning that it should not be taken as a precedent for military intervention in conflicts that do not involve equivalent economic and strategic interests. Nevertheless, even such thoughtful commentators as Anthony Lewis, Madeleine Albright, and Leslie Gelb were quick to cite the Gulf War as a precedent for a United States–led coalition against the Serbs in Bosnia. In fact, Bosnia was from the outset a leading, though extremely troublesome, example of the very change of attitude that put on the international agenda internal conflicts not involving the vital interests of any major country.

We have now completed a circuit that, starting with a description of the aforesaid change, sought to account for its occurrence and touched on the consequences of failure to create wide recognition of its unprecedented challenges. Then, in order to get a better understanding of the scope of those challenges, we looked at factors that have influenced the behavior of the United States in the course of reaching its present unique position. And so we arrived, together with the rest of the world, at a point where moral standards and humanitarian values pose the issue of sacrifice. In the pages that follow I shall approach this last issue by examining the manner in which choices among competing claims for international intervention get made, the current available means of dealing with the conflicts that are thus singled out, the essentiality of risk sharing, and future possibilities offering the hope of practical solutions.

Reverting once more to the new humanitarianism, I'm struck by the thought that generously motivated nations are in the same position toward coping with conflict as they are toward coping with poverty: too many mouths, too little food. As this is being written, estimates of the number of small wars currently under way ranges, depending on the definition being applied, from 27 to 71. Only a few of these conflicts can hope to attract much international attention. The rest are victims of scarcity: political leaders don't have time to deal with them; the United Nations Security Council agenda doesn't have room for them; there aren't enough relief supplies to send them; there isn't enough disposable military power to suppress them. And even if all of these deficiencies could somehow be overcome, neither the news media nor the general public would be able to keep track of them.

As to how or why some few conflicts get selected for attention, the most often cited explanation is "the CNN factor": the emotional impact generated by the TV screen's iterated images of starving children, mutilated bodies, and bombed-out buildings. This factor did undoubtedly have a lot to do with Bosnia's and Somalia's getting on the United Nations Security Council agenda when Afghanistan and Liberia did not. But the CNN factor was not purely capricious. The networks and newspapers did not completely lack objective and communicable reasons for zeroing in on Bosnia, Somalia, Haiti, and—later—Rwanda. In each case there were discernible differences of degree in such things as the virulence of hate, the visibility of human suffering, or geographic proximity to the viewing audience.

Although the United Nations Security Council is no better able than the media to deal simultaneously with every conflict that could legitimately appeal to humanity's conscience or enlist its compassion, it has greater need to be publicly accountable for its allocation of resources. This puts a premium on the identification of objective criteria. Among the most obviously relevant are the scale of death and destruction, the extent to which the loss of life is limited to combatants or includes the slaughter of civilians, and the risk of spillover into neighboring areas. Others are the degree to which power is abused, human rights are violated, due process is denied, and tolerance is suppressed. For purposes of peace enforcement, though not of news coverage, another criterion is the prospect that intervention will achieve a positive outcome. Since the relative significance of all these factors will vary not only from situation to situation, but within each of them, it must therefore be their combined weight that determines the outcome. And if in the end the process of choice has not been wholly objective, the conflicts that reach the top of the international agenda will at least have been selected on a defensible basis.

Of course, the fact that a conflict is not quite shocking enough to qualify for peace-enforcement measures does not need to mean that it will be totally neglected. Even while Bosnia-Somalia-Haiti-Rwanda preempted the headlines, the United Nations continued to seek negotiated settlements, cease-fires, and political compromises in many other places. Among the United Nations' successes in that period were Nagorno-Karabakh, where United Nations mediators negotiated a tenuous solution two years after this ugly flare-up of ancient enmities had dropped from the headlines. Other little-noticed mediating efforts continue to go forward in Sudan, Liberia, and Soviet Georgia. But the United Nations' greatest recent successes, because they were successes, have been all but forgotten. These have been in Angola, Cambodia, Mozambique, and Nicaragua, where, because each was a victim of the Cold War, its ending made the healing process easier. Afghanistan, indeed, is the only Cold War victim within whose territory conflict still goes on.

As to the conflicts that do get to the top of the priority list, the only assured result is high-level attention. Unfortunately, as we all know, such attention carries with it no assurance of peace. No one has yet discovered a cheap or easy way of bringing an outlaw regime to heel. From mildest to strongest, the options start with diplomatic pressures and go on to the encouragement of negotiations leading to a cease-fire that can then be the subject of a United Nations peacekeeping role. But if these initiatives fail, the coercive mechanism then most readily at hand and least costly to the rest of the world is the application of economic sanctions—the blocking of bank accounts, an arms embargo, the cutoff of food supplies, and the imposition of a blockade. But economic sanctions, though cheap for the rest of the world, are not merely a blunt but a cruel instrument.

During a visit to Baghdad in the summer of 1991 as members of a United Nations humanitarian commission, several of us spent most of a day visiting randomly chosen families. The babies lacked milk, the old people lacked medicine, and no one had enough to eat. During the evening of that same day I sat next to Deputy Prime Minister Tariq Aziz at an official dinner. His tumbler of Johnnie Walker Black Label was regularly replenished. He was constantly lighting and discarding enormous Cuban cigars as if to demonstrate that, for him, the supply was endless.

This example of the bosses' insulation from the pain inflicted by sanctions brought to mind the months when, as under secretary of state, I was responsible for coordinating the delivery of food to the starving people of Biafra, a province of Nigeria that was attempting to secede. This tragedy was made all the more poignant by the evident determination of General Odumegwu Ojukwu, the Biafran leader, to hold out until the last of his people had starved to death. I get angry all over again whenever I think about the ordinary people in Iraq and Haiti and Cuba who have suffered under sanctions brought on or perpetuated by the egocentricity of their rulers. Higher priority needs to be given to devising targeted ways of inflicting pain on the Saddam Husseins, Raoul Cédrases, and Fidel Castros of the world.

To deter or punish particular conduct unaffected by the sustained pressure of sanctions, air strikes are both a means of signaling an escalation of pressure and of delivering pinpointed damage. Also relatively cost-free for the peace enforcers, air strikes in Bosnia have from time to time brought periods of respite from bloodshed. Their limitation, however, is that they can neither inflict defeat on a stubborn enemy nor force a brutal regime to abdicate. As postwar aerial bombing surveys have found, neither the massive bombing of Germany in World War II nor the even more concentrated use of airpower against North Vietnam was notably successful in breaking the will of those regimes. In Iraq the bombing of military targets was so precise that the number of civilian lives lost in proportion to the tonnage of the bombs dropped was much smaller than in any previous war. While we'll never know for sure, it seems improbable that airpower alone would have been able to induce Iraq's capitulation even if the bombing had been less discriminating.

But when no combination of these measures is sufficient and when successive efforts to promote a permanent cease-fire have been exhausted, the only remaining recourse is the use of ground forces. And where peace enforcement is their purpose, this necessitates their employment not simply to maintain relief supply lines or to protect enclaves, as in Bosnia, but also to destroy the fighting capacity of the offending side. The only two peace-enforcement actions that have thus far fulfilled their missions—those against Iraq and Haiti—both resorted to the use of ground forces. For the reasons previously noted, however, these precedents have little applicability to other situations.

Where no country has any unique interest in a particular conflict and where its geographical proximity to the conflict is not a factor, nations united by humanitarian aims have shown little inclination to risk the lives of their own citizens. The United States is no exception. Three days after twelve American soldiers were killed when two U.S. helicopters were shot down in Somalia, we announced our intention to withdraw all American troops from the country within six months. Neither we nor our allies have squarely faced such questions as how many servicemen's lives we would be willing to put at risk if such an action would assure the survival of a hundred thousand Rwandans or prevent the murder of twenty-three Maryknoll nuns. For a nation that prides itself on its moral values, the answer can hardly be "None."

But no nation is likely to face squarely the question of how many casualties it is willing to accept as the price of peace enforcement before it has been assured that the burden of potential sacrifice will be fairly distributed. For the United States, given its superior strength in trained military manpower, this is a particularly sensitive point. Our leadership role does not in itself require us to accept once again in some future multilateral military action a share of the blood risk anywhere so much out of line as the one we assumed in the Gulf War. And certainly other countries will have similar concerns about the fairness of burden sharing.

As to how a given country's appropriate share might be determined, the answer would be straightforward enough if the mere availability of manpower—which is to say population size—were the only pertinent factor. Where modern weapons systems are concerned, however, the number of such systems a country possesses is in large part determined by the number it can afford. That number—and how many it chooses to buy—will in turn determine the number of its military personnel who are trained to operate them. In proportion to population size, therefore, an optimally effective force would have a higher ratio of personnel from rich countries than from poor countries. The fair apportionment of blood risk would thus require training the personnel of the poor countries in the use of weapons owned by the richer countries. And this, of course, would further complicate such problems as the need to overcome language barriers, develop necessary skills, work out acceptable command and control arrangements, and so on.

Assuming that difficulties of this kind could be overcome, it would be necessary to consider what weight should be given to past military experience and present military strength. But as NATO continues to demonstrate, the assignment of missions and the allocation of burdens can be done fairly. The equitable sharing of economic costs and blood risks would be reflected in an agreement prescribing both the composition of combat task forces and the sequence in which they would be called upon for action. The task forces thus composed could meanwhile engage in joint training exercises. In fact, Chapter VII of the United Nations Charter contemplates just such agreements.

Where standby capacity to deal with the infrequent cases of flagrant aggression is concerned, there remains a sticky problem for which I have no solution. This is the impracticability of planning to meet a specific foreseeable threat. If this is difficult for our Defense Department in seeking to anticipate MRCs, it approaches impossibility for an international organization with universal membership. The designation of national units for peace-enforcement duty without reference to any particular conflict cannot take into account the political repercussions of an actual crisis. In the event, therefore, each designating nation must be allowed to decide whether or not to make its contingents available. And since, for the same reason, the United Nations' Military Staff Committee cannot make realistic plans for the use of national units without offending somebody, joint training exercises cannot be given concrete objectives.

These problems are not significant, however, in the case of lesser conflicts of the kind that engage the new humanitarianism. The ubiquity of ancient hatreds assures that the latter will not be infrequent. They can be anticipated, therefore, if not in particular places at particular times, at least generically. The United Nations has long been successful in assembling peacekeeping forces partly because the localized quarrels whose antagonists need to be kept apart seldom engage the direct interests of countries outside the immediate vicinity. A great many countries are thus potential suppliers of peacekeeping units. In the course of time more and more countries, in anticipation of being called upon for this purpose, have been willing to designate and train such units. Indeed, the United Nations itself now provides such training. Although peace-enforcement units would have to be larger and their training would be different, there is no reason I can see why the same considerations should not apply to them.

In the course of time, supplying international units for peace-enforcement duty may come to be regarded as an obligation of global citizenship. The assurance of fairness in the sharing of risk could go a long way toward building acceptance of that obligation. The designated units, moreover, might come to develop an esprit de corps like that of the United States Marines or the Royal Air Force. But to guard against the possibility of indefinite escalation induced, as in Vietnam, by the illusion that just a little more effort will turn the tide, there should be agreement in advance that there will be no additional sacrifice beyond a specified level. If failure to achieve success before reaching that point made it necessary to admit defeat, so be it: there is a point after all, at which it makes no sense to spend lives in order to save lives.

Should it appear that the leading nations are prepared to think seriously about going forward along these lines, it will then become realistic to take another look at the desirability of creating a highly trained international volunteer force under the control of the United Nations Security Council that could quickly move into and stabilize a deteriorating situation. This was, in fact, an idea considered when the United Nations Charter was being drafted. Although dropped then, it has recently received thoughtful reexamination by Brian Urquhart. A paratrooper in World War II who was at the San Francisco Conference that gave birth to the United Nations, he immediately went to work for it, taking part in its earliest peacekeeping efforts, and later, in his position as under secretary general, overseeing its peacekeeping operations until his retirement in 1968.

As Urquhart visualizes the role of a "relatively small but highly trained force," it would "be willing, if necessary, to fight hard to break the cycle of violence at an early stage in low-level but dangerous conflicts, especially ones involving irregular militias and groups." And since such a force would be composed of volunteers and paid for under the regular United Nations budget, its commitment to a peace-enforcement mission would bypass most of the problems associated with the ad hoc allocation of costs and risks among member states. Assuming that such matters as recruiting, training, and logistics could be worked out, there would remain the stickier issues of command and control (Urquhart's suggestion that the force be "under the day-to-day direction of the secretary-general" scarcely seems feasible) and provision for air and naval support. And though the force might in time become a kind of international counterpart of the French Foreign Legion, in every case where its use was contemplated, there would arise the question of whether or not there needed to be a prior agreement on its reinforcement, if necessary, by pre-designated national contingents. These are, to be sure, formidable difficulties, but that's all the more reason to get on with the job of thinking them through.[3]

The effective use of any form of military force when other means have failed to bring a conflict to an end will lead, of course, to another troublesome set of problems: putting together a government that can run the pacified country, restoring its social infrastructure, and restarting its economy. Rather than let these burdens be transferred from Saddam

---

[3] Brian Urquhart, "For a UN Volunteer Military Force," *New York Review of Books,* June 10, 1993, p. 10. For comments on the Urquhart proposal and his responses, see the *New York Review of Books,* June 24, 1993, p. 58 and July 15, 1993, p. 52.

Hussein to the rest of the world, Operation Desert Storm stopped short of Baghdad. In Haiti, on the other hand, the United States, together with numerous international organizations and nongovernmental organizations, deliberately elected to take on the task of nation-building. This is a role which in principle will often seem to be inescapable. When a multilateral force has undertaken the use of force to prevent the loss of life, ensure respect for human rights, and maintain the order without which neither of the former is possible, it can hardly avoid undertaking as well responsibility for the necessary follow-up actions.

But no matter when, whether, or how these issues are resolved, peace-enforcement measures of any sort will always be both costly to apply and uncertain in effect. This being so, the highest possible priority must urgently be given to preventing latent conflicts from erupting into war. It is essential for this purpose to strengthen the ability of the United Nations to detect the signs that smoldering enmities may be on the point of bursting into flame. At that early stage some combination of well-prepared diplomatic initiatives, offers of conciliation or mediation, and stern warnings of possible sanctions may be able to avert bloodshed. Teams of individuals with expertise in the languages, cultures, and politics of volatile areas could be assembled in advance, develop contingency plans, and remain on call. Representatives of each side who show potential for responsible leadership could be given the opportunity to discuss their differences at meetings abroad in which disinterested parties would put forward constructive suggestions. Meanwhile, the focused application of resourcefulness and ingenuity will, I'm sure, turn up other and better preventive techniques.

The effort to head off incipient conflicts should also make use of regional organizations. The members of such organizations are more familiar than outsiders with the roots of potential conflict, the probable antagonists, and the possible avenues of compromise. The Security Council and secretary-general of the United Nations need, however, to give more energetic leadership to strengthening the willingness and capacity of regional organizations to deal with breaches of the peace in their own areas. The "Soccer War" between Honduras and El Salvador that broke out in 1969 provided an instructive example of what can be accomplished by this approach. As acting secretary of state at the time, I encouraged Galo Plaza, then secretary-general of the Organization of American States, and Foreign Minister Alfonso López-Michelsen of

Colombia to take advantage of this opportunity to demonstrate the effectiveness of the OAS. The resulting plan gave it the lead in bringing the parties together, with the United States playing only a supportive role. The execution of this plan brought the war to an end in a matter of days, and the OAS did get the credit.

Pluralistic democracy should also be recognized as an important contributor to conflict prevention. I had never clearly focused on this relationship until I happened to be in Iraq as a member of a United Nations humanitarian commission. Our chairman, Prince Sadruddin Aga Khan, arranged for us to meet with the Iraqi leaders of the Kurdish minority. In the course of a long discussion one moment stood out. This was when Jalal Talbani, the senior member of the group, said, "We Kurds have come to understand that for us democratization is a higher priority than autonomy."

Democratization a higher priority than autonomy? I suddenly saw that for minorities like the Kurds this must of course be so: no group identified by bonds of family, culture, and religion can sensibly regard its confinement to small and economically nonviable enclaves as a desirable means of preserving its cultural and religious identity. The Jews managed it in the Middle Ages, but only with great discipline and at great cost. A far better solution, clearly, is a pluralistic society in which differences are accorded respect and protected through the very kinds of safeguards written into our own Constitution over two hundred years ago.

Gidon Gottlieb, a professor of international law and diplomacy at the University of Chicago, has gone further. His recent book *States-Plus-Nations*[4] highlights the need to adapt concepts like sovereignty, territory, and citizenship to ethnic realities. In proposing new kinds of links among nations and peoples and between nations and states, he exposes the insufficiency of approaches to ethnic strife that rely merely on promises to protect human rights.

When preventive efforts have failed and fighting breaks out, whatever peace-enforcement actions are then initiated must be accompanied by every possible effort to bring about a negotiated solution. For though deep-seated hatreds, once they have flared into violence, resist rational

---

[4] *States-Plus-Nations: A New Approach to Ethnic Conflicts, the Decline of Sovereignty, & the Dilemmas of Collective Security* (New York: Council on Foreign Relations, 1993).

accommodation, the situation in Bosnia attests to the potential of pressures, threats, destruction, exhaustion, and the cumulative loss of life to yield a political settlement. Whether or not the resulting federation, oddly subdivided as it is along religious lines, can outlast the presence of an occupying military force may depend upon the degree to which world opinion encourages the development of a civil society transcending those subdivisions. But come what may, both the ordeal by trial and error from which the settlement emerged and the process of its implementation will have been uniquely valuable tests of the new humanitarianism. The outcome may also test the occupying powers' resolve to withdraw on schedule. I for one hope that they will not let the resumption of violence draw them in so deeply as to risk the forfeiture of public support. To my mind, it would be far better that they should cut their losses and get out than for them to allow another Vietnam to foreclose the option of future interventions.

To strengthen early-stage prevention and follow up peace enforcement, there is a need for another important contributor to a more peaceful world order. This is the role of laws and legal institutions not simply as instruments for punishing war crimes but as means of deterring bloody conflicts. Such conflicts, whether arising from ancient enmities, political ambitions, or clashes over territory and resources, should in principle be treated in the same way that domestic law treats quarrels between individuals and smaller groups—that is, by proscribing conduct incompatible with generally accepted norms. What I have in mind would go beyond the Nuremberg precedent now being applied in Cambodia and Rwanda and leapfrog as well the permanent international criminal tribunal recently proposed by the United Nations International Law Commission. While such tribunals can punish violations of compacts like the Geneva Conventions on the laws of war and the Genocide Convention, they reach only the most conspicuous offenders—a provincial governor, a prison warden, or a military commander—and have no means whatsoever of establishing collective responsibility for violations of these compacts.

More than once in recent years I've referred to this limitation as a "black hole in the law." I've also suggested that there might be an analogy here to the gradual extension of the "King's Peace" in England after the Norman Conquest. This extension came about because William the

Conqueror and his successors were determined to maintain dominion over their French possessions. For this purpose they would need England's manpower and productivity, and both were being sapped by incessant bloody quarrels among the local gentry. As a countermeasure, therefore, the kings created a system of courts with authority to enforce the law throughout the realm. It soon came to be said that the King's Peace extended as far as "the reach of the King's writ"—the range, in other words, within which a summons to appear in court could effectively be served. By the reign of Henry II, a marauding baron and his henchmen could not hope to escape prosecution merely because the owner of the property they pillaged was the grandson of the villain who raped the baron's great-aunt.

Today's counterparts of quarreling feudal lords are warring tribes, antagonistic sects, and militant political movements. Why should these groups be indulged greater freedom to engage in acts of frightfulness than is allowed to feuding families, squabbling villages, or terrorist organizations?

There are, I admit, problems with this analogy. One is that in many civil conflicts it may be impossible to ascribe greater fault to one side than the other. Yet this problem might be dealt with by invoking another domestic analogy, this time to the long-established practice of attaching equal culpability to all the participants in a barroom brawl. A more serious obstacle lies in the difficulty of imposing collective penalties for collective crimes. To begin with, at any rate ad hoc tribunals could be charged with finding the facts, determining culpability, and recommending appropriate sanctions, which might include massive fines. These tribunals, if they prove effective, could be followed in due course by a worldwide system of international peace-enforcement courts.

As it happened, the interval between the Norman Conquest and the reign of Henry II was a hundred years. It would be a monumental achievement if within half that time there could be established the global equivalent of the King's Peace. The peace-enforcement process will meanwhile need to be part of a comprehensive system resting on the United Nations Charter in addition to implementing Security Council decisions.

But any prospect that the United Nations will be able to develop such a system is already seriously weakened by its members' failure, in violation of the Charter, to make timely payments of their dues and assessments. As of January 1995, 101 countries owed $2.5 billion. The U.S. share of this total is just over $1 billion.

Being the United Nations' foremost deadbeat undercuts U.S. national interests in three obvious ways. First, though we profess to be a stalwart champion of the rule of law, we expose ourselves as willing to fulfill this role only when it suits us. Second, it undermines the credibility of our leadership in the eyes of those whom we aim to lead. Third, it reduces the value to us of involving the United Nations where, as in the Persian Gulf and Haiti, a U.S. initiative needs multilateral vindication.

But even after all arrearages have been liquidated, the United Nations system will still require greatly increased funding. A substantially augmented peace-enforcement role would require large amounts in addition to those demanded by all the many other claims on United Nations resources. Various ways of meeting these demands have been proposed. One—the international taxation of air travel or currency transactions—is resisted in the United States by the same neo-isolationist mentality that still inhabits a one-dimensional unilateral world.

As to the value of the struggle for these goals, let me relate a World War II experience. In 1944, while training for the Normandy invasion, my regiment was headquartered in Exeter, the county town of Devonshire. That spring I attended the Easter service in Exeter Cathedral. Speaking without a public-address system from a lofty pulpit in the echoing space of the bomb-damaged nave, the Bishop of Exeter intoned his words so that his sermon could be heard. I shall never forget the ringing chant of his high-pitched voice as it repeated the words, "My text is taken from chapter fourteen, verse twenty, of the Gospel according to Saint Matthew: *Gather up the fragments that none may be lost.*" The bishop turned first to the belief that well-intended but unsuccessful efforts are worthless. It is not the road to hell that is paved with good intentions, he said, but the road to heaven. The human pursuit of lofty aspirations must inevitably fall short. Our very striving for them is nonetheless precious. Hence, gather up the fragments that none may be lost. When I'm discouraged about the frustrations and failures of the struggle to create peace, I think of that sermon.

The human beings who make up every ethnic group and every political entity share common bonds with all the other human beings on this planet. All of us want a safer, more orderly, and more humane world not simply because such a world is better for ourselves but because we recognize our kinship—however distant—with those others. Is this idealistic? Realistic? Practical? It doesn't matter: any or all will do. What matters is that we get on with the task of building safety, order, and peace.

Ethics in Government

L ike a Minnesota winter, the Cold War had warm spells. One followed Soviet premier Nikita Khrushchev's meeting with President Eisenhower at Camp David in 1959. In "the spirit of Camp
David" the United States sent a delegation of American educators on a
tour of the USSR, and not long after that a group of their Soviet counterparts made a reciprocal visit to the United States. A chance encounter
during that visit highlighted for me the vital link between trust in government and ethics in government.

The encounter took place at a reception for the Soviet educators
hosted by the Department of Health, Education, and Welfare. While
standing in the receiving line I fell into conversation with the cultural attaché at the Soviet embassy. "You know," he remarked, "we in the Soviet
Union believe that the people exist to serve the state, while you in the
United States believe that the state exists to serve the people. But aren't
these, after all, merely different ways of saying the same thing?" While
not doubting that he meant to be gracious, I couldn't let this go unchallenged. "I'm afraid I can't agree," I said. "For you, the 'state' is an entity
with purposes of its own that the people can be required to serve. For us
the word is only a label for the arrangements by which we the people

delegate to some among us responsibility for things that concern us in common."

Although my words were spontaneous, I have never been able to improve upon this way of describing the basis of ethics in government. We the people are the public. Those to whom we delegate responsibility for the tasks that concern us in common are serving us. The delegation of responsibility to them necessarily implies our trust in them. Public service is therefore a public trust. This is the premise from which the principles of ethics in government are derived.

Although not different in kind from the obligations that bind all human beings to one another, the obligations that arise from the acceptance of trust are more direct and specific. To trust someone else is to put some part of your life in that person's hands. All of us put significant parts of our lives in the hands of public employees whom we hold accountable for the faithful performance of tasks vital to our security and well-being. That's why, in the absence of trust, free representative self-government is impossible.

Because trust in government and ethics in government are inseparably linked, most of this essay will deal with aspects of that linkage: the ethics of government, ethics in government and the confusion between principles and appearances, the legislation of morality, and the need for a counterattack against cynicism. But what I have to say about ethics in government will be clearer if I begin with some more general observations about moral behavior. So that I shall do.

Cynicism corrodes trust. Here at home the corrosive process began with the "credibility gap" that grew out of our role in Vietnam, the rancid duplicity of Watergate, and the disdain for accountability displayed by the illegal diversion to the Contras of the proceeds of arms sales to Iraq. Augmented since then by the disappointment of unrealistic expectations, the sensationalism of the media, and the negativism of political campaigns, cynicism toward government has become endemic. So deeply has it bitten into the foundations of trust that it is now widely supposed that any public employee who has the opportunity to do the wrong thing probably will.

One manifestation of the spread of cynicism is the ascendancy of the view that all human behavior is reducible to self-seeking motives. Common decency is unfashionable (or at best uninteresting). Idealism is out. Rather than be regarded as naïve, well-intentioned Washingtonians lean on maxims encapsulating shrewd, practical reasons why doing the right thing is the smart thing. The hardiest perennial, of course, is "Honesty's the best policy." This is the kind of adage I associate with Benjamin Franklin, but its author turns out to have been that greatest of phrase makers, Miguel de Cervantes. A similar piece of advice that has gained currency in our own day is "When deciding whether or not something is ethical, ask yourself whether you would want to see it on the front page of the *New York Times*." But by all odds the most delicious such reminder is H. L. Mencken's "Conscience is the inner voice which warns us somebody may be looking."

Is there a difference between behavior consistently and intelligently guided by Cervantes's advice and the actions of a genuinely honest person? Would conduct calculated to escape criticism by readers of the *New York Times* be indistinguishable from conduct conforming with high ethical standards? And if everything everybody did could withstand the scrutiny of everyone else, would all forms of lying, cheating, and stealing virtually disappear? A community in which these axioms were consistently observed would certainly be hard to differentiate from a community of genuinely ethical people. Indeed, the only difference between the two might be that the members of the latter would feel more comfortable with themselves than the members of the former. As Ernest Hemingway put it, "What is moral is what you feel good after and what is immoral is what you feel bad after."

But if people who *are* honest feel good about it, perhaps people who start out merely pretending to be honest will come in time to find satisfaction in honesty for its own sake. Max Beerbohm's fanciful tale *The Happy Hypocrite* wonderfully conveys this thought. It's about Lord George Hell, a "Regency rake" who falls deeply in love with a sweet and innocent young maiden. Dissipation has so ravaged his face that he repels her; she would marry, she tells him, only a man with a saintly countenance. He seeks out a gifted mask maker, who creates for him the utterly lifelike mask of a loving and virtuous youth. Wearing this mask, Lord George Hell woos and wins the maiden. Wildly happy, he repents of his sins and redresses past wrongs. A rejected former mistress tracks him down and rips off the mask. Lo and behold, his face—his *real* face—now looks exactly like the masked face!

Could this be an answer to cynicism? Perhaps if we wear the mask of morality long enough we'll become truly moral people. It can work for children. Taught to say "please" and "thank you," share their toys, and greet guests courteously, they are likely to turn into adults who genuinely *feel* courteous to others. Although a step beyond courtesy, consideration for others can also, I think, be taught. I remember being told as a boy that compared with that nice boy Charley Goodshoes, I was thoughtless and inconsiderate. I received this observation not as a challenge to emulate Charley but as merely informing me that consideration for others was a quality that, unfortunately, I simply did not possess. Rather than being allowed to make this assumption, I should instead have been told that I could learn to be considerate simply by taking the trouble to try to grasp the other person's situation.

But if genuine morality is satisfying and the semblance of it rewarding, why is immoral behavior so prevalent? The obvious answer: lack of self-control. People *want* things, sometimes desperately. They indulge their greed, pursue their ambitions, unleash their libidos, lie about all of these things, and shove aside anyone who gets in the way. If that's all there were to human behavior, the cynics would be right. It's what they leave out that proves them wrong. In fact, by the time we reach adulthood most of us have learned to curb our selfish impulses. This is the largest part of what we mean by "maturity."

The most decent of us successfully control our self-centered impulses and consistently act on our generous feelings. We call saintly the individual whose daily life is wholly given to others. Meanwhile, the self-indulgers who will not discipline their selfishness are known by the manner of its indulgence: thief, embezzler, grafter, pusher, shoplifter, rapist, addict, arsonist, traitor, blackmailer, con man, mugger, and the like. The common denominator: injury to other people.

That our achievement of self-discipline is seldom perfect is illustrated by the most omnipresent form of such injury. That, of course, is cheating—inflating insurance claims, padding expense accounts, peeking at someone else's examination paper. Ironically, the usual excuse for cheating—"everybody does it"—is an acknowledgment of its immorality. If, as La Rochefoucauld observed, "Hypocrisy is the homage that vice pays to virtue," so also is the care with which cheating is concealed. While I hate all forms of cheating, in my Inferno tax evaders occupy a circle of their own. I see them not only as backsliders on their own civic responsibility but as stealing from their fellow citizens: the more successfully they escape what they owe, the more the rest of us have to pay.

I take satisfaction, therefore, in the fact that during my tenure as U.S. attorney for the District of Massachusetts, every tax evader we prosecuted was convicted, and all of them went to jail.

Have you ever wondered, by the way, why social scientists haven't taken more interest in trying to quantify the propensity to cheat? It wouldn't be easy to do, of course, given the inevitable secretiveness surrounding such matters. Still, surveyors of sexual behavior seem to be able to get people to reveal the extent of their cheating on their spouses. The key is assurance that anonymity will be protected. Given such assurance, why shouldn't the survey subjects be equally ready to answer questions about other forms of cheating?

At the opposite pole from cheating other people is treating them kindly. This leads to the assumption of personal obligations toward them. Such obligations accumulate. None of us is free to start a new day by exchanging our existing obligations for new ones. Old promises, long-standing relationships, prior commitments on which others have relied, claims arising from long-past services, ties bequeathed from a still more remote past—all these burden the present as the present will burden the future. Only a fraction of the claims on my time that I have no option but to honor are claims I would choose if I could start all over again. These persisting demands compel me again and again to pass up activities more interesting and more useful than many of those to which I'm already committed. My situation, in fact, is like that of the Boston lady who, when asked where she purchased her hats, replied, "In Boston we don't purchase our hats. We *have* them."

And so we come, not yet to ethics *in* government, but to the ethics *of* government. Like individuals, governments also have continuing obligations. Some are benign and caring; they reflect society's moral responsibility toward the victims of brutality, injustice, poverty, and sickness. The origin of others is stern and judgmental; they stem from violations of moral standards serious enough to warrant prohibition and punishment.

For the government of the United States both kinds of obligations present acutely difficult issues. The benign obligations fall under domestic as well as foreign headings. The domestic issues are not new, but they are plagued both by painful budgetary constraints and by the inadequacy of the proposed solutions. The foreign issues, on the other hand, present wholly unprecedented challenges. In distant places where we have no vital interests at stake we are nevertheless called upon to find ways of preventing conflict, restoring peace, and strengthening democracy. American reactions to these challenges range from "None of our business, we've got problems enough of our own" to "Common decency requires that we try to help."

The extent and character of our national government's responses to both domestic and foreign claims are an outcome of interaction between political leadership and public opinion. Relevant factors include the proximity of the claimants, the merits of their claims, and the force with which their needs are communicated. The political leader who seeks to widen our horizons must be able to bring to bear a high order of vision, eloquence, and determination. In the cases of health-care reform, fiscal policy, Somalia, and Haiti we have seen varying degrees of adequacy in meeting these requirements. It has also been strikingly obvious that relative distance made a literal difference.

In our society, there is no fundamental difference between the ethical obligations of government to its citizens and those of citizens to one another. Social Security is a good example of these interrelated obligations. Its funding is supplied by a payroll tax shared equally by employers and employees, but with immunity for income above $62,000 (a cutoff which rises as wages rise). The tax rate has been set at a level deemed adequate to provide benefits pretty much on a pay-as-you-go basis and to create a contingency reserve sufficient to see the system through any unexpected short-term financial problem. Implicit in this longstanding compact between and among the American people is the understanding that all contributors have a right to benefits: the wealthy participant and the poor participant alike are entitled to feel that their benefits have been earned.

Despite this social compact, Social Security's size (outlays of $353 billion in fiscal 1996) and rate of growth (only the medical programs are growing faster) make it an obvious target for budget balancers. If it had been decided when the payroll tax rates were set, however, that benefit payments should be lower, that the age of eligibility should be higher, or that the annual cost-of-living adjustment need not keep pace with the rate of inflation, the rates would have been set at a lower level. Hence, the terms of the compact would require that a reduction now in any of these three numbers should result in a reduction, not in the deficit, but in the tax rates.

Some budget balancers would even go so far as to make benefit amounts depend on total income at the time of eligibility—a welfare-style means test. But this would subvert the primary aim of Social Security and other social insurance programs—to obviate the necessity for determining eligibility for public charity. The importance of that aim will for me always be associated with a conversation in 1957 or 1958 on the way back to Boston from an American Public Welfare Association meeting in New Hampshire. My companions were a trio of welfare caseworkers, one from Massachusetts and two from Rhode Island. One of the Rhode Islanders recalled an elderly man who had recently come into the Pawtucket welfare office to apply for old age assistance. In response to a question about his assets, the applicant disclosed that he had a fairly substantial savings account. "What for?" asked the caseworker. "For a rainy day," retorted the old man. "Brother," said the caseworker, "when you apply for welfare, it's *pouring!*"

Reducing Social Security because of other income would send the wrong message to young Americans. It would say, "If you're a saver, you will be penalized by having your Social Security reduced." As a base to be supplemented by private pensions and other savings, Social Security is an important part of retirement income for just about everyone. If, therefore, it's necessary to raise taxes in order to reduce the deficit, this should not be done indirectly through tapping the Social Security payroll tax but directly by means of a tax that employs a positive means test—the income tax. That way, the more you have, the more you pay.

Government's stern and judgmental role also illustrates the inseparability of public and private ethical obligations. This role is brought to bear where, but for that role, assaults on another person's dignity, rights, or property would be likely to provoke the injured party into taking the matter into his own hands. Governmental sanctions against violations of accepted moral standards thus attach to the lower half of a continuum extending all the way from a frown of disapproval to the death penalty. At the top of the nongovernmental half we find the phenomenon of "political correctness." While easily, and sometimes deservedly, ridiculed, it responds to a real lack of sensitivity toward fragile components of other people's self-esteem. In a society composed of many diverse cultural, ethnic, and religious groups, the mild pressure exerted by the requirement of political correctness is not unlike that resulting from parental insistence on politeness. Further along the continuum are offenses like malicious gossip and demeaning insults. Verbal assaults that amount to a "slap in the face" or a "kick in the teeth" can be almost as provocative as their physical counterparts.

Deficiencies of moral sensitivity shade in a similar way into harmful behavior. A typical sequence starts with lack of consideration and goes via egocentricity to utter self-absorption. Or again, from lack of generosity through parsimony to stinginess. Thus do people slide into progressively increasing insensitivity to their fellow human beings. To be made aware of how blind they have become they need, like Scrooge, to be confronted with their past, present, and future selves.

A society's instinct as to when to call upon government to enforce moral standards is the product of historic experience, cultural influences, reactions to recent happenings, and seat-of-the-pants judgment. Different cultures mark the outer fringe of criminal law in different places. In colonial New England it was a crime to be a "common scold," and a person found guilty of this offense would be strapped to a ducking-stool and repeatedly doused in the chilly water of a nearby pond. In Singapore today, the sale of chewing gum can draw a fine of up to $2,000; an importer can be fined three times as much and sentenced to a year in prison.

In every society punishments are matched to wrongdoing on a graduated scale from petty offenses through increasingly serious misdemeanors and felonies to heinous capital crimes. This makes good practical sense because the swifter, surer, fairer, and more even-handed the sentence, the greater its deterrent value. It also makes good moral sense because punishment that fits the crime is punishment commensurate with society's moral condemnation of the offending conduct. In this country, unfortunately, such commensurability is being undermined by the cynical assumption that to aim at rehabilitation is to be soft on crime. Insofar as the demand for tougher sentencing is driven by the raw desire for retribution, it substitutes vengeance for justice as the motivator of government's coercive power.

Cynicism toward the ethics of government leads to cynicism toward ethics in government. An unmistakable sign of this progression is the perversion of the word "ethics." In today's Washington the distinction between the actuality of unethical conduct and the appearance of such conduct has almost disappeared. The press, the public, and the politicians (in that order) take off after questionable appearances with the same noisy outcries with which they once pursued real wrongdoing. It

195

will soon be "ethically questionable" for a person with strong opinions on civil rights to be assistant attorney general for civil rights. This logic would also prevent a stockbroker from heading the Securities and Exchange Commission, an African American from heading the Equal Employment Opportunities Commission, or a rancher from being secretary of the interior. Carried a step further, it would disqualify from every job anyone with relevant experience.

Now, I am not saying that appearances are never important. When on April 29, 1973, President Nixon asked me to leave the Department of Defense and go to the Department of Justice he left it up to me whether or not there should be a special prosecutor for Watergate. The more I thought about it, the clearer it seemed to me that public confidence in the investigation would depend on its being independent not only in fact but in appearance. And though I believed I could fulfill the first of these requirements, it was clear that I could not meet the second: I had from the beginning of his administration been the appointee of a president whose staff was being investigated and who might himself be implicated. I would, moreover, once again be serving at his pleasure.

Seven days after my meeting with Nixon I announced at a press conference that I would, if confirmed as attorney general, appoint a special prosecutor and give him all the independence, authority, and staff support needed to carry out the tasks entrusted to him. I assumed that future occasions to appoint a special prosecutor would be rare—no more frequent, perhaps, than two or three in the balance of the century. Only twice before in our history, after all, had such an appointment been thought necessary: the Teapot Dome scandal in 1925 and the investigation of Justice Department officials in the early 1950s. It would have amazed me to be told that two-thirds of the way through the century's next-to-last presidential term *six* special prosecutors would be serving simultaneously, with one looking into the Reagan era's Department of Housing and Urban Development, three investigating current cabinet members, one the actions of individuals in the Bush administration, and one transactions involving Bill Clinton that occurred long before he became president.

In addition to conceding the need for public confidence in the handling of highly visible situations, I recognize as well the desirability of rules governing the conduct of day-to-day government business. Public employees should avoid, for example, placing themselves in situations that could reasonably be regarded as exploitable for their own benefit or as putting them under obligation to someone whose interests could be affected by their actions. The problem is not with the rules but with the reinforcement of cynicism that results from confusing them with ethical principles. By 1992 I had begun to regard this as a deeply disturbing trend. When, therefore, early in that year, the Council for Excellence in Government invited me to chair a working group on ethics in government, I was happy to accept.

The members of the working group had all served in one or more responsible government positions. Each of them had struggled with such questions as when the appearance of a conflict of interest should require recusal, the applicability of financial-disclosure requirements, and the length of the interval before a political appointee should be allowed to deal with her old agency. No doubt expecting that questions of this kind would be at the top of our agenda, the working group may have been surprised when I began the first meeting by asking how many of them thought it was unethical to have a conflict of interest. Many of them thought it was. "Do you realize," I said, "that if you said this to a conscientious trustee he would be insulted? You would be accusing him of putting his personal interest ahead of his fiduciary obligation. In fact, he would be more likely to bend over backward in order *not* to do so."

Using a position of trust for personal gain is a flagrant breach of ethics. To have a conflict of interest is merely to be exposed to temptation. (Conflicts of duty—representing both sides in the same case, for example—are quite another matter.) In most private situations—membership on a corporate board, for instance—it is sufficient merely to disclose a conflict of interest and to abstain from voting. In the case of government, it has been thought desirable to prohibit conflicts of interest. I have no quarrel with the proposition that this is necessary to maintaining public confidence. Indeed, I agree with it. "Thou shalt not have a conflict of interest," however, is not an ethical principle; it is a rule of public policy.

By the end of that first meeting the group had pretty well accepted these points. I accordingly suggested that at our next meeting we discuss the ethical guidelines in actual use by a government agency. One of our members had served as associate general counsel of the Securities and Exchange Commission. She got for us copies of an SEC manual setting forth "the standards of ethical conduct required of members, employees and others." It turned out that everything this forty-four-page manual had to say about ethics added up to only a page and a half. The remainder dealt with such matters as when, if at all, you may allow someone else to pay for your lunch, give you an honorarium, or reimburse your travel expenses.

The eventual product of the working group's deliberations was a brief statement entitled "Ethical Principles for Public Servants." Signed by more than four hundred members of the Council for Excellence in Government, the statement called attention at the outset to the distinction between moral standards and rules of conduct. Proscribing the latter without understanding the former was like trying to build a house before the foundation is laid. It was essential, we said, to refocus attention on the central role of the principles underlying the rules.

The substantive part of our statement began with a summation of core values:

> Public service is a public trust. The highest obligation of every individual in government is to fulfill that trust. Each person who undertakes the public trust assumes two paramount obligations:
>
> —to serve the public interest; and
> —to perform with integrity.
>
> These are the commitments implicit in all public service. In addition to faithful adherence to the ethical principles enjoined upon all honest and decent people, public employees have a duty to discern, understand, and meet the needs of their fellow citizens. That is, after all, the definition of a public *servant*.

To some, perhaps, these thoughts may seem self-evident, but it's hard for me to believe that they will be so regarded by anyone who has made a serious effort to understand what public service is about. They're too general, of course, to be the basis for resolving concrete ethical problems. Recognizing this, the working group attempted to spell out the practical implications of these core values. We said, for example, that "integrity requires of you the consistent pursuit of the merits." This, for those who occupy senior positions, obliges them to invite ideas, encourage debate, and accept criticism. By the same token, it demands of their subordinates the willingness to speak up, to argue, and to question. Most fundamentally, public servants must have the courage to insist on what they believe to be morally right and the fortitude to refuse to go along with what they believe to be morally wrong. The aim of being right, however, calls for persistent effort to weigh competing interests and values and to understand the relevant facts.

We recognized, of course, that hard ethical questions involve tough choices. Loyalty to one's organization can conflict with respect for authority, dedication to programmatic goals with deference to the policy role of political appointees and responsiveness to the public's right to know, and sensitivity to the need for confidentiality. The ultimate test of a public servant is how well and how honorably he or she balances these claims.

If you had to judge by the media coverage of unethical behavior in public service, you would think that the principal instigator of such behavior is greed. We felt it necessary, therefore, to observe that greed is a far less common corrupter of public servants than ego, envy, timidity, ambition, or a craving for publicity. To resist these seducers demands character and self-discipline. With a view to fortifying the good instincts of government employees, we undertook to specify the distinctive attributes of the "true public servant." We said that this ideal person:

- will not act out of spite, bias, or favoritism;
- will not tell the boss only what she or he wants to hear;
- respects the competence and views of others;
- does not succumb to peer or political pressure;
- contributes to a climate of mutual trust and respect;
- refuses to let official action be influenced by personal relationships, including those arising from past or prospective employment;
- has the courage of his or her convictions;
- is not seduced by flattery;
- unflinchingly accepts responsibility;
- does not try to shift blame to others;
- can distinguish between the need to support an unwelcome decision and the duty to blow the whistle;
- and never forgets that she or he is working for the people—all the people.

For a public servant faced with a difficult ethical dilemma, the ultimate recourse is to consult one's colleagues, listen to one's conscience, and think hard. But better preparation for public service could help. To that end we recommended that employee training sessions include, in addition to briefings on laws, regulations, and rules, case studies illustrating the precepts we had just set forth. We also urged that employees with specific ethical dilemmas be given easily accessible sources of sensible, sympathetic, and reliable advice.

But it's going to take more than this statement of principles to reverse the present perverted order of things. Government agencies continue to refer to rules of conduct as if they were ethical principles. When, for example, my appointment as the president's special representative for the Philippines came up for renewal early in 1994, I had to certify that I had watched a videotape produced by the Office of Government Ethics with the title *Integrity in Public Service: Earning the Public's Trust.* The videotape barely touched on integrity in public service. In one scene a civil servant tells his brother-in-law that he will not inquire into the status of a benefit payment. In another a young woman is having lunch with a man who has just won a contract with her agency. She politely refuses to let him pick up the check. And so on. In short, it was a video version of the SEC manual.

Again, the point is not that rules of this kind are unnecessary. As in the case of conflicts of interest, it is desirable to deny the cynics the opportunity to indulge their suspicions. But to treat a public servant's acceptance of a free lunch as a matter of integrity is to imply that he or she has no ethical principles at all. Hence the importance of reasserting the distinction between a role of conduct and an ethical principle.

For a long time now the public reactions to actual wrongdoing have been almost equally shallow. Instead of leading to higher standards and better enforcement of existing laws, they have spawned new laws, new penalties, and new policing devices. Watergate produced the Ethics in Government Act of 1978. Since its premise is that no one in government can be trusted (it requires upper-level federal employees, for example, to disclose all earned income exceeding $200), it might more appropriately have been called the "No Ethics in Government Act." Two years later another law mandated the appointment of inspectors general throughout the government. These officials perform functions that departmental comptrollers, general counsels, and the preexisting investigative agencies were already performing. Finally, to remind government employees that it can be dangerous to do the right thing, we gave them an updated "whistleblower" statute to protect them from reprisal if they turn in a corrupt colleague. It's time we took seriously the question first asked by the satirist Juvenal in the early years of the Roman empire: *Sed quis custodiet ipsos custodes?* But who is to guard the guards themselves?

The assumption that public officials are too weak, too greedy, or too unprincipled to wish or be able to do the right thing permeates this whole roster of "reforms." Bans on dealing with your former agency, requirements for the divestiture of investments, restrictions on communication, and "recusal" for the mere appearance of a conflict of interest all presuppose that public servants have neither backbone nor integrity. Again, the point is not that rules of this kind are valueless. It is that they foster the illusion that morality can be legislated. This is an illusion that needs to be destroyed, and I would like to think that these words will help to sharpen the stake that will eventually be driven through its heart.

The truth is that most public servants who have been around a while have become expert at maintaining their integrity. They know, for example, the value of the Brandeis axiom "Daylight is the best disinfectant." One young bureaucrat of my acquaintance disarmed a whole battery of highly paid lawyers and lobbyists for several huge companies simply by giving a *Washington Post* reporter a hint of what they were up to. A well-connected influence peddler is, of course, better able than an unknown to get his phone calls returned. More often than not, however, the only result of his influence is that the decisionmaker takes extra trouble to bulletproof the outcome she believes to be right. For a public servant, the equivalent of grace under pressure is being right under pressure.

Speaking of pressure, Richard Kleindienst, my predecessor as attorney general, was about to appeal a federal district court's dismissal of an antitrust proceeding against the International Telephone and Telegraph Company when he got a telephone call from President Nixon. Nixon told Kleindienst not to file the appeal. Sometime later a congressional committee asked Kleindienst if he had ever been subjected to "White House pressure." He said no. Indicted for lying, he pleaded guilty—why I don't know. He wouldn't have felt under pressure if he'd been confident that he could get Nixon to change his mind. And, in fact, he did eventually persuade the president that the appeal should go forward.

It's a mistake to overreact to an order you think is wrong. I remember particularly well a phone call from presidential assistant John Ehrlichman. He was passing on Nixon's instruction that I immediately fire the commissioner of mental health. Why? Because the commissioner had suggested that the decriminalization of marijuana should perhaps be considered. "Please tell the president," I said, "that I would be glad to discuss the matter with him at his convenience." That was the last I ever heard of it.

Similar calculations enable executive-department employees to maintain their ethical equilibrium under the pressures emanating from Capitol Hill. Civil servants take it for granted that a congressional office will do its best to win a desired contract or grant for the folks back home, and the congressional office assumes that the executive branch will say no if that's the right answer. If the Hill office isn't exerting "pressure," it isn't doing its job, and the executive-branch office is equally remiss if it rolls over when it shouldn't.

For the executive branch to expedite action on a meritorious application from a friendly source has always been considered legitimate. So also has been giving a supportive senator or congressman the opportunity to announce a favorable result. It is equally well recognized, however, that bending the applicable standards under congressional pressure is beyond the pale.

I can recall only one situation in my own government services in which it seemed necessary to take special precautions against foreseeable charges of political manipulation. This was in 1976, a presidential election year. I was secretary of commerce. The economy was in bad shape in the early months of that year, and Congress wanted to stimulate a recovery by giving the department $2.5 billion to fund job-creating municipal projects. The Ford administration opposed the appropriation on the ground that the money couldn't be spent quickly enough to produce the intended result. Congress, however, appropriated the money anyway, and President Ford decided not to veto the bill. Commerce's job in the circumstances was to get the money out as fast as possible while at the same time making sure that no one could accuse us of using it as a political slush fund.

The only thing to do, I decided, was to set up a system under which all projects would be rated on the basis of their readiness to get under way, the amount of unemployment in the area, the poverty level, and other such criteria. Each project's rating was fed into a computer, the weighted average was calculated, and all the projects were ranked accordingly. We got a few calls from congressmen and gave them the answers dictated by the computer. And then I got a call from President Ford. He hoped that we could see our way clear to funding a project in Grand Rapids, his hometown. I had to tell him that there was nothing we could do: the Grand Rapids project did not meet the eligibility standard.

Washington's obliviousness to any corrupting influence other than money is almost as oddly skewed as its substitution of appearances for principles. Conflict-of-interest laws, "revolving-door" restraints, lobbying registration, campaign-contribution limits, and any number of other restrictions have an almost exclusively economic focus. But these barriers impede only a fraction of the pressures that bend the merits out of shape. Those who seek high elective or appointive office are more likely to be seeking recognition, influence, or prestige than a pecuniary reward. True, winning a political campaign may hold the prospect of achieving all these aims, and money is a key to winning. The regulation of campaign financing—spending limits, contributions limits, and a ban on "soft money"—is thus essential.

I wish it were also possible to restrict the ability of the very rich to buy elective success: the $36 million spent by Michael Huffington in his 1994 campaign for a Senate seat in California constituted 93 percent (!) of his total campaign war chest. Still, I can't argue with the Supreme Court's ruling that the Constitution protects a candidate's freedom to spend his own money. The public financing of campaigns, on the other hand, bothers me not so much because I think it's a bad idea in itself, but because the collection of large numbers of small contributions is, I've always thought, a good way of encouraging grass-roots participation in the political process. Where I come out is with the view that public funds should be used to buy radio and television time provided that the time is devoted to explaining the candidate's positions on substantive issues.

Having said that, I still think that there is less than meets the eye in the impression that money is a powerful distorting influence on an elective officeholder's substantive positions. Most campaign contributions come from sources whose interests the candidate already supports for reasons that have nothing to do with money. In Massachusetts, for example, fishing has been an important economic interest ever since colonial

times. When I worked for Leverett Saltonstall, then the Commonwealth's senior senator, I spent a lot of time on his behalf trying to help
the fishing industry. While I hope that the fishermen gave financial support to Senator Saltonstall's reelection, he and his staff would have done
for them whatever we did whether or not they ever contributed.

Further diminishing the power of money is the candidate's right to
take it for granted that no one could possibly regard him as for sale. A political action committee, in any case, is not allowed to contribute more
than $10,000 to any one candidate, and it would be a pretty cheap politi-
cian who would sell his soul for one-fourth of 1 percent of the cost of his
campaign. PACs, to be sure, do not often go shopping for souls. They
don't expect a complete switch of positions from, say, pro-choice to pro-
life. Their prime targets are candidates who have not yet taken a position
on their issues or who could be moved to support a seemingly narrow or
innocuous amendment. It is also conceivable that a PAC might have disinterested reasons for supporting a candidate who disagreed with its positions. Even the NRA should have wanted to help Chuck Robb beat
Ollie North!

A PAC, in any case, must be cautious about extracting a pledge of
support in return for its contribution, lest the transaction shade into
bribery. But quid pro quos aside, there is a flip side to the ethical issue.
Can a candidate appropriately accept a contribution from a PAC whose
known interests he does not believe in and, if elected or reelected, will
do nothing to advance? Should he be free, despite having taken the
money, even to oppose those interests? Should it make a difference that
his opposition to them was already publicly known before the contribution was made? Should he, even without being asked, have told the PAC
people where he stood? These are questions that can't be answered without more facts, but they obviously concern real ethical problems.

But it's the prospect of obtaining an interest group's endorsement,
not its money, that exerts the *real* pressure. In a close election the endorsement of a large membership organization—a veterans organization,
an environmental lobby, or a labor union, for example—can make a significant difference. But such an endorsement is seldom given except in
return for explicit agreement with the organization's positions on substantive issues. I remember as a candidate for a U.S. Senate nomination
twelve years ago sweating over how to say what I honestly believed in a
way that would not forfeit a major endorsement. The money that would

also be forthcoming if I got a passing grade was incidental—and not because I didn't need it.

Of course, managing, reconciling, mollifying, neutralizing, fending off, and avoiding a host of competing and conflicting interests while at the same time trying to serve the general public interest is what a working politician's job is all about. Meanwhile, no politician ever forgets that elections are won or lost by narrow margins. They are obliged to seek support wherever it may be found. The hope of enlisting it makes them want to respond positively to other people's requests, needs, or importunities. And then there are the opinion polls—one way by which constituents tell politicians what they want to hear. No other occupation subjects its practitioners to such a constant flow of difficult, demanding, and sometimes painful choices. It isn't news that many politicians are in varying degrees and combinations weak, vacillating, manipulative, devious, and/or deceptive. The noteworthy fact is that so many keep their integrity and humor in the midst of all these pressures. Few of the voters who badmouth and belittle them have either the experience or the imagination to know whereof they speak. They deserve worse politicians than they get.

Though being too responsive can get a politician into trouble, helping people is satisfying for its own sake. This accounts for the most telling difference between a businessman and a politician. If you ask a businessman to do something, he will say no unless he can see a good reason for saying yes. If you ask a politician to do something, he will say yes unless he can see a good reason for saying no. As a sometime politician who still gets a great many requests, I say no quite often these days but not often enough. Had I been more successful at doing so, these essays would have been completed quite a lot sooner.

It is perhaps to be expected that a society prone to ascribe the meanest of motives to its public servants should also assume that maintaining integrity must take more than ordinary courage. Having myself been accorded excessive credit on this score, I have good reason to be aware that this assumption is widely shared. While true heroism may be called for in exceptional circumstances—John F. Kennedy's *Profiles in Courage* assembled some dramatic examples—doing the right thing is not ordinarily difficult. As I have repeatedly emphasized in these pages, the key to dealing with most hard problems is to stick with the merits and persist in seeking the best and most workable approach. Once you have found this approach, pursuing it seldom requires tensing your muscles or gritting your teeth. In most situations it's the most direct and defensible course of action.

The individuals whose integrity looms largest when I look back are all people who made it look easy. One was Marion B. Folsom, a former senior executive at Kodak and pioneer in developing the Social Security Act. He was my first boss at the Department of Health, Education, and Welfare in the Eisenhower administration. An unassuming man who never raised his voice, he listened carefully to all sides and always made sure he had all the facts on any matter at issue. He kept himself free to deal with urgent problems by delegating day-to-day functions to his senior colleagues in a manner suitably adjusted to their strengths and limitations. When he reached a decision, he would stick with it unless given some good reason why he should change his mind. If he did not do so, it was not because he was immovable but simply that he was not persuaded. He could tell you why not, moreover, in such a way that if it did not induce you to abandon your own position, it reinforced your respect for his. More to the point, he dealt the same way with the president, a cabinet colleague, a congressional committee chairman, the head of a national organization, or the CEO of a giant corporation.

Arthur S. Flemming, who succeeded Folsom at HEW, has maintained the same approach throughout a career of public service that began under FDR as a member of the Civil Service Commission. Never moved by pressure, never compromising his convictions, and never putting a foot wrong, he has retained for more than five decades the respect and affection of countless others whose primary allegiance is to the public interest. Now over ninety, he's still going strong.

Having in several capacities had the good fortune to become acquainted with many of the men who have risen to the top in the uniformed services, I'm deeply impressed by their consistently high quality. For that we owe a tremendous though unacknowledged debt to the continuing perspicacity of the armed services' selection and promotion systems. These views were reinforced when, during the events in June of 1994 commemorating the fiftieth anniversary of the Allied landings in Normandy, I had the chance to talk with quite a few of our most senior officers.

On the flight back from Normandy I sat across from General John W. Vessey, Jr. Now retired, he enlisted in the army at the age of seventeen, received a battlefield commission at Anzio in 1944, commanded the Fourth Division in Vietnam and U.S. armed forces in South Korea, became vice-chief of staff of the army, and ended up as chairman of the Joint Chiefs of Staff. Since then he has given large chunks of six additional years to bringing about a final accounting for those missing in action in Vietnam. In all these capacities Jack Vessey was too astute to bamboozle, too strong to push, too courageous to intimidate, too patient to outlast, and too unassuming to flatter.

In Shakespeare's *Julius Caesar* Brutus says to the conspirator Cassius:

There is no terror, Cassius, in your threats;
For I am arm'd so strong in honesty
That they pass by me as the idle wind,
Which I respect not.

I can easily imagine Folsom, Flemming, or Vessey saying something like that. The unscrupulous schemer who thinks he can co-opt, circumvent, or con such a person is—well, the only word for it is "stupid."

The schemer has few options, none of them likely to succeed. If he lets himself be drawn into the merits, he will come out in the end with no more and no less than he deserves. If he tries to invoke threats or pressure or hold out special inducements, he's likely to end up with nothing. And he has small chance of gaining an edge by cultivating the top man's subordinates because they will have been chosen with an eye to the boss's own standards. In these circumstances, even the most inveterate schemer soon discovers that he has only two real choices: either to play the game in accordance with the rules or to pick up his marbles and go home.

Though the requirements of integrity do not vary with the nature of the assignment, there are distinctions among the ethical principles applicable to political appointees, career public servants, and legislators. Political appointees serve three masters: the president, their departments or agencies, and the public interest as they personally perceive it. In the best of circumstances they see their obligations to each as identical. Ordinary divergences of view are readily smoothed over by loyalty and team spirit. In a case where the president's final decision goes against the appointee, it is usually not difficult for him to respect the basis on which it was made. It is only rarely that a clash between loyalty and principle forces a political appointee to think about resignation. Walking off the stage is an act that has no encore. In such a situation it behooves the appointee to search his conscience carefully before concluding that resignation is the only honorable course.

For the career public servant, objectives and priorities are established by the political process, and the resources they require are provided in the same way. The civil servant's obligations to this process demand the responsible input of expert knowledge, sound judgment, and institutional memory. When this input collides with the policies of the incumbent administration, the civil servant has a duty to make sure that his views are fully considered. And where higher authority takes an action that the civil servant believes to be wrong, he has to choose, in the words of the Council for Excellence in Government, "between the need to support an unwelcome decision and the duty to blow the whistle." As to other relevant standards, I can't improve on the council's statement of ethical principles for public servants.

What distinguishes a legislator's role from that of a political appointee or a civil servant is, of course, her direct accountability to the people who elected her. While responsive to her constituents' needs and problems and ready to speak up for their interests, she should not be blind to the merits of competing claims. A senator or representative is no less entitled than a lawyer to make a forceful case for her own side of an issue, but she should be held, as should he, to high standards of integrity in assembling and presenting the pertinent facts. If, in addition to carrying out these obligations, she demonstrates fair regard for other views and appropriately balances national priorities against local interests, she truly deserves to be called "Honorable." Who would not want to reelect her again and again?

But the seeker of elective office cannot postpone her ethical obligations until she takes the oath of office. A would-be president, governor, or legislator assumes obligations merely by virtue of seeking office. Do you remember the presidential election of 1984? That was the year when Vice President Walter Mondale, the Democratic standard-bearer, warned that new taxes would be needed to hold down the deficit. That was also the year in which I was a candidate for the U.S. Senate in the Massachusetts Republican primary. I said quite a lot—too much, perhaps—about the dangerous consequences of letting supply-side economics dictate the nation's fiscal policy. It seemed to me clear that, in addition to holding down spending increases, we had to find new sources of revenue, and I said so repeatedly. In the last two weeks of the campaign my opponent, a wealthy businessman, spent a barrel of his own money on radio and TV ads asserting that "Richardson Wants to Raise Taxes." All I could say in self-defense was, "I don't *want* to raise taxes, but we've got to deal with the deficit!"[1]

We all know what happened to Mondale. Since I, as a candidate for a Republican nomination, was implicitly criticizing an incumbent president beloved by my party's rank and file, I lost by a larger margin than Mondale did. No doubt there were other equally incautious losers in 1984. Four years later it was clear that President Reagan's prudently loyal vice president had been right the first time when, as a candidate for the Republican presidential nomination in 1980, he denounced Ronald Reagan's "voodoo economics." But in 1988 it was also clear which way the wind was blowing. The result: "Read my lips: No New Taxes."

Though one of the more conspicuous examples of accommodation with political necessity, George Bush's pledge was hardly precedent-setting. He could have cited the example of Theodore Roosevelt. As a prospective candidate for the governorship of New York in 1898, TR was faced with the necessity of paying homage to the state's powerful Republican boss, Senator Thomas C. Platt. Since Roosevelt's greatest political asset was his reputation as a reformer, he could not afford to let it be known that he had met with a machine politician of Platt's ilk. If he failed to pay a call on Platt, however, he could not hope to get the latter's all-important support.

What to do? As Roosevelt's friend, the muckraking journalist Lincoln Steffens, tells the story, Roosevelt agreed that he had no choice but

---

[1] Too bad I didn't know then what I know now about the views of David Stockman, President Reagan's first budget director. In a book published in 1986, Stockman confessed that by 1983 he knew that taxes would have to be raised. "The deficit had now already come in at $208 billion," he wrote. "The case for a major tax increase was overwhelming, unassailable, inescapable and self-evident. Not to raise taxes when all other avenues were closed was a willful act of ignorance and grotesque irresponsibility. In the entire twentieth-century fiscal history of the nation, there has been nothing to rival it." David A. Stockman, *The Triumph of Politics: Why the Reagan Revolution Failed* (New York: Harper & Row, 1986), p. 373.

to see Platt and then to deny that he'd done so. Roosevelt accordingly made the necessary pilgrimage. On his return he set to work in Steffens's presence on composing a denial. Having watched Roosevelt draw up and reject a whole series of drafts, Steffens eventually spoke up. "There is no known literary form for denying a fact without lying," said Steffens, "and that you don't want to do. Why not pick out one of those statements . . . and read it before and after meals, till, in a day or two, you come to believe it yourself? Then give it out. It will be true then."

Two days later, Steffens saw Roosevelt again. "Well, Colonel," he asked, "have you got that lie so that you believe it yourself?" Roosevelt was furious. He had been almost ready to give the statement out. This "insulting question," Steffens recalled, "had set him back, probably a day or two."

Before and since TR and George Bush countless politicians have swallowed hard and said what they thought they had to say. For two centuries, nevertheless, our political process has been able to assimilate this kind of misrepresentation tolerably well, perhaps because its usual function was to conform the candidate's declared position to the prevailing popular view. Such deference to the populace, indeed, might be rationalized on the ground that it furthers a form of democracy purer than the Burkean variety. It's more forgivable, certainly, to suppress a belief in gun control when running in a rural district than to promote a worthless remedy for a serious problem.

It would be hard to say where in the world of politics lies leave off and some combination of simplemindedness, wishful thinking, and eagerness to please takes over. The "don't just stand there, do something" syndrome produces a lot of this kind of fakery—the "war on crime," for example. Rather than face up to really hard problems like the self-perpetuating cycle of inner-city poverty, despair, joblessness, and violence—we allow ourselves to be diverted by such secondary issues as abortion, school prayer, or term limits. During the interval in which our attention is absorbed by these political sideshows the serious problems continue to get worse. And when, on top of all these, we're told we can have it both ways—a balanced budget *and* tax cuts, global leadership *and* the avoidance of sacrifice, better government *and* contempt for the bureaucracy, the disconnection between representation and reality has become all but unbridgeable.

What I've said up to this point began with basic ethical principles and went from there to the ethical obligations of government. Then came a discussion of ethics in public service, followed by some observations on ethics and politics. But to stop here would leave out the ethical responsibilities of the most important actors in the whole drama—the responsibilities which, at the end of the day, belong to us, the people.

By October 1973, when I resigned from the Department of Justice, I had became deeply concerned with the question of how, in an increasingly complex society, to preserve a creative relationship between government and the individual. I therefore welcomed the opportunity to become a fellow of the Woodrow Wilson International Center for Scholars so that I could start work there on a book addressing this question. A good place to begin, I thought, was with the framers' conception of the role of the citizen. It was my good fortune that two of my colleagues at the center were professors of American history. The original sources to which they introduced me made clear that the framers' primary concern with the citizen was with his rights, not his responsibilities. The framers were well aware, nonetheless, that the nation they founded would have to depend on its citizens for the performance of essential functions. Citizens would need, for one thing, to be vigilant in maintaining the liberties guaranteed to them. For another, theirs would be the duty of selecting those to whom they would delegate responsibility for dealing with common concerns. A third function of citizenship would be to participate in the shaping of government policies. And while it was obvious that no one person could have an informed opinion about everything, it was equally inescapable that people could—and if the system were to succeed, they must—be collectively capable of contributing to an intelligent consensus about basic choices.

In the light of these functions it is not an exaggeration to call citizenship a "public office." Indeed, as my great teacher Felix Frankfurter was fond of pointing out, citizenship is in a real sense a democracy's highest office. The holders of powers delegated to them by their fellow citizens are answerable to those same citizens. The latter thus retain a duty to hold their surrogates to account. This duty may or may not be fulfilled, but a citizen can shed it only by renouncing citizenship itself.

Throughout this nation's history there has been recurring reason for anxiety over whether or not the American people would justify Madison's confidence in their capacity to fulfill the duties of citizenship. Were they not too uninformed, too independent, too narrow in outlook, too self-seeking, too apathetic, and so on, to make sensible judgments? I have no doubt that at almost any time in the last two hundred years there has been reason for concern that the American people would prove incapable of summoning the understanding and the will to grapple successfully with the most urgent crises of the time. They have again and again proved the doomsayers wrong.

And yet our present crisis is different from those we have heretofore surmounted. It does not stem primarily from the problems we face. It derives, rather, from our reactions to government's failures to solve those problems. "We have nothing to fear but fear itself," said FDR. Today we have nothing to fear but the disillusionment, the cynicism, the resentment, the frustration, and the anger evoked by those failures. And yet "the government" toward which we direct those reactions is not a "thing." Like the word "state," it is, as I said to the Soviet cultural attaché, "only a label for the arrangements by which we the people have delegated to some among us responsibility for things that concern us in common." Our ethical obligation to fulfill that responsibility is inseparable from the rights and privileges of citizenship.

That "government"—those to whom we have delegated responsibility—has often failed at the national level is clear. This book touches on many such failures. But it is equally clear that we the people are in substantial part to blame. This book points to those failures also: The "don't just stand there, do something" syndrome, the narrowness and egocentricity of our attitude toward our elected representatives, our unwillingness to face up to unpleasant facts, and our insistence on being told what we want to hear.

Compounded by the inexorable increase in complexity, the first three failures intensify the fourth. But a single remedy faithfully applied would go a long way toward overcoming all four. That remedy is honesty: Honesty on the part of our elected officeholders—president, vice president, senators, and representatives—and honesty with ourselves. Honesty can be the cure of these failures if, but only if, it attaches to the way we perceive things, the way they're represented to us, and the way we face up to them.

Interaction

Sweeping across national boundaries and overwhelming the capacities of sovereign states, the worldwide impact of social, demographic, economic, technological, and environmental change is the most striking phenomenon of our time.

The usual name for this phenomenon is, of course, "interdependence," but I've never found it satisfactory: its connotations are too static and too passive. To my mind, the word "interaction" better conveys the thrust and counterthrust of transnational forces. Every country's domestic actions—economic, political, social, cultural, and ecological—impinge on other countries. These effects cause reactions, and the reactions cause repercussions. Hence "interaction."

The changes driving interaction are for the most part so large and pervasive as to be impervious to governmental influence, unilateral or multilateral. We tend, in fact, to think of the agents of interaction the way we think of changes in the weather or the seasons: to be welcomed or endured, but beyond our control. Among these agents, none is more autonomous than technology. Springing from patterns of behavior imprinted by primordial necessities, technology increases the productivity of human labor, fuels economic growth, and supports higher levels of well-being. Most of us would not want to slow it down even if we could. Technology does, however, have irrevocably damaging side effects— among them, degradation of the environment, depletion of nonrenewable resources, and the destruction of species.

Driven by imperatives even more basic than those propelling technology, population growth has always been affected by cultural traditions and religious teachings as well as by the ebb and flow of famine, pestilence, and war. Late in the nineteenth century it, too, began to be influenced by technology. Since then sanitation, immunization, and antibiotics have radically reduced death from infectious diseases, particularly among children. Fertilizers, irrigation, and higher-yielding seed grains have enabled food production to keep abreast of population growth. In the poor countries the combination of high birth rates and higher rates of survival to childbearing age have added to pressure on arable land, strained water resources, and increased urban sprawl. More people cut down more trees, burn more wood, cause more erosion, produce more greenhouse gases, and generate more waste.

The ups and downs of the struggle to make this a more civilized world have held my interest ever since, as a teenager, I rooted for the League of Nations in its hapless attempt to stop Italy's brutal conquest of Ethiopia. In my college years, a course on the League of Nations and, at law school after World War II, Louis Sohn's brand-new seminar on international organizations were signs that this enthusiasm was still alive. Thirty years later Cyrus Vance, the new secretary of state, noticed that I was about to be unemployed and asked me if I might be interested in heading the U.S. delegation to the United Nations Conference on the Law of the Sea. "By all means!" I said. As you will see, that experience has made a large contribution to my understanding of the ways in which the world community responds to the forces of interaction.

For we are not helpless before the forces of interaction. We are capable of coping with at least some of the problems they create. Just as in our own countries we build levees against floods, insulate our houses against the cold, and install traffic lights, so on the international plane we promote family planning, take steps to prevent the depletion of the ozone layer, and regulate international flights. And since the international consequences to be addressed are the product of forces that disregard every kind of boundary, the necessary responses have to be cooperative rather than unilateral, practical rather than ideological.

Having manufactured the myth that today's pervasive network of legal constraints on national autonomy is the product of a sinister conspiracy, isolationists, "domesticists," and America-firsters take pleasure in denouncing this network. The truth, as we shall see, is that because each new multilateral undertaking has to overcome the inertia of the status quo, the political, bureaucratic, and practical result of the commitments undertaken by states is no more comprehensive or onerous than strictly necessary to the purpose at hand.

Of course, the need to deal with the consequences of interaction is not new. In the case of international commerce, for example, the means of facilitating its flow began to be fashioned a long time ago. It was no accident that the great Dutch pioneer in international law, Hugo Grotius, wrote at a time in the seventeenth century when the Netherlands was on the threshold of becoming Europe's foremost trading nation. Since the publication in 1609 of *Mare Liberum,* the famous treatise on freedom of the seas in which Grotius laid the foundations of modern ocean law, the rules governing the uses of ocean space have steadily evolved in comprehensiveness and sophistication.

Like the slow accretion of a coral reef, analogous rules governing other areas of international conduct have also been accumulating for many centuries. Although the reef's core was elaborated by custom, its most recent layers are the deposit of multilateral agreements adopted by common consent. As the elements of interaction have become more complex and more far-reaching, so has the scope of such agreements. Starting with nonbinding standards, sovereign states have gone on to mutual obligations to take or refrain from taking certain actions, finally arriving at the delegation to international organizations of specified functions.

As to be expected, the most patently undesirable consequences of interaction have been the first to evoke a multilateral response. Jammed airwaves point directly to the need to allocate the radio spectrum, destructive oil spills to the construction of double-hulled tankers. Other consequences of interaction are more insidious and may take a long time even to elicit agreement that a problem exists. In this category belong the pollution of the Mediterranean and the depletion of the ozone layer, which led, respectively, to 1976's Convention for Protection of the Mediterranean Sea Against Pollution and 1987's Montreal Protocol on Substances that Deplete the Ozone Layer. And where, as in the case of global warming and the destruction of biodiversity, the cost of remedial action is extraordinarily high, so also is the demand for proof that action is necessary.

As in the case of domestic law, a primary function of mutual agreements is the prevention of conflicts. In this respect, a key indicator of their value is the regularity with which treaties provide for dispute settlement. Some disputes, to be sure, involve only questions of interpretation or application that would not have arisen but for the existence of the rule. A country would hardly complain, for example, of being denied most-favored-nation status if the GATT did not have rules creating eligibility for such status. Dispute settlement does avert conflict, however, when it mediates a clash of interests that would not otherwise have been peacefully reconciled. In this connection I'm once again reminded of Francis Plimpton's observation that "The history of civilization is the history of myriads of solved conflicts."

But the good accomplished by solving conflicts cannot be measured merely by adding up the outcomes of individual cases. Even more important is what the resolution of a particular conflict teaches about how to diminish the incidence of future conflicts. The precedent thereby established is valuable in proportion to its future utility. In the domestic sphere this is the true measure both of judge-made law and of the laws enacted by legislatures, just as in the international sphere it is the true measure both of customary law and treaty law.

The key to the observance of domestic as well as international law is broad acceptance. Enforcement is secondary. As Louis Henkin, a leading authority on international law, has pointed out, the Supreme Court of the United States had no way of enforcing its order for delivery of subpoenaed Oval Office tapes to the Watergate special prosecutor. Yet Richard Nixon nevertheless did obey the order, thereby bringing about his resignation from the presidency. "Why," asked Professor Henkin, "did Mr. Nixon comply with the court's order?" Henkin's answer:

> . . . Mr. Nixon was induced to obey by a combination of internal (personal) motivations and external pressures, and by a complex of forces that added up to what one might call a "culture of compliance," an element in a "culture of Constitutionalism."

In the case of international law, the "culture of compliance" is by far the most important factor contributing to its general observance. But when treaty obligations are given the force of domestic law, individual states do on occasion bring to bear more direct measures. As United States Attorney for Massachusetts I once embarked from Boston on a U.S. Coast Guard cutter bound for Georges Bank, then (but alas, no longer) the richest fishing ground in the world, on just such a mission. Having spotted a trawler on the radar screen, we'd put out at night from the cutter on a pitching lifeboat and climb onto the trawler's slimy deck in order to check the mesh size of the nets for compliance with the Northwest Atlantic Fisheries Treaty. Here was a small but unforgettable demonstration that nation-states can where necessary call upon one of their number to serve as a surrogate on their joint behalf.

There is no better example of the process by which universal rules become accepted than the evolution of the Law of the Sea. By the middle of this century technological innovation had overtaken the evolutionary process launched by Hugo Grotius. Factory ships operating in international waters far from home were rapidly depleting fishing grounds formerly accessible only to adjacent countries. Marine mammals were being decimated by ever more deadly methods. New methods of recovering oil and gas at steadily increasing water depths were already making obsolete the recently extended limit of coastal-state jurisdiction over the continental shelf. A growing volume of pollutants was reaching the sea via rivers and air currents. Oceanographers and marine biologists were pressing for access to remote coastal waters for the conduct of their research. On top of all this, multinational consortia were rapidly developing the capacity to lift mineral-rich manganese nodules from the ocean floor.

In reaction to these technological changes, a tendency known as "creeping jurisdiction" had begun to challenge the freedom of the seas. In 1945 the United States asserted jurisdiction over the seabed and subsoil of the continental shelf, leaving the high seas above undisturbed. In 1952 Ecuador, Peru, and Chile asserted sovereignty over the waters all the way out to two hundred miles from shore. Their seizures of American tuna boats soon became a source of chronic friction with the United States. Upon my arrival at the State Department in 1969, I found awaiting me a new rash of tuna-boat seizures that had to be dealt with under a 1954 law for which, coincidentally, I had been the principal staffer when it was making its way through the Senate.

As I soon learned, other coastal states were on the point of abandoning the historic three-mile limit of the territorial sea and substituting a new limit of twelve miles. When this extension became universal, it would close the high-seas corridor through every important strait since all of them are less than twenty-four miles wide. Meanwhile, archipelagic states like Indonesia and the Philippines had declared their intention to convert all the waters embraced by their islands into the equivalent of national lakes.

By 1969 these developments had created a serious national security concern for the United States. For us simply to let it be known that we would use force if necessary to maintain our traditional high-seas freedoms would not have been a satisfactory option. We had cordial relations with virtually all coastal states, and the threat or use of force would be bound to create resentment. New universal rules accommodating their and our interests would be far preferable. Surmising that for once the United States and the Soviet Union might see eye to eye, my Defense Department counterpart, David Packard, and I took steps to enlist their cooperation in an international negotiation where such rules could be worked out.

Spurred by these interacting circumstances, a new United Nations Conference on the Law of the Sea convened in January of 1973. Meeting twice a year until finally adjourned in 1982, the conference was a legislative assembly of 156 nations called upon to address every human concern pertaining to the oceans. As an ambassador at large and special representative of the president, I headed the U.S. delegation from early 1977 until late 1980 (my longest and most demanding tour of duty in any government job).

The Law of the Sea Convention, having finally secured the necessary sixty ratifications, entered into force in 1994. Such innovations as "transit passage" through straits, designated sea-lanes and air corridors for "archipelagic waters," and high-seas freedom of movement in, over, and under the "exclusive economic zone" (EEZ) resolved the differences between coastal and maritime countries. And as it turned out, the greatest beneficiary of the EEZ, which protects international traffic while giving coastal states jurisdiction over all living and nonliving resources within two hundred miles from shore, was the United States.

Prolonged and difficult bargaining went into these and many other issues, but the prize for convoluted compromise belongs to the deal defining the outer limit of coastal-state rights to the oil and gas where the outer limit of the continental margin extends beyond the EEZ. This remarkable concordat combines the U.S. proposal (sixty miles beyond the foot of the continental slope) with an Irish alternative (the line where the depth of the sediment overlying the earth's crust is 1 percent of the distance from the foot of the slope) subject to a Soviet limit (three hundred and fifty miles from shore) as modified by a British option (one hundred miles beyond the two-thousand-meter isobath), a Soviet exception to that modification (an absolute three-hundred-and-fifty-mile cutoff for ridges), and a proviso important to Australia, New Zealand, and the United States (making clear that caps, elevations, spurs, and rises are not ridges).

The last distinction was significant, by the way, because caps, elevations, spurs, and rises may overlie hydrocarbons. When, therefore, the broad-margin countries, known collectively as the "margineers," submitted their baroque masterpiece to a plenary session of the Conference for approval, I had to make a statement for the record. My statement was brief and had been cleared in advance with our neighbors in the Arctic. The provisions that had been agreed upon were acceptable to the United States, I said, because the Chukchi Plateau (a vast sedimentary expanse north of the Bering Strait) is not a ridge. Who knows? The Chukchi Plateau may someday be found to contain zillions of dollars' worth of oil and gas.

In keeping with the Law of the Sea Convention's unprecedented breadth are its unprecedentedly comprehensive provisions for binding dispute settlement. With only a few narrow exceptions, all disputes arising under any of its seventeen parts and nine annexes are subject to compulsory and binding adjudication settlement. The parties have a choice between the International Court of Justice, generally known as the World Court, and a new Law of the Sea Tribunal. If they can't agree on one of these options, they must accept binding arbitration. For this outcome great credit goes to John Stevenson, the first head of the U.S. delegation, who insisted on the inclusion of strong dispute settlement provisions, and Louis Sohn, who was both a senior member of the U.S. delegation and the conference's principal adviser on this subject.

Like other recent accretions to the coral reef I referred to earlier, the Law of the Sea Convention is an agreement setting forth principles, rules, and standards. These are the world community's principal means of modifying the impact of interaction. But the application of principles, rules, or standards is not an adequate response to every situation. This may be because it is necessary to act promptly in the light of considerations not covered by the agreement's general language. Or it may be because the circumstances call for a determination better suited to administrative supervision than formal adjudication. Some unforeseen development may have created an urgent necessity for a new kind of approach. In all these cases the common denominator is a need for a response that ought not to be deferred until the states parties can come together. The only way to meet such immediate requirements is through some kind of duly empowered multilateral body.

One group of multilateral bodies not classifiable as "international organizations" has come into being for the purpose of responding to various widely recognized needs. Not purporting to impose obligations on subscribing states and not being required to administer some regulatory function, the United Nations affiliates that perform this role are called "programmes." The best-known is the United Nations International Children's Emergency Fund (UNICEF), followed closely by the United Nations High Commission for Refugees.

The services that these affiliates provide range from supplying emergency care (for example, the Office of the Disaster Relief Coordinator) to preventing infection (for example, the International Drug Control Programme), and providing chronic care (for example, the United Nations Environmental Programme). Where the consequences of interaction are concerned, programmes are to multilateral bodies what doctors and nurses, firefighters and social workers are to legislatures and regulatory agencies.

Counting the "programmes," there are now some thirty-two members of the United Nations family. All were brought into being and received their mandates through a process of upward delegation. Each such organization embodies a unique adaptation of structure to function. Its mission defines its membership, determines the manner of its governance, and shapes the powers it will need to have. Still lacking, however, is adequate means of assuring the integration of their functions; overcoming the deficiency should be the prime objective of United Nations reform.[1]

---

[1] From 1986 to 1987 I chaired a task force of the United Nations Association of the USA that addressed this problem in considerable depth. Our report was published as *A Successor Vision* (New York: UNA/USA, 1987).

If all that is required of an international organization is that it collect, exchange, and disseminate information, that will be the only mandate its charter confers. Typical of groups in this category is the World Meteorological Organization, which promotes the exchange and standardization of meteorological information through its World Weather Watch. In the next category are organizations empowered to develop and propose standards or regulations that will take effect only when ratified by member states. The International Labor Organization is one of this sort. Since its founding in 1919 the ILO has proposed 174 conventions covering everything from hours of work to protection against occupational hazards; of these some have been almost universally adopted, some have been adopted by a handful of countries, and a few have never taken effect anywhere. On the next rung of the ladder are organizations authorized to promulgate standards or regulations binding on member states without any further action on the states' part. In the last and strongest category are organizations with the power to make all the decisions and take all the actions incidental to the performance of specified functions. These are "supranational" organizations—in the eyes of the ultranationalists, the worst kind.

The practical and nonideological character of the factors that determine the roles of worldwide organizations are well illustrated by the evolution of the International Telecommunication Union. Its predecessor, the International Telegraph Union (headquartered in Madrid in 1932), was the very first such body. The latter's founding in 1865 came about because of the obvious need for a more effective way of extending the telegraph beyond national borders than by means of a bilateral treaty. There was a need as well both for uniform standards, codes, and tariffs and for up-to-date information on technical developments. These requirements could be met only by a regularly convened international organization.

The ITU's successive adaptations to advancing technology dealt with wireless telegraphy (1903), the allocation of radio frequency bands to government stations (1906) and other classes of users (1920), standards for regulating long-distance telephone service (1925), adoption of the Radiotelegraph Convention (1927), and merger of that convention and the original Telegraph Convention (1932).

At Atlantic City in 1947 the ITU's jurisdiction caught up with technological advances making possible the use of the upper reaches of the frequency spectrum. The ITU also received increased authority to grant vested rights in radio frequencies and modify their allocation among individual stations. The World Administrative Radio Conference in 1971 further enlarged the ITU's role, this time extending it to the assignment of satellite positions in the geostationary orbit and the allocation of rights to the increasingly crowded radio-frequency bands. Since then, conferences at several-year intervals have similarly kept the ITU abreast of evolving technology.

Based in Geneva, the ITU now has one hundred eighty-four members, all of whom are represented in the Plenipotentiary Conference. The Administrative Council, with forty-six members, supervises the General Secretariat and coordinates the activities of the ITU's three specialized agencies. With just over seven hundred employees worldwide, the ITU is quite a large bureaucracy, but the leaders of the information revolution do not seem to regard it as too large. A leading American industrialist, in fact, has called the ITU "the best managed and most cost effective" of all international organizations.

The sparing hand with which supranational authority has been delegated to the ITU is noteworthy but not exceptional. Given the intense nationalism that coexists with the necessity for responding to interaction, no sovereign state can be induced to delegate supranational authority until and unless it is satisfied that there is no other way to deal with an urgent problem. Indeed, I'm not aware of any international organization that possesses a single dyne of nonessential power. The International Civil Aviation Organization, for example, has no authority over flights exclusively within the boundaries of a single country; its rule-making power attaches only to international aviation. Moreover, bureaucratic power is typically subject to political control over virtually all significant decisions. Even the World Bank, which has to have broad discretion to decide where and how to lend its money, must submit every loan to a vote of its executive directors, of whom five are appointed by the largest shareholders and seventeen are elected by the governors representing the other members.

The true ultranationalist, however, does not live in the real world. To him, any and every delegation to an international bureaucracy is an affront to national sovereignty. As of the mid-seventies, however, all the bureaucracies eligible for such an outburst had long since faded into the international landscape. Just then, the Law of the Sea Convention's International Seabed Authority came into view. Here was a made-to-order

target. True, the deep-seabed mining regime as originally adopted wt have required the authority to administer certain provisions (a techr, ogy transfer clause, for example, and a ceiling on the production seabed minerals) disrespectful of free-market principles. Legacies of th "New International Economic Order," a socialistic vision of economic progress that gripped the developing countries in the seventies and eighties, these blemishes were the basis for President Reagan's decision that the United States should not sign the convention. But even after all his objections were met by a U.S.-supported supplementary agreement adopted in 1994, the ultranationalists were not appeased. The Seabed Authority is still a supranational body, and one, moreover, that has no legitimate role: any person should be just as free to mine the ocean's floor as to catch fish on its surface.

In fact, catching fish is as different from seabed mining as deer hunting is different from dairy farming. Fish are free-swimming; manganese nodules are black, more or less potato-sized objects scattered on the ocean floor and containing, in addition to manganese, nickel, copper, and cobalt. To exploit these objects, you need a vessel equipped to collect the nodules from the seabed, lift them through three or four miles of water, and transport them to a shore-based processing plant. But first you have to survey and record the manganese-nodule distribution in an area of at least 150,000 square kilometers. By the time your mining operation gets under way you will have spent upwards of $1.5 billion. Moreover, to make any money, you must have an exclusive right to the area for the twenty years or so it will take to strip it of manganese nodules.

If seabed mining is a high-seas freedom, how can a would-be seabed miner acquire such a right good against the rest of the world? Certainly not from his own country: it would be unthinkable in this semi-enlightened age to the world to subdivide sovereignty over large tracts of the deep seabed the way the great powers carved up Africa in the nineteenth century. That being so, the only workable alternative is to treat the seabed as a global commons and empower an international organization to act on behalf of the world community as a whole in granting the right to mine a portion of it for a period long enough to justify the necessary investment. Fairness requires that the international organization be able to assess an applicant's technical and financial qualifications before awarding a long-term contract. It must also set environmental and safety standards and collect and allocate fees and royalties comparable to

those collected on land. These and only these are in fact the functions of the International Seabed Authority. Whenever metal prices recover enough to make seabed mining worthwhile, the investors in seabed mining will be glad it exists.

Of course, an international organization like the Seabed Authority is no better able than any other entity to exercise authority without making decisions. In the case of corporations, nonprofit institutions, and governments, a variety of decisionmaking procedures have by now become pretty well standardized. The question, however, of how a new international organization is to make decisions has to be tackled from scratch. The framers of its charter need to know as precisely as possible what kinds of decisions the organization will be called upon to make. That knowledge will govern their choices both as to the body or bodies to be charged with those decisions and as to who or what should be represented in these bodies: people, political entities, or both? Should such factors as wealth, power, production, or trade volume be taken into account? By what majorities will decisions be made?

When at the end of the day these questions have been answered, the result will be a structure balancing political and practical considerations. Two large and familiar examples are the Constitution of the United States and the United Nations Charter. In Philadelphia, the question of how to balance each sovereign state's claim to equality against the inequalities in their size and importance deadlocked the convention until Roger Sherman of Connecticut broached his famous compromise. This, of course, was the arrangement under which the House of Representatives would be popularly elected and apportioned according to population and the Senate would consist of two members from each state elected by the state legislators.

In San Francisco fifty years ago, the framers of the United Nations Charter faced a similar problem. They too opted for two representative bodies, both representing states The larger one would be a General Assembly in name as well as in fact in which all member states, large and small alike, would have one vote. The smaller one, called the Security Council, would have only eleven members (later increased to fifteen), with five seats permanently allotted to the five principal victors in World War II and the remainder rotating for two-year terms among other United Nations members. Decisions on substantive matters would require the concurring votes of all five permanent members.

Although both documents were compacts among sovereign states, their legal effect was dramatically different. The Constitution of the United States created, as Samuel Eliot Morison put it, "what every earlier political scientist had thought impossible, a sovereign state of sovereign states." And since the new nation derived its power through its constituent states from their citizens, it was only right that both the states and the citizens should be represented in its government. Sharing, moreover, similar values and institutions, speaking the same language, and secure in the powers retained in their own hands, the states and their people were willing to give extensive powers to their new national government.

The sovereign states that formed the United Nations shared no such common bonds and were not about to let themselves be governed by the vote of their peers. But even if for limited purposes the founding states had been willing to do so, their adherence to the doctrine of sovereign equality would have imposed a one-nation, one-vote decisionmaking system despite the gross disparities in their populations, economic weight, and military strength. It would have been completely unrealistic, on the other hand, to allow a majority of small states to outvote a minority with, say, three times their aggregate population and ten times their combined national product. Conversely, not to give a dominant role in matters involving international peace and security to the new organization's most powerful members would have been equally unrealistic.

In the case of the General Assembly, the only solution consistent with these realities was to restrict its power to such matters as the approval of the United Nations budget and questions involving its own organization. In all other matters its votes are purely recommendatory. The Security Council, on the other hand, has full authority to act within its sphere on behalf of the United Nations as a whole. All members are bound to carry out its decisions regarding the maintenance and restoration of international peace and security and enforcing judgments of the International Court of Justice.

Throughout the fifty years since the San Francisco conference every debate on the charter of a new multilateral organization has been obliged to readdress the "sovereign equality of states." Though the protagonists of this doctrine attempt each time to dress it in the language of "democracy," the clothing does not fit. China's *demos*, after all, is 120,000 times larger than Nauru's. As Hans Kelsen remarked, "Members of the society of nations may be presumed to be equal as a general principle; but when it appears that in certain aspects of legal equality they are organically unequal, it would seem that the law must either take cognizance of the facts or else admit its unreality."

The law does in most cases eventually take cognizance of the facts. Often, however, particularly in the case of decisionmaking, this occurs only after a considerable struggle. A good example is the World Bank's resolution of the impasse which had long frustrated its attempts to create a multilateral agency to insure investors against political risks. In the early eighties a voting formula weighted according to financial contributions, which the developing countries opposed, collided with a one-state, one-vote approach, which was favored by the developing countries. The negotiations broke down. Several years later, however, the parties were able to work out a solution allotting an equal number of votes to a small group of capital-exporting ("home") countries and a much larger group of capital-importing ("host") countries. The resulting Multilateral Investment Guarantee Agency (MIGA) made commitments in fiscal 1994 involving approximately $1.3 billion in total direct investment.

But negotiations on the decisionmaking issue have never been more contentious than the struggle over the voting system for the International Seabed Authority. It had been agreed early on that the Authority would have two governing bodies. Its assembly would represent all states parties on a one-nation, one-vote basis. Its council, a much smaller body responsible for day-to-day management, would have a membership representing four groups: seabed-mining countries, countries producing the same minerals on land, developing countries, and geographic regions. The council would also exercise the supranational powers previously discussed.

By 1977, when I became involved in this issue, the industrial countries had given up on weighted voting, and the developing countries were getting nowhere with a one-nation, one-vote approach. Other proposals were being talked about, but none commanded broad support. Hoping to break the deadlock, the Soviet Union floated a scheme requiring affirmative votes in three of the council's four interest groups provided that no geographical region was unanimously opposed. Since one of these recognized geographical regions—Eastern Europe—was in the Soviet Union's pocket, this meant, in effect, that it would always have a veto. Nobody else wanted that result, and so the stalemate dragged on.

In August 1980, just before leaving for Geneva, I taped into my wallet a fortune-cookie motto a friend had given me. It said, "This is the month when ingenuity stands at the top of the list." Tommy T. B. Koh, Singapore's ambassador to the United Nations, had become president of the conference after the death of Hamilton Shirley Amerasinghe of Sri Lanka. Koh convened a small group to explore new possibilities. Late in August the group came up with a solution requiring a consensus on the most sensitive issues, a three-fourths affirmative majority for a second tier of issues, and a two-thirds majority for the remainder. When no one objected, ingenuity had indeed arrived at the top of the list.

Being accustomed to voting as a clean-cut way of resolving disputed issues, the American delegation had misgivings about the workability of the consensus requirement. If on sensitive matters every member of the council could block actions adverse to its own interest, how could the council get anything done? We were aware, however, that most international organizations were somehow able to operate by consensus most of the time. The Law of the Sea Conference itself had up to then resolved every substantive question by consensus. Even in the case of highly complex and controversial issues it was able, through unspoken understandings as to the weight appropriate to the views of given delegations on particular issues, to avoid the necessity for voting. It turned out, in fact, that the conference never did take a formal vote until its final session.

Consensus and unanimity are not the same, but the distinction between them is not easy to explain. At one of the conference's Geneva sessions, Constantine Stavropoulos, head of the Greek delegation and former United Nations legal counsel, got it right, I think, when he quoted his successor, Erik Suy, as remarking, "You have a consensus when the presiding officer says, 'Is there any objection? Hearing none, it is so decided,' and only after the gavel falls does anyone object." Such an outcome occurs because the need for consensus has created a climate in which holding out to the bitter end would be perceived as unreasonably obstructing an otherwise acceptable solution. In my own less elegant version, achieving consensus depends on the "horse's ass principle": it's better to go along in the end than to be so regarded.

Looking back over this discussion of decisionmaking, I can see two major variables. The first is the international organization's ability to affect its members' interests. The second is the degree of importance they attach to those interests. When the organization has the power only to

227

consult and recommend, it is relatively easy for member states to accept an outcome determined by a one-nation, one-vote majority. When, on the other hand, the organization's actions can directly affect its members' interests, they will insist on a decisionmaking process that they and other like-minded nations can strongly influence or at least obstruct. This is all the more true if, as in the case of the International Seabed Authority, the organization has been granted some operational autonomy as well.

Some highly desirable outcomes can be achieved only by giving a majority the power to override objections, but each member's concern that its own most sensitive interests may be the ones sacrificed is likely to stand in the way of granting that power. Where that concern exists, not even provision for weighted voting by a special majority will induce the members to subordinate their autonomy to a collective purpose. In such circumstances the only achievable solution is likely to be one that withholds powers essential to the organization's effectiveness. A conspicuous example is the Big Five's veto in the United Nations Security Council.

Paradoxically, multilateral cooperation tends to reinforce nationalism. For one thing, multilateral agreements are negotiated and carried out by sovereign states, and the international organizations thereby created are for the most part composed of sovereign states. Moreover, as Edward C. Luck, former president of the United Nations Association of the USA, has pointed out, by helping states to address problems that would otherwise be beyond their individual control, the United Nations system has reinforced the basis for national sovereignty. Thus, feeding national pride, a little multilateral cooperation may diminish a nation's appetite for more cooperation.

But the reluctance of states to give their creations sufficient power is not the only obstacle to making them more effective. They could be amply empowered and still come up against the inherent limitations of bureaucratic capacity. The disintegration of the Soviet Union and the transformation of communist China, not to mention the Republican "revolution of '94," supply ample warning that the accumulation of centralized functions can reach a point where simplification and decentralization are essential to the relief of bureaucratic constipation. Indeed, these examples should make us wary of any scheme, however well-meaning, that aims in the direction of "world government." It would be foolish to ask an international organization to regulate some large aspect of interaction. Were this attempted with regard to such complex and pervasive components of interaction as the transnational flows of trade, investment, and technology or the deterioration of the environment, the organization's bureaucratic capacity would be exhausted even sooner than acquiescence in its officious intermeddling.

The lesson implicit in the limitations of bureaucratic capacity turns out in the end to be the same one taught by the accommodations with national autonomy previously discussed. In applying limited resources, whether bureaucratic or political, the questions that always have to be addressed are these: What exactly needs to be done? What minimal combination of measures will be sufficient to get it done? Where will the needed support come from? Whose concurrence is necessary? In the discussion of large interactive processes that occupies the remainder of this essay, the importance of these questions will become obvious.

International trade is the first such process I want to discuss because it has been conducted within the boundaries of a firmly established multilateral framework for nearly half a century. At Bretton Woods in 1944 the International Trade Organization was one of three entities envisaged by the nations represented there. Two of the three—the World Bank and the International Monetary Fund—were agreed upon then, but the ITO was deferred. Three years later, when negotiations on the General Agreement on Tariffs and Trade were concluded at Geneva, it was still assumed that formation of the ITO would soon follow. Always regarded as a merely interim arrangement, the GATT never became a duly constituted international organization. In the course of a long career, nevertheless, it proved to be remarkably successful.

At the outset subscribed to by only twenty-three relatively homogeneous nations, the GATT had by 1994 attracted more than one hundred contracting parties with wide disparities in their stages of economic development, types of economic system, and forms of government. What was the secret of its success? How was it able to operate for so long with so much support from so many countries without a charter spelling out its powers and duties? Why did it have no apparent need to address the structural issues whose resolution is ordinarily so crucial to the effectiveness of an international organization? Had I not been trying to understand the ways in which such organizations contribute to coping with interaction, I doubt that I would even have recognized the importance of these questions.

The answers, I believe, are implicit in two basic propositions. The first is that the GATT was given a clear aim validated by long prior experience: to assure that comparative advantages are optimally exploited through the freest possible exchange of goods and services. The second is that the GATT pursues this aim in a straightforward way: through reducing or removing barriers to this kind of exchange. When the GATT was formed the world had already learned the hard way that beggar-thy-neighbor practices lead to beggaring thyself. Still Exhibit A is the Smoot-Hawley Tariff Act of 1930, which increased duties on more than a thousand items and precipitated a drastic reduction in American exports as well as imports.

Once having subscribed to these basic propositions, all that the parties to the GATT had to do next was decide what barriers to lower over what periods of time and provide means of resolving any disputes that might thereby be engendered. This accomplished, the parties could then get out of the way and let market forces do the rest.

Significantly, the two propositions basic to the original GATT have never been questioned at any time since 1986, when the Uruguay Round started on its roundabout course. What made the negotiations arduous was applying these propositions to new purposes (the elimination of quotas and the lowering of domestic-content requirements) in areas of great political sensitivity (agricultural subsidies and textile import restrictions). Largely at the urging of the United States, the dispute-settlement procedures were substantially strengthened and streamlined. To back up all of this, the parties put in place an expanded and remodeled administrative structure.

Crowning these achievements was the revival in only slightly different form of the name first proposed at Bretton Woods. Instead of being referred to merely as "the GATT," the whole apparatus is now known as the World Trade Organization. In a formal sense, however, the name World Trade Organization applies only to a ministerial conference that does not have to meet more than once every two years. The General Council meets monthly to oversee the operations of the subsidiary bodies that track trade in goods, trade in services, and the trade-related aspects of intellectual property rights and investment. Interestingly, these bodies make decisions in accordance with a definition of "consensus" that could have been drafted by Suy: a decision results "if no member, present at the meeting where the decision is taken, formally objects to the proposed decision." (The horse's-ass principle is not mentioned.)

I could now understand why the GATT's success depended so little on its institutional framework. Indeed, I should have seen the explanation in the very name—"General Agreement." Once the parties carried out their pledges to lower tariffs and eliminate quotas, all that they then had to do was to create means of resolving the inevitable disputes over compliance with these commitments. The GATT has thus always been and, despite its change of name, still remains, an agreement on a set of rules coupled with dispute-settlement procedures. As such it is an important part of the coral reef I spoke of earlier. In this respect, indeed, its role is analogous to that of the Law of the Sea Convention except the part on seabed mining. And finally, the reason why the GATT–WTO puts little strain on the limitations of bureaucratic capacity is that its function is not to control but to free up economic forces.

It is striking that by comparison with trade, remarkably little multilateral attention is devoted to other aspects of the global economy. Take, for example, transborder flows of direct investment. In recent years such flows have grown even faster than trade itself and the annual volume for all countries now exceeds $200 billion. Although obliged to observe the requirements of domestic law at the originating and receiving ends, the transactions comprising this aggregate are not subject to any comprehensive, binding multilateral agreement or regulation.

Does it seem anomalous that there should be such a gross disparity between the domestic and international treatment of direct investment? That, I confess, is how the contrast struck me until I reminded myself that the burden of proving the need for governmental intervention at any level must necessarily rest on the proponent. There is no evidence, certainly, that barriers to such investments are a significant problem for the international community as a whole. One country's tariff barriers hurt all its trading partners, but one country's investment barriers hurt no one but itself. Not long ago, to be sure, a few holdouts like India and the Philippines were still retarding their own economic development by making things difficult for foreign investors. During the late eighties and early nineties a sharp rise in foreign direct investment into the United States, particularly from Japan, aroused uneasiness even here. Alarmist bestsellers like the Tolchins' *Buying into America* and Pat Choate's *Agents of Influence* called for immediate remedial action. Reacting to these same fears, a number of senators and congressmen introduced restrictive legislation.

In that apprehensive period I dealt with foreign investment issues in two part-time capacities. I was the special representative of the president for the Multilateral Assistance Initiative in the Philippines (how's that for a title?). I also headed an organization called the Association for International Investment. The same sermon on the job-creating virtues of foreign investment served equally well both in Washington and in Manila, and I delivered it many times. Since then even the economic isolationists have been forced to recognize that the supply of capital available to productive enterprises is finite and that competition for it fierce. So important, however, has a physical presence in overseas markets become to business success that in May 1995 the twenty-five member countries of the Organization for Economic Cooperation and Development began the negotiation of the Multilateral Agreement on Investment. The MAI's role will be to further the liberalization of investment restrictions, protect investors from discriminatory treatment, and provide for dispute settlement. The MAI would thus do for investment essentially what the WTO does for trade.

But what of the immense economic power of transnational corporations? Isn't that in itself a sufficient reason for making their investment decisions subject to some kind of international supervision? That they do play a large role in the global economy is, of course, obvious. One indicator is that the aggregate sales of the world's hundred largest companies are currently three times the combined gross national product of all the countries in Africa and South America. Notwithstanding this, the behavior of these companies is consistent with having the sole aim of maximizing the return on their investments. It's in the interest of a transnational enterprise, therefore, to give any investment-seeking country the opportunity to put forward the best case it can make for its unique advantages as a place in which to invest. Any country that wins out in the competition for such an investment has ample power to see to it that the operations conducted within its territory comply with the local laws and customs.

So long as these incentives hold, the international community has no reason to be concerned. And while it is conceivable that one or more corporate managers of capital may someday conspire to divert it into a sinister scheme unrelated to a bona fide business purpose, we have no reason to suspect that this is happening now. Until we do, we can safely proceed on the assumption that the decisions of transnational corporations will be guided by a perception of self-interest that appropriately recognizes the role of responsible corporate citizenship. And so long as that perception prevails, the international community would be well advised to proceed on the basis that when it is not necessary to act, it is necessary not to act.

That brings us to another category of global economic activity even larger in dollar volume and even further outside the range of international supervision. This is the arcane world of round-the-clock financial transactions. Every second of every hour stocks, bonds, currencies, and commodities are traded and swapped, pledged and hedged, credited and debited, discounted and indexed among all the world's financial centers. Amounting to trillions of dollars a day, these transactions take place without anything approaching the same level of supervision, regulation, or even information routinely required of purely national transactions. Yet any glitch in the simultaneity with which accounts are credited and debited could trigger a panic. As in the case, moreover, of Mexico in the third week of January 1995, the overnight dumping of a nation's currency and bonds can precipitate a disastrous devaluation.

Transactions identical with these but for the fact that they take place within the boundaries of a single country are governed by an extensive web of state and local regulation. The Federal Reserve Board, the Office of the Comptroller of the Currency, the Securities and Exchange Commission, the Commodities Futures Trading Commission, and state Blue Sky commissions all have their own sets of regulations and all keep a watchful eye on the transactions that take place within their statutory mandates. In addition to all this oversight, the stock and commodities exchanges prescribe their own detailed rules for the conduct of the transactions that take place on their trading floors. Other nations have similar regulatory bodies. Yet the aggregate value of all the transactions conducted daily through all the stock and commodities exchanges throughout the world is no more than a fraction of the face amount of the off-the-floor transactions occurring somewhere in the world during the same twenty-four hours.

For a decade or more, knowledgeable observers have pointed to the need for greater international supervision of cross-border financial transactions. Henry Kaufman, long the chief economist of Salomon Brothers and now head of his own company, has long advocated the creation of a board of overseers of major international institutions and markets that would serve as the focal point for regulatory harmonization. Consisting of central banks and other governmental agencies as well as members drawn from the private sector, this new body would set mutually acceptable minimum capital requirements for all major institutions and establish uniform trading, reporting, and disclosure standards for open credit markets. It would also monitor the performances of institutions and markets under its jurisdiction. His concern—that the volatility of financial markets will otherwise lead to a major financial crisis—seems to me persuasively argued.

We come finally to the most far-reaching consequences of interaction. Markedly different from all the others, these consequences are inflicted not only on every form of life supported by this earth of ours but also on the earth itself. The product of many other compounded effects of interaction—population growth, the increasing consumption of food, fuel, and industrial products, and the spread of pollutants—they destroy forests, enlarge deserts, wash away topsoil, diminish biodiversity, and promote climate change. By comparison with other such consequences, their cumulative impact is almost wholly destructive rather than benign or neutral. Although it remains uncertain how much harm will eventually result, it is clear most of it is irreversible. The economic and social costs, moreover, of trying to slow down or halt these effects of interaction will be enormous. Climate change is just one of their potential outcomes, but it so well illustrates the difficulties surrounding the task of prevention that I shall let it serve as my only example of them.

To begin with, then, we know that there has long been under way a steady increase in the fraction of the earth's atmosphere composed of gases that slow down the rate at which heat is radiated from the earth into space. Among these gases, which include methane, nitrous oxide, and the chlorofluorocarbons, by far the largest contributor to this insulating effect is carbon dioxide. Its concentration in the atmosphere, which remained relatively stable throughout history up to the eighteenth century, has increased by 27 percent since then and is now higher than at any time in the last 160,000 years. If this rate of increase continues, carbon dioxide's fractional share of the atmosphere will nearly double by the middle of the twenty-first century. The concern thereby aroused, as most people know, is that this increase, together with corresponding increases in other greenhouse gases, will result in global warming that melts the polar icecaps and raises the level of the sea, thus threatening the inundation of coastal areas in Bangladesh, Florida, and many other places. Warming sufficient to cause this oceanic rise would also be likely to move the wheat belt northward in Canada and Russia, make India even hotter, enlarge existing deserts, and create new ones.

If the long-term threat of climate change is enormous, so will be the short-term cost of averting it. Manifold and omnipresent, the processes that generate greenhouse gases are integral to an astonishing variety of activities all over the world. They include wood fires, dairy farming, rice growing, power generation, grass burning, automobile travel, and countless others. Even moderate steps toward reducing greenhouse-gas emissions could lead to large economic dislocations. It is inevitable, therefore, that industrial countries will resist constraints which impair their competitiveness even as developing countries will resist constraints which impair their growth.

To be sure, some of the actions that can help slow down the buildup of greenhouse gases will also yield other benefits. Energy conservation and reforestation are in this category. Greatly expanded reliance on nuclear power, whose environmental risks are minimal by comparison with those stemming from fossil-fuel combustion, would bring about a large reduction. So too would the substitution of flywheel batteries for internal combustion engines in automobiles. Such independently justified efforts to protect the atmosphere as reducing smog and curbing acid rain will also help to offset the warming trend. But the fact that it is in every nation's—or most nations'—interest to combat climate change does not make it likely that enough will be done. The results of independent national action are bound in any case to be highly uneven. From the standpoint of impact as well as equity, there is no alternative to a broad-based multilateral commitment to take additional and more painful measures.

By 1990 all of these considerations were well recognized. In that year the United Nations General Assembly directed an intergovernmental committee to prepare a framework treaty on climate change for adoption by the Conference on Environment and Development, otherwise known as the "Earth Summit," when it convened at Rio de Janeiro in 1992. It would have been impossible in that short interval to obtain agreement on a document that, like the GATT or the Law of the Sea Convention, imposed binding multilateral obligations. From preparation to completion the Uruguay Round took eight years, the LOS Convention, starting in 1969 with the UN Seabeds Committee, thirteen years, and a dozen more to affect corrections necessary to promote widespread ratification. But those efforts, demanding though they were, faced no such formidable difficulties as those that permeate climate change: the enormity of the potential harm, the likelihood that this harm will not occur at all for a generation or more, a lack of complete certainty that it will occur, but certainty that preventive measures will cause severe economic disruption.

So low were the expectations aroused by the General Assembly's mandate that the Framework Convention on Climate Change produced by the Earth Summit disappointed no one. Only one of its articles calls for "commitments," and these are merely undertakings to "promote and cooperate" or "communicate." Its closest approach to a concrete obligation is aimed only at developed countries and does no more than direct them to "adopt national policies and take corresponding measures on the mitigation of climate change." Each of the developed countries accordingly chose as its target for the year 2000 the stabilization of greenhouse-gas emissions at its own 1990 level. The developing countries, whose annual rate of increase in emissions is 6 percent versus 1 percent in the developed countries, were not called upon to set any targets.[1]

The first formal review of the Framework Convention's accomplishments was held in Berlin in the spring of 1995. It emerged that except for Germany, no developed country was meeting its target. It appeared likely, moreover, that in the remaining years of the century stronger than predicted worldwide economic growth would lead to greater energy consumption and thus to higher than projected emissions. The developing countries' share of worldwide energy consumption, which amounted to only 25 percent in 1985, could be nearly 50 percent by 2025. But even if the developed countries' emissions were brought down to the 1990 level and held there indefinitely while the developing countries cut their rate of increase in half, this would only slow the rate of accumulation of greenhouse gases. It would defer but not prevent whatever disasters the greenhouse effect may eventually cause.

---

[1] If energy use in 1990 by countries not belonging to the Organization for Economic Co-operation and Development had been at the same level as the OECD countries, their greenhouse-gas emissions would be more than quadrupled and worldwide emissions would be nearly tripled (*Resources for the Future*, Winter 1995).

Over the past decade, scientists have become increasingly certain that the earth is undergoing a warming trend at least partially caused by human activities. Evidence has been mounting that this trend will result in significant global changes with adverse and potentially permanent consequences. The scientists also agree that the accumulation of greenhouse gases, if not irreversible, will be very slow to decline.

In December 1995, the Intergovernmental Panel on Climate Change, a body representing 120 governments and including 2,000 of the world's leading environmental scientists, reached a consensus on these findings. The IPCC agreed, moreover, that the earth's mean surface temperature, which is now only 5 to 9 degrees Fahrenheit warmer than that of the last Ice Age, will be between 1.8 and 6.3 degrees higher by 2100 than it is now. The scientists' best estimate of this increase is 3.6 degrees. It is probable as well that the level of the ocean's surface will have risen a half meter by 2100. Additional research will be needed to determine the fractional share of future global warming attributable to human activity, the amount by which the average global temperature will thereby be increased, and the extent of the net resulting harm. It follows, however, from the accepted estimates that the possibility of large-scale devastation is substantial.

It would be hard to imagine a more striking disparity than that between the world community's low-keyed response to these projections and its agitated reactions to remote risks of far less harm. Take, for example, the prevailing reluctance to make greater use of nuclear energy in place of fossil fuels for the generation of electric power. Notwithstanding that such a move would reduce carbon dioxide emissions, it is nevertheless resisted because of worries about another Three Mile Island–type of accident and the resulting increase in the rate of nuclear waste accumulation. Yet Three Mile Island caused no fatalities, and none have thus far been attributed to nuclear waste storage. According to the Nuclear Regulatory Commission, the safeguards that now surround reactors in this country have diminished the risk of another such accident to less than one in one hundred thousand over the life of each reactor. The possibility, meanwhile, that nuclear wastes stored at the proposed Yucca Mountain facility will give rise even to a small localized risk sooner than ten thousand years from now is close to zero.

Optimism toward the possible outcomes of future research cannot justify this ostrichlike behavior. Suppose, for example, that ten years from now the IPCC has reduced its best estimate of a mean-surface temperature increase by 2100 from 3.6 degrees Fahrenheit to 2.5 degrees. Suppose also that the probability of this new best estimate is midway between a high estimate of 5.6 degrees and a low estimate of 1.25 degrees. There is a fifty-fifty chance that the best estimate will prove correct, and for both the high and low estimates the chances are one in ten. Suppose, finally, that the IPCC agrees that an increase of 9 degrees would be virtually certain to cause catastrophic devastation. With one chance in ten of a 5.6-degree increase, the chance of a 9-degree increase is likely to be about one in a hundred.

A one-hundred-to-one possibility of massive devastation is several orders of magnitude higher than some of the remote risks we take enormous pains to avert. If we reacted to that projection the way we react to those minuscule risks, we would now be throwing into the preventive effort every weapon that might conceivably work and frantically looking around for new ones. Why, in the case of climate change, aren't we doing that? Not, surely, because we lack concern for the well-being of future generations: witness our anxiety to avoid passing on our fiscal deficit. And not because we are unconcerned about the potential for environmental degradation: on the contrary, the great majority of Americans regard themselves as environmentalists. At some point this anomaly will sink in, and when that happens the 1992 Convention's flimsy framework will no longer serve as a substitute for more definitive action.

In a 1990 op-ed piece for the *New York Times* I wrote, "Environmentalists and politicians can argue the costs and benefits of international action on global warming from now until doomsday, and they probably will. But nothing will get done without an institutional mechanism to develop, institute, and enforce regulations across national boundaries." You may well ask: What kind of mechanism? At the time I assumed that it would be something like a global Environmental Protection Administration. It was not until several months later when I began to write a paper on what a framework treaty on climate change might look like that I saw the flaws in this assumption. No international organization can realistically be expected to impose uniform prohibitions, constraints, controls, and standards on 150-plus sovereign states. Any such attempt, moreover, would also be certain to provoke sharp reactions against the global EPA's intrusions on national sovereignty since, to ensure compliance, it would be forced to deploy a legion of inspectors and enforcers. This, rather than achieving greater conformity with international standards, could well have the opposite effect.

A more realistic option would be to seek binding commitments to specific obligations. More demanding than the "best efforts" called for by the Framework Convention but less onerous than multilateral regulation, this is the approach embodied in the GATT and the LOS Convention. Nations would go about reducing greenhouse-gas emissions in accordance with an agreed timetable in the same way they have reduced tariffs. An international organization would assist them in preparing plans spelling out how they proposed to fulfill these obligations. For developing countries, technical assistance and financial support would be made available. Meanwhile, the organization would monitor and report the progress of all its members.

If and when broad-based agreement has been achieved, the international organization administering the agreement will be in a very different position from that of a national regulatory agency like the EPA. An international body has no need to ensure compliance with its rules by thousands of corporations or millions of individuals. It is concerned only with the compliance of governments. This observation, which is so obvious that it long eluded me, goes a long way toward explaining why international organizations work as well as they do. Despite the recent increase in the number of sovereign states, United Nations membership is still under two hundred. Given a sufficiently compelling cause, that's not too many from which to hope for the acceptance and observance of necessary obligations.

Still, there is a radical difference between lowering a quota on textile imports or respecting another country's freedom of navigation and reducing carbon-dioxide emissions. The quota reduction's harm to domestic textile manufacturers will tend to be offset by larger exports to the countries benefiting from the reduction. Acquiescing in freedom of navigation is almost entirely painless. A rapid and substantial cutback of fossil-fuel consumption, on the other hand, would force staggering write-offs of capital equipment and require enormous investments in alternative electricity-generating and automotive technologies. Developing countries struggling to improve their standards of living could be especially hard hit. Moreover, the benefits of curbing the greenhouse effect would be very unevenly distributed.

While climate change is, no doubt, the most difficult of the environmental dilemmas that now confront the world community, it is only one item on a long list. The Earth Summit's showcase achievement was a document called Agenda 21. A call for action in the century ahead, Agenda 21 exhaustively catalogs the interactions between economic activity and the environment and puts forward a broad array of recommendations. Some of these recommendations are directed toward existing multilateral agreements and organizations. One calls for the early entry into force of the United Nations Convention on Biological Diversity, another for the drafting of a convention to combat desertification. Several propose guidelines or standards with regard to such matters as the safe management of biotechnology, the treatment and disposal of solid wastes, and discharges into fresh water. Most, however, speak merely of what governments "should do." Tied to each recommendation is an estimate of the annual cost of its implementation together with a suggestion as to the share of this cost that should be in the form of grants or soft loans. For the developing countries alone, the projected total in each of the years 1993 through 2000 is $600 billion, of which $125 billion would come from soft loans. And while there appears to have been no dissent at the Earth Summit as to the ballpark validity of these numbers, neither was there any serious attention to the question of where the money was to come from.

There are, of course, several ways in which the international community can respond to Agenda 21's recommendations and estimates: we can look the other way and pretend they were never made; we can address them squarely and say we can't afford to do much about them; or we can acknowledge their compelling urgency, seek the most cost-effective ways of dealing with them, and then set about mobilizing the necessary resources. If we were to do the latter, we would also be obliged to take a harder look at the proposals for more adequate funding of the United Nations system as a whole that are now at last beginning to receive serious attention.

And so we come once more to a question that waited for us at the end of many of the roads these essays have traveled: How much are those of us in a position to do so morally obligated to help others whose only link to us is our common humanity? We encountered this question as it applies to such concerns as alleviating poverty, preventing illiteracy, providing job training for welfare mothers, and rehabilitating drug addicts. We encountered it again when we came to helping developing countries to free themselves from poverty, ignorance, and oppression. And, of course, we have seen it starkly posed by the issue of individual nations' responsibility to share the burdens and risks of enforcing peace.

As I wrote in the first of these essays, our ties to other people, though attenuated by distance and time, never completely disappear. We are, to quote John Donne once more, "involved in mankind." But where this generation's neglect of global warming or education or economic development will harm its own children and grandchildren, the circumstance that the harm will not be manifest until after we are gone in no way diminishes the quality and kind of our moral obligations toward them. It is also natural that we should feel a sense of responsibility toward grandchildren and great-grandchildren not yet born. And since the descendants of *every* human being now alive will suffer from consequences of interaction that we disregard now, does it not follow that we must act now?

Gather Up the Fragments

A t many points in the foregoing pages I have touched on the need to shed illusions, renounce wishful thinking, and look at the world with a clear and steady gaze. The facts that most need to be seen clearly are those bearing on the state of democracy in America.

Because what I think I see is disquieting, I remind myself that we the American people have always been able somehow to overcome threats to our fundamental values. We have again and again succeeded in calling on just enough common sense, just enough determination, and just enough moral strength to surmount our crises. We did it in the American Revolution and in the struggle for ratification of the Constitution. We did it again in the Civil War, the Great Depression, World War II, and the Cold War. And all the while we have been adjusting to vast increases in population and territory, technological changes that have radically altered our ways of life, and the inescapable demands of global leadership.

To guard against a loss of perspective I continually tell myself that any projection of current trends is inherently fallible. None of us can so far transcend our own geographical, historical, and social circumstances as to be able to gain a truly detached vantage point, yet without such a vantage point we cannot gauge objectively the direction and velocity of change. Though we no longer take for granted that its net result will be progress, one doesn't have to be a chronic hoper to believe that most things balance out over the long term or to recognize that the pessimists are often wrong. And if, despite these reassuring thoughts, I'm still worried, perhaps that's the product of a healthy impulse. The foolish man who built his house upon the sand could have used a tendency to view with alarm. Besides, should it later appear that the grounds for alarm were exaggerated, well, a bit of exaggeration can be forgiven when it's the only way of waking up the complacent, getting the ear of the preoccupied, or catching the eye of the unobservant.

Even so, even so, I do not think I exaggerate the current dangers to democracy in America. They arise from our failure to achieve the balance of realism, honesty, and moral responsibility that our situation demands. The warning signs tell us that the democratic process is being overwhelmed by complexity and betrayed by excessive expectations. Ducking the hard choices, we refuse to recognize the shortfall between our aims and our capability. When the inevitable disappointment sets in, the cynicism thereby induced eats at the underpinning of our most essential values and institutions. Let down by lack of leadership and stampeded by populism, we are increasingly torn by divisiveness.

The "Revolution of '94," whose advent was accompanied by the trumpet sound of the Contract with America and a Tofflerian fanfare on the Gingrich organ, reinforced my apprehensions. Not that the revolution was all bad. The good parts of the Contract were its promises to reduce the concentration of government functions in Washington, get rid of unnecessary regulation, and move toward a balanced budget. However, insofar as it pitched term-limit and balanced-budget amendments to the Constitution as treatments for serious ailments, it had the aroma of an old-time medicine show. And insofar as it proposed to transfer cuts in assistance to the poor into tax relief for the well-off, it retreated from long-established standards of fairness and compassion.

Much of the inflated rhetoric surrounding the Republican revolution took me back to the days when I was new to politics and enjoyed improvising parodies of political speeches. I liked the phrase, "I yield to no man. . . ." To this phrase I would append some such impeccable sentiment as "in my abhorrence of waste, fraud, and abuse" or "in the conviction that this nation's prosperity depends upon fiscal prudence" or "in my faith that the strength of America lies in the moral fiber of its people." I always suspected that these parodies were more eloquent than my real speeches, but this was never confirmed until I delivered one of the former at a Republican rally in Boston during my ill-starred 1984 primary campaign for the Senate. Swallowing the parody whole, my supporters cheered my oratory for the first and only time in the whole campaign.

The noisy cheers that greeted the Contract with America's "conservative" virtues in early 1995 were scarcely better deserved. In fact, nothing in the Contract was distinctively conservative in the true sense of the word. If, indeed, the term applied at all, it was only because, as in the case of the word "ethics," its usage had been debased. Take, to start with, the two highly advertised constitutional amendments whose curative pretensions have already been mentioned. Both sought to make substantial changes in the carefully balanced system constructed by the framers. Any good these changes might have done would be marginal at best, and the harm could be considerable. Their inevitable embroilment in the courts, for example, would be bound to be confusing if not disruptive. But these concerns were insignificant beside the glaring defect common to both proposed amendments: both ignored the two hundred years of experience vindicating the framers' confidence that we the people can be trusted to hold our elected representatives accountable to us. And yet the protagonists of the Contract portray themselves as advocates of returning power to the people! The appropriate adjective for such revisionism is "presumptuous," not "conservative."

Then there were the Contract's cutbacks in the federal programs whose common aim is to help the poor. Since when has it been conservative for Americans to turn their backs on the poor? They are not the faceless "masses" that Marx talked about. They are not an alien "lower class." They are people like us. They are our neighbors. Although our communities have greatly expanded, there is still much truth in what Tocqueville wrote in the 1830s:

> These Americans are the most peculiar people in the world. You will not believe it when I tell you how they behave. In a local community in their country a citizen may conceive of some need which is not being met. What does he do? He goes across the street and discusses it with his neighbor. Then what happens? A

committee comes into existence and then the committee begins functioning on behalf of that need.

This was the tradition—this was the outlook—that guided the domestic policies of President Eisenhower's administration when I came to the Department of Health, Education, and Welfare at the beginning of his second term. It was summed up by Abraham Lincoln in a sentence that became almost a mantra for the "New Republicans" of that era:

> The legitimate object of government is to do for a community of people whatever they need to have done but cannot do at all or cannot do so well for themselves in their separate and individual capacities.

It followed, of course, that with respect to things people can adequately do for themselves, government should stay out.

Many of today's "New Republicans," I suspect, think Eisenhower was too pragmatic and aren't really comfortable with Lincoln. Eisenhower was in fact a true conservative, though some of his cabinet members—notably Secretary of the Treasury George Humphrey, and Secretary of Agriculture Ezra Taft Benson—were more opinionatedly so. Having as acting secretary of HEW attended a good many cabinet meetings during that period, I had the opportunity to observe its members at close range. It was clear that all of them supported in principle the government's duty to respond to basic human needs.

An assignment that came my way in 1958, my second year at HEW, reaffirmed the consistency between conservatism and compassion. By May of that year a sudden, sharp recession was beginning to exhaust unemployment compensation benefits in many states. No one, of course, could be sure how long the recession would last or how far down it would go. It was in any case highly uncertain whether the states would or could extend the benefits. I was accordingly asked to produce a bill authorizing federal support for all needy families of unemployed workers—in essence, a dole. When the bill was ready, Sherman Adams, President Eisenhower's chief of staff, convened a meeting to discuss it. All the concerned department or agency heads were present or represented. They decided that the bill should go forward unless, as did in fact turn out to be the case, an upturn in the economy made it unnecessary. No one dissented. "Think of it," I said to myself. "The war against the New Deal is over! From now on, whenever it's clear that only the federal government can meet a compelling human need, all that's left to argue about will be how, not whether, to respond."

The Lincoln proposition as a whole—the explicit affirmative half together with the implicit negative half—encapsulates a political philosophy that has dominated the American political system from the earliest days of the Republic. Putting it into effect can, of course, require difficult judgments about where to draw the line between the things that people cannot do for themselves and the things that they can and should do. The Republican or "conservative" side has traditionally taken a more restrictive view of the necessity for helping people, and the Democratic or "liberal" side a more inclusive one. There have accordingly been historic shifts in the locus of the line depending on which party was in the ascendancy for the time being.

The basic differences between the two sides have always been—and still are—no more than differences of degree. True, the new majority's language often has a strong ideological cast. In the summer of 1995, for example, House Majority Leader Dick Armey mailed out a fund-raising appeal hailing "the freedom revolution that booted out the 'liberal Tax and Spend' establishment." But the notion that the Revolution of '94 overturned a "philosophy of big government" was a triumph of hype over reality. The revolutionaries, far from launching a "dead-aim assault on the welfare state," as even David Broder described their strategy, have not challenged any essential component of our domestic version of the "welfare state." The welfare state's defining feature is social insurance. This country's largest social-insurance program is, of course, Social Security. Far from assaulting it, all of the Republican Party's presidential candidates have sworn to keep it intact. The third-largest social-insurance program—unemployment compensation—isn't even mentioned. In the case of the Supplemental Security Income program, which was the one Nixon welfare-reform proposal adopted in 1972, the critics have limited themselves to attacking the inclusion of children under fourteen and the classification of alcoholics and drug abusers as "disabled." The most visible welfare program—Aid to Families with Dependent Children (AFDC)—is slated for extensive overhaul in respects I shall come to soon but the alterations would not change its central purpose. The only welfare programs that postdate the New Deal are Medicare and Medicaid, and as to these, concern about cost containment is shared by both parties. What welfare state, then, do the "revolutionaries" think they're attacking?

In fact, both Republicans and Democrats have always agreed that the best government is the least government. It is an axiom that had already been implanted in our national ethos when in New York on April 30, 1789, George Washington took the oath of office as our first president. The government he headed had only such powers as experience with the deficiencies of the Articles of Confederation had shown to be essential. The activist side has ever since had the burden of proving a practical need for the augmentation of centralized authority.

Between the onset of rapid industrialization in the 1880s and the Depression years in the 1930s, the necessary proof was supplied by the evident fact that in an increasingly wage-dependent society millions of workers were shamelessly exploited. They were vulnerable both to layoffs compelled by a downtrend in the business cycle and to the obsolescence of their skills. Few of them, moreover, would be able to save enough to maintain a minimal level of subsistence in their old age.

For half a century, nevertheless, virtually every legislative response to these growing concerns was challenged either as violating "substantive due process" or as exceeding the federal government's power to regulate interstate commerce. A Supreme Court insulated from the nation's recent experience upheld most of these challenges. In 1937, however, even the Supreme Court yielded to the cumulative impact of social and economic forces. In a case challenging a Washington State minimum-wage law for women, Justice Owen J. Roberts, until then identified with the conservative majority, shifted his position, and the law survived. From then on, the way was cleared for measures to regulate wages and hours, assure a minimum level of subsistence for retirees, cushion the joblessness caused by downturns in the business cycle, regulate the securities markets, set rules for collective bargaining, and a host of other measures whose justification has never since been seriously questioned.

After the end of World War II and throughout the fifties and sixties the federal role continued to expand. Some of this expansion was a necessary response to damaging side effects of industrial development and technological innovation. Much of it, however, came about for no better reason than that turning to the federal government was easier than having to deal with scores of state governments, thousands of local governments, and hundreds of thousands of voluntary organizations. For activists driven by such categorical imperatives as "End poverty!" "Stop drug abuse!" or "Prevent crime!" the ready answer, the direct route, was to exert pressure at a single point, call upon federal funds, enact a new federal law, and set up a new federal agency. Paradoxically, marches on Washington were often led by state and local officials whose primary allegiance was not to their own level of government but to the aims and needs of their own professions or constituencies. Even big business had an interest in the federal preemption of inconsistent state and local regulations.

In the first decade after World War II the concerns aroused by the growth of the federal establishment centered on problems of manageability and efficiency. The corrective actions were thus confined to measures like structural reorganization, the reduction of regulatory burdens, and the elimination of red tape. Presidents Truman and Eisenhower both called upon Herbert Hoover to lead national commissions charged with just such aims. Almost every succeeding administration has convened similarly instructed commissions, cabinet committees, or task forces. In these respects, the Contract with America followed a well-traveled trail.

More serious signs of strain began to show when LBJ's Great Society unleashed a new burst of federal activity. The Nixon administration continued the trend, though at a less frantic pace. Recognizing, for example, the urgency of arresting environmental deterioration, it created the Environmental Protection Administration and the Council on Environmental Quality. Nixon's welfare reform initiative, the Family Assistance Plan, proposed work incentives similar to those now being debated and would also have extended benefits to all families with incomes below a certain level, even though the father lived with the family and had a job. In a special message to Congress in February 1971, Nixon also proposed a comprehensive "national health strategy" that included a "guarantee that all workers will receive adequate health insurance protection." The employer mandate on which this guarantee rested, though anticipating Clinton's similar proposal by twenty-two years, was no better received.

As secretary of HEW from 1970 to 1973, I was deeply involved in the latter two initiatives. I was also becoming aware that Washington had made promises and taken on tasks that it lacked the capacity to fulfill. This made me a strong supporter of Nixon's New Federalism, which, by means of revenue sharing and the substitution of block grants for narrowly drawn federal mandates, sought to give states and localities greater flexibility in setting their own priorities. We at HEW meanwhile developed an ambitious plan to condense more than three hundred narrowly drawn programs into less than a third that number. The Allied Services Act was a companion piece aimed at getting the states to consolidate administrative functions and integrate their services to families and individuals. Although never adopted, the proposal played an influential part in encouraging most states to create comprehensive human-resources agencies.

Although so far as I know, no one (other than on occasion myself) has ever labeled me a conservative, I did write a book which, according to one reviewer, "sounded just like Ronald Reagan." That ambiguous compliment was presumably won by statements pointing out that "It is a simplistic assumption that more money and more government are infallible cures for whatever ails us";[1] and that the Great Society's attempt to conquer "poverty, deprivation, and suffering in all their still lingering forms" generated promises from which "grew expectations which flourished uncontrollably."[2] And, yes, I did conclude that the time had come to reverse the long-term trend toward enlarging the federal role. The indicated remedy was decentralization:

> It will make government more responsive, more accessible, and more manageable. By dispersing power, decentralization will diminish our vulnerability to its abuse. And because the dispersal of power reduces the size and increases the proximity of the units which possess power, the individual thereby gains greater opportunity to exert an impact on the way it is exercised. Individual liberties and the individual's control over his own destiny will both be strengthened.[3]

---

[1] *The Creative Balance* (New York: Holt, Rinehart and Winston, 1976), p. 125.

[2] Ibid.

[3] Ibid., p. 195.

But none of the above reflected a conversion to conservatism. I was comfortable with the Eisenhower and Nixon administrations' conception of the national government's appropriate role. Nor did I see any inconsistency between that conception and the belief that the demands being placed on the federal government had become excessive. Indeed, I do not believe that the task of curbing this excess is advanced by letting it be supposed that it is a uniquely "conservative" mission, as Irving Kristol seems to assume, or a "radical" departure, as Newt Gingrich is fond of asserting. To the extent that a monolithic majority has recently succeeded in putting a Republican stamp on initiatives that in fact have no partisan content, they have created controversy where consensus would better serve the public interest. The new majority's militancy risks counteraction or at least a loss of momentum if and when the Republicans lose their control of Congress. A sustained effort needs broad-based support. Moreover, to represent a functional realignment as an ideological crusade is at best misleading and at worst deals yet another blow to the credibility of the political process.

Side by side with the hoary old axiom about "the least government" belongs a parallel axiom about "government closest to the people." And here again we reach back to an affirmation broader and deeper than any partisan difference: the opportunity to participate in the public choices that affect our lives is a means to individual dignity as well as mutual respect. It's an opportunity neglected by many who would nevertheless fight to preserve it.

To my way of thinking, therefore, the need to cut back federal functions springs only in part from a bureaucratic concern with manageability and efficiency. Ever since my second tour at HEW in 1970–73, what has troubled me more is that an unwieldy and almost impenetrable structure stands in the way of the citizen's opportunity to play a part in value-related choices. Simplification and decentralization will make these choices more accessible to democratic direction and control.

It is also important to keep in view the principles composing the framework within which our national debates have traditionally been conducted. This various and volatile nation of ours has survived because, under stress, the center has held. We have been able to outlast men of passionate intensity because—perhaps only because—the best retained conviction. I am disturbed, nonetheless, by the degree to which the new

Republican leadership consciously sought to capitalize on the meanest of the electorate's fears and resentments.

That the voters who shifted to Republican candidates in the 1994 midterm election were alienated by government-as-usual can scarcely be doubted. This attitude came through loud and clear in the reports of pollsters and journalists in the election's aftermath. Typical of such reports was a *Washington Post* story quoting a teaching consultant in St. Joseph, Michigan, a police sergeant in New York City, and an electrician in Elk River, Minnesota. "It's time for the government to stop trying to rescue everyone," said the teaching consultant. The police sergeant said, "I don't want to see a lot of time and money spent on expanding government programs where we're not necessarily getting our bang for the buck." The electrician said his vote meant "Get government off our backs."

How should these comments have been interpreted? Did they actually convey a demand for radical change? That's how most of the media and all of the new majority's spokesmen chose to interpret them. But then, it was in their respective interests to do so. The *Post's* first two quotes were in fact quite restrained and perfectly reasonable. Even the third might have been no more than an impatient reaction to pervasive government regulation. All three, indeed, could have been treated simply as expressing a demand for more effective government. But this would have been pallid fare both for the consumers of news and for zealous Republicans. It is hard, therefore, to escape the inference that the Republican strategists saw an opportunity to mobilize a populist force that would sweep the nation in 1996 and assure Republican congressional majorities for a generation to come. Their message came across as aimed at deeper-lying resentments than those revealed by the *Post's* trio of interviewees. Its apparent target was typified by the white male attitude "I'm sick of working my butt off so that a bunch of liberal clowns can use my money to pay teenagers for breeding more illegitimate babies."

Teenage mothers also had another use. In addition to being the focus of particular resentment, these mothers also symbolized a fatter target—the "welfare state." Judging by the new majority's rhetoric, you would think that teenage motherhood had been *caused* by the welfare state rather than by such basic needs as solace for an existence that offered no opportunity, no hope, and no self-esteem. As Senator Pete

Domenici of New Mexico, the Republican chairman of the Budget Committee, put it in 1995's debate on the "family cap," "If you believe that curbing cash benefits to welfare mothers will prevent more births you believe in the tooth fairy."

For a given volume and mix of federal functions, neither reflexive lashing out at "big government" nor an automatic preference for state and local governments will yield the maximum feasible reduction in total government. Today's allocation will in any case have to be readjusted in the light of tomorrow's requirements. To ensure that new problems will at the outset be assigned to the appropriate levels of government, we should begin now to spell out criteria for choosing which of them—federal, state, or local—can best perform what kinds of functions. Moreover, in applying these criteria, we should make sure that only clear and convincing evidence is allowed to overcome a consistent preference for the lowest workable option.

Despite this preference, one factor that justifies reliance on the national government is the need for uniformity. Two clear examples are civil aviation and acid rain: both transcend state boundaries, and both require uniform nationwide standards. Another factor that may call for the same result is efficiency. In the case of Old Age, Survivors, and Disability Insurance (Social Security), efficiency demands federal administration because payroll contributions into the system have to be recorded throughout an individual's entire working lifetime, and benefit payments must go to the retiree wherever she or he is living. The system is in fact so efficient that the administrative outlay is only eight-tenths of 1 percent. For similar reasons Nixon's welfare-reform program proposed that benefit payments to families be administered at the national level. Full control of the family budget, on the other hand, would be given to the family as a result of cashing out such benefits in kind as food stamps and housing subsidies. Social services, meanwhile, would be provided by neighborhood agencies.

Whether or not government should undertake a given function and at what level that function should be performed appear at first to be sharply distinguishable questions. And yet a strong public demand that something be done readily translates into a strong demand for sweeping action. Hence national civil rights laws and a national "War on Drugs." A recent—and irrational—example was the 1994 crime bill's extension of the death penalty to several dozen federal offenses. In those and other analogous cases the federal government itself has a direct enforcement role. Quite commonly, however, Congress has responded to the demand for action by passing a law requiring the states to do something but has not given the federal government a role of its own and has not authorized federal financial support for state action. Hence the governors' success in pushing through, as one of the Contract with America's first accomplishments, the repeal of "unfunded mandates."

Where the principal impetus for calling upon the federal government comes from a broadly shared public concern, at least three significant considerations should be kept in view. The first is that states, localities, or private entities (for-profit or nonprofit) may be better equipped to carry out the national policy than the federal government itself. Indeed, as in the case of education, housing, and social services, the federal government may have no such capacity at all. Where, nevertheless, a vital national interest such as civil rights is at stake, a federal mandate may be the only means of obtaining a nationwide response. In that event even an unfunded mandate can be justified as a way of telling the states to give a higher priority to a national interest than it would otherwise receive.

The second consideration suggested by broadly shared demands for national action is that leadership capacity, human resources, and public support need to be prioritized and budgeted like tax dollars. The magnitude and number of the initiatives thus launched must accordingly be kept within manageable bounds. The least compelling claims will have to be deferred. And when the need for national action is no longer acute, full authority should revert to the states. The cumulative result will otherwise be to re-create the same kind of unwieldy and inaccessible superstructure that we are now scaling down.

The third consideration is that in allocating resources we should strive to balance the treatment of symptoms against the need for prevention, the relief of pain against the pursuit of a cure. This very effort will, by focusing our attention on underlying causes and conditions, lead us to do a better job in setting priorities. Doing that well demands defining those priorities in such a way as to encourage the most effective possible use of available resources. And that brings us back to the need for tough-minded evaluation.

Judged by this last consideration, our existing national agenda does not stand up well. That is true, moreover, notwithstanding everything I said earlier about the intrinsic difficulty of rank-ordering competing claims for government action. It should, for example, be possible quite easily to agree that the pollsters' standard questions about the relative seriousness of such things as violent crime, drug abuse, teenage pregnancy, and welfare dependency are addressed to symptoms rather than causes. There is a vital need for a national dialogue on the latter. As a contribution toward encouraging such a dialogue, here is my list of what I regard as the nation's five most critical problems. Although these too may be drearily familiar, I do not think that enough of us adequately grasp the degree to which they overhang the present and shadow the future.

First on my list is the ebbing of the confident belief that things are going to be better, if not for ourselves, at least for our children. The purchasing power of American families in the middle-income range has declined in real terms over the last twenty years while the participation of wives in paid employment has nearly doubled. Further increasing the strain on family life are two other factors. One is the unrelieved necessity of coping with an increasingly complex world. The other is the bewildering range of choices, particularly for our children, consequent upon the weakening hold of long-accepted conventions. It was inevitable that these changes would lead to a greater preoccupation with personal concerns and a more limited outreach of compassion. Their combined effect has been to make all the other problems on this list more difficult to deal with.

Second comes the widening gap between the rich and everyone else. Middle-income families are trapped on an escalator that has ceased to move while the rich are carried to ever higher levels of affluence. The disparity in income between rich and poor in this country is greater than in any other industrialized country: 40 percent of the nation's wealth is concentrated in only 1 percent of American households. During the 1980s, 100 percent of the increase in wealth went to the top 20 percent of American families. The proportion of the population living in poverty grew from 12.5 percent in 1971 to 14.5 percent in 1994. We have double the child poverty rate of any other industrialized country, and there are now almost twice as many poor people living in crowded inner-city ghettos as there were in 1980. And though productivity has been soaring in recent years, the "trickle down" process is inoperative, and workers have not been sharing in the benefits. Turning this around should be an aim not simply of a revitalized labor movement but of intelligent employers as well.

In addition to discouraging the American dream, the rich–poor gap has fostered the by now firmly established habit of referring to the majority of Americans as "the middle class." This implies that there must be an "upper class" and a "lower class." It troubles me that we have slipped into this way of thinking. The fact that our society used to regard itself as nearly classless was, I have always believed, the greatest source of our strength. These trends too compound the difficulty of addressing the other four problems.

Next is education. We constantly hear, of course, about the damage to U.S. competitiveness foreshadowed by the inferior test scores of American schoolchildren. While the recent downsizing of our big corporations has deferred the economic impact of this competitive disadvantage, it will eventually occur if we don't do more to prevent it. Of still greater concern, as has also been pointed out many times, is the disqualification of inadequately educated young people from the jobs demanding substantial levels of literacy and basic knowledge that constitute an ever larger fraction of all employment opportunities. Most troubling of all is the mounting cost to society of leaving these young people behind. Large discrepancies in educational achievement widen the gap between a highly educated "elite" and a barely educated "underclass." This is bad for our social health.

Fourth, race relations. The most demanding test of the American dream is the extent to which it has been brought within the reach of descendants of people—Native Americans, Africans, and Mexicans—who never sought to belong to this country. The early generations were made to suffer by the actions that subjugated or uprooted them, and their descendants have been demeaned by the denial of dignity and equality. Americans have good reason, nevertheless, to take considerable satisfaction in the degree to which we have succeeded in creating a free society embracing every color, creed, and culture on the face of the earth. This should not be forgotten even as those of us who cherish this ideal struggle to overcome the lag in its fulfillment that now gives reason for increasing concern and even alarm.

This country also has much to celebrate in the achievements of the civil rights movement in the last four decades. Of all indicators, the most dramatic is the gain in the number of African-American officials elected throughout the South—from 72 in 1965, when the Voting Rights Act was adopted, to 4,294 now—a 68 percent increase. But unless we deal effectively with the underlying causes of racial tension—persisting strains of racism and bigotry on the one hand and lack of educational and employment opportunity on the other—it is likely to increase.

The lingering effects of past discrimination is not the real issue. The significant reality in the black community is the awareness that it is being discriminated against now. To pretend that this feeling no longer exists is no less hypocritical than the pretense that our society is color-blind because it ought to be. Affirmative action still has a lot to accomplish.

Speaking to the Joint Center for Political and Economic Studies shortly after the 1995 Million Man March, Vernon E. Jordan, Jr., a prominent Washington, D.C., lawyer and former president of the Urban League, quoted from Ralph Ellison's *Invisible Man*: "Our fate is to become one, and yet many. This is not prophecy, but description." Jordan added, "We are a long way from that goal, and the path to it is an arduous one. There will be diversions along the route from both white racists and black separatists. But it is the only route that leads to the attainable goal and to a goal worth attaining." I share that view.

Finally, the resources crunch. This is the product of a three-way collision of the need to shrink the deficit, the desire to offer tax relief, and the urgent demands for increased government spending. The impact of the first two has not gone unnoticed. The power of the third is less apparent. To gain an appreciation of its strength, one should eliminate at the outset any unmet demand for which a strongly appealing case has not been made. The next step should be a rigorous test of cost-effectiveness. This will further reduce the number of eligible claimants. Even so, to satisfy in full the remaining certifiably critical needs could easily double the aggregate deficit projected for the next five fiscal years. Suppose, for example, that we gave Head Start enough money for all eligible children, guaranteed adequate medical care to all those who cannot now afford it, and did what it takes to make sure that our least advantaged children get an adequate education. These steps alone would add some $350 billion to total government spending over the same five years.

Pervading these five excruciatingly difficult problems are persuasive moral claims. For families with little prospect of a significant increase in purchasing power, tax reduction offers a measure of relief from acute financial pressure. For the next generation of taxpayers the burden of huge interest payments on a public debt incurred by their parents could well be thought unfair. For the homeless, the mentally ill, the elderly who do not qualify for Social Security, the fatherless children of teenage mothers, and all those others who cannot help themselves, a helping hand is a moral imperative. And even such needs as law enforcement, transportation safety, a clean environment, and national security have their places in the moral order.

This moral contest might in a way be easier to umpire if it were a zero-sum game. But of course it is not. Many financially hard-pressed families would prefer adequate defense spending, crime prevention, better public education, deficit reduction, and even public broadcasting to a marginal tax cut. Instead of resenting an inherited deficit, the next generation may have good reason to be grateful that this one invested in such things as protecting the environment, strengthening international peacekeeping capability, and seeking a cure for AIDS. And many citizens—perhaps even a majority—may feel as I do that the true test of a civilized society is not its art or its manners, but its treatment of the least advantaged.

As this is written, the battle over government's responsibility toward the poor is reaching a climax. The potential outcomes are both less and more crucial than commonly portrayed: less so because the changes in the welfare system now being urged would not in themselves compel a radical result; more so because these changes might well lead to an outcome that faced the American people with a stark moral choice. To make this distinction clear I need first to say a word about the implications of "reform," "entitlements," "devolution," and "block grants."

Reform, we are told, is necessary because the system has "failed." But the system's primary mission is simply to see to it that poverty does not force children and their mothers to go without food, shelter, or medical care. By and large and in varying degrees from state to state, some combination of Aid to Families with Dependent Children (AFDC), food stamps, disability benefits, housing subsidies, and Medicaid does in fact protect some five million mothers and ten million children from total destitution. To this extent the system is not a failure: it is doing what it is supposed to do. Where it has failed is in preventing dependency and promoting self-sufficiency. But these are aims that the welfare system has never been adequately equipped to fulfill or specifically charged with carrying out. Filling this gap has been the aim of every welfare-reform program proposal since Richard Nixon put forward the Family Assistance Plan in 1969. In the meanwhile, however, spending targeted on helping the poor escape poverty has been falling even as benefit payments have been rising.

The farther right you go in the political spectrum the more firmly embedded the assumption that welfare mothers are lazy sluts who would rather live on the dole than work for a living. To the contrary, survey after survey has shown that with few exceptions welfare mothers would much rather work than depend on handouts. Although the average duration of welfare dependency is about six years, many recipients go on and off welfare and in and out of jobs. Moreover, women stay on the rolls year after year for many reasons other than unwillingness to work: because a low-paying job would bring in less money than the aggregate of current benefits, because too many other distractions get in the way, or because they are basically unemployable. For an untrained person, moreover, seeking employment must be deeply discouraging where, as in Harlem today, there are fourteen applicants for every fast-food job paying the minimum wage.

Standing by itself, a work requirement has never gone far toward reducing persistent dependency, and it has no realistic chance of doing so unless it is backed up by provision for day care, effective job training, help in job placement, and—where the normal job market cannot supply a job—some kind of publicly supported work. To be worthwhile, these measures would have to be well designed and administered and, even if they reached only the most readily employable, this would add a minimum of $3 billion over and above present spending for income support. If, in addition, we are determined to cut off beneficiaries after a specified number of years, the least we can do is try to make sure that they are capable of surviving, and that will cost a lot more. Meanwhile, cuts in the earned income tax credit for the working poor would discourage anyone from seeking work whose take-home pay, without the credit, would be less than the total amount of means-tested benefits.

As to devolution, it should be noted that less than 1 percent of the people who work in the welfare system are federal employees. The federal government neither administers welfare benefits nor determines their amounts, but merely matches whatever the states choose to spend on a basis inversely proportionate to state per capita income. In place of this open-ended matching formula, block grants would annually allocate a fixed sum to each state.

AFDC is an "entitlement" because, once a state elects to have an AFDC program, federal law requires that benefits be paid to all those found eligible. If this requrement is eliminated, the states will, of course, be free to determine whether or not to maintain existing standards and benefit payments. The real problem with the replacement of federal matching funds by a block grant will arise when the state begins to cut off payments to eligible applicants because it has exhausted its block grant and does not choose to raise the necessary additional revenue. Just such a shutdown is likeliest to occur, moreover, when unemployment is high, jobs are scarce, state revenues are down, and the number of applicants is up.

The genuinely crucial question, then, is how in those circumstances the American people will respond. Will they tolerate a situation in which some states raise their taxes in order to maintain welfare benefits while others turn their backs on the needy? Will they conclude that federal block grants should be supplemented in proportion to each state's increased caseload? Or will they decide as they did in 1935, when the Social Security Act was adopted, that the federal government should virtually guarantee minimal assistance to the poor? If we assume that reform will by then have made possible everything that can feasibly be done to enable welfare recipients to find jobs, there will be no way of ducking the moral choice between the first option and the other two. The American people have not, I trust, retreated so far from their transitional values as to leave that choice in serious doubt.

There are many other situations, meanwhile, in which the provision of jobs is crucial in the role of reducing welfare dependency. During nearly twelve years in social services and law enforcement, again and again I came across the frustrations resulting from a lack of employment opportunities. In the case of criminal offenders, for example, study after study confirmed both that jobs were the key to escape from crime and that jobs were seldom available. Attempts to break the cycle of addiction, rehabilitation, and relapse all too often arrived at the same dead end. Indeed, I shall never forget the dedicated black doctors at a rehabilitation center in Detroit who appealed for my help in persuading the Labor Department to support their effort to stop this revolving door.

The difficulty, of course, with relying on general job creation as the preferred remedy for social ailments is that macroeconomic policies capable of expanding the job market enough to enable it to absorb marginal workers are also likely to exact an unacceptable inflationary price. The only alternatives are creating community-service jobs outside the regular labor market and delaying entry into it of individuals who can benefit from the upgrading of their knowledge and skill. But for someone who has no prospect of a better job, washing the floors of municipal restrooms is scarcely less demeaning than welfare itself. Community-service job programs that provided better, more developmental, work opportunities, while expensive in the short term, could pay handsome dividends later on. Meanwhile, reducing the high school dropout rate and increasing the number of high school graduates who go on to college or technical school will reduce dependency and enhance self-respect, while at the same time drawing down the excess supply of low-skilled workers. It will also yield a rich array of other rewards from lifting productivity and increasing our competitiveness to reducing the breakup of families.

It would be hard to think of any investment that offers the potential for such a splendid return. And yet have you noticed that those who protest most loudly against "saddling the next generation" with this generation's fiscal deficit tend to be the same people who show no concern about passing on the social costs of our current neglect? Could this be because they'd rather enjoy lower taxes than put more money into making the most of our human resources?

If the question could be looked at in isolation, I would bet on the next generation's good sense. Unfortunately, however, the problem is not that simple. Steady, noninflationary economic growth can be the single most important contributor to coping with all of our most serious problems. Given the enormity of the federal government's existing debt, borrowing even for the worthiest of long-term purposes tends to increase interest rates and to absorb capital that might otherwise be invested in new job-creating enterprises. In fact, the General Accounting Office has estimated that per capita growth of gross domestic product (GDP) between 1994 and 2025 would be 34 percent higher per capita if the budget were balanced from and after the year 2002 than it would be if present trends persisted.

We have no choice, then, but to conclude that the allocation of resources is not a zero-sum game but an exercise in optimization, how do we break out of the circularity that this implies? Does it follow that no important claim is more important than any other? Not in my view. Our moral obligation to relieve suffering and help the helpless comes first. A society whose per capita consumption is nearly two and a half times what it was in 1950—and most of us were pretty comfortable then—can surely afford common decency. Moreover, we need to address our moral obligation toward the helpless directly, before we invoke pragmatic forebodings about the cost of neglecting sociopathological conditions.

But what does common decency demand of us? Before trying to answer that question, we need to be reminded of two facts. The first is that compared with other leading industrial countries, we are not heavily taxed: in 1991, the most recent year for which the figures are available, the average fraction of GDP that went into taxes in the twenty-four leading industrial countries was 38.7 percent; in the United States it was 29.8 percent. The second is that only a small fraction of our tax dollar can appropriately be regarded as a "sacrifice" for the benefit of others. The remainder pays for services that directly benefit our personal security or well-being. A few examples are police and fire protection, national defense, public education, public parks, biomedical research, meat inspection, and weather reports. Even the justification for farm price supports rests not on what they do for farmers but on what they do to assure a cheap and adequate food supply for everyone else.

But accepting in principle our obligation to the neediest does not tell us how much more than the bare minimum is required. Nor are there objective standards by which to calculate what share of tax dollars should go to each of the government services beneficial to everyone. These are issues that can be resolved only by balancing value-related claims, and that, as I have previously observed, is what the political process is for. And again, the very purpose of making this process a democratic one is that we, the people, can participate in making those choices. But if the most important objective of greater reliance on state and local government is to enlarge the opportunity for such participation, shouldn't we be seeking additional ways of giving people a larger voice in making these choices?

This is the sort of thinking that could, I suppose, explain all the talk we've been hearing lately about "power to the people." It's not at all clear, however, what it entails. *The Creative Balance* had quite a lot to say things that could be done to give citizens more influence on governmental decisions, but most of them involve the empowerment of community-based groups. What we're hearing now sounds more like a wake-up call for "populism": as such it's hard to take seriously. Although the word derives from the name of the short-lived political party which in the 1890s brought together farmers made desperate by persistently low farm prices and a distressingly high rate of mortgage foreclosures, it no longer signifies an identifiable movement, program, or idea. It is now no more than a label for the amplification by political means of public resentment, frustration, or anger. Today's populist is an exploiter—a feeder. People aren't the populists; the politicians are.

To be sure, the venting of anger or frustration is not all bad. Some resentments and frustrations are justified and should get a response. The farmers who formed the core of the original Populist Party had every right to be angry. But today's populists exaggerate, and their remedies tend to be simplistic, if not misguided. When circumstances change and the anger evaporates, the "populism" that fed on it disappears. Thus, populism is to democracy what Rush Limbaugh is to Jim Lehrer.

But if narrowly focused frustration, resentment, or anger is not a sufficient foundation for a workable democracy, there are other ways of giving efficacy to broader and less intemperate expressions of the popular will. As it is, many politicians depend heavily on polling data to determine what positions they should take on matters of concern to their constituents. If a majority are for abortion and against gun control, so is the politician. While the politician has been motivated in most cases, no doubt, by the desire to get elected or reelected, why shouldn't such responsiveness to the electorate's views be regarded, not as spineless conformity, but as a model of democratic accountability?

In this information age it would not be hard to take another long stride toward even more faithful compliance with public opinions. We might, for instance, beam into people's homes on Saturday mornings a series of policy questions accompanied by a paragraph or two of explanation such as you find underneath a referendum question on a ballot. Each of us would have an identification number and could record our individual responses to the questions simply by calling an 800 number. Those who wished to do so could also communicate their individual views via the Internet to a center where they would be electronically processed and tabulated.

At the outset, to be sure, it would scarcely be feasible to make the results of such a weekly catharsis binding on Congress. Indeed, so long as the Senate maintains its traditional rules, the pace of congressional action is such that public opinion might reverse itself more than once in the time it takes to pass a bill. But the talk shows have opened the door to something like this, and Ross Perot once floated a similar proposal. Even a start in this direction would supply Congress with more authoritative guidance than ever before.

Here at last would be real people power. But is it a good idea? Of course not. Even Jefferson would have gagged on it. Hamilton, Madison, and Jay would have been horrified. *The Federalist* breathes distrust of "popular governments": their "mortal diseases" have everywhere been "instability, injustice, and confusion." Far better to rely instead on "a chosen body of citizens, whose wisdom may best discern the true interest of the country" and whose pronouncement of "the public voice . . . will be more consonant to the public good than if pronounced by the people themselves."

Though still far short of a pure democracy, our system has moved a considerable distance since those words were written. The elimination of property qualifications for voting, the direct election of senators, successive extensions of the right to vote, and easier modes of registration have progressively enlarged the electorate. The best term for what we now have, I think, is "representative democracy." We take it for granted that our elected officeholders should want not only to be aware of how their constituents feel about things but also to convey in return the perception that they have fully understood and recognized those feelings. But we should not want their passive conformity; there are better ways for an officeholder to show respect for a constituency's views. If the voters back home have made a wise choice, they have learned to trust the member's integrity and good judgment. If the member also takes the trouble to explain in clear, understandable terms why, on balance, she concluded that her constituents' views or interests were outweighed by other meritorious considerations, this trust will predispose them to accept her judgment. Such interaction between a constituency and its elected representative can be good for the district as well as the nation.

We count, as I have said before, on the political process to choose among incommensurable values and interests, but there must, on the face of it, be some way of defining the choices submitted to that process.

If every individual citizen and member of Congress were left at large to come up with their own lists of choices, nothing would get done. Political parties help to narrow the range by pointing directions and identifying priorities. News analysts and editorial writers also play useful parts. But there is another ingredient without which the system cannot work. That ingredient, of course, is leadership.[4]

For the president particularly, it is not enough to be far-seeing and intelligent in setting the right goals, choosing the right priorities, and finding the right solutions. As the leader of a democracy he must also seek and obtain broad public support. He must be able, moreover, to discern the limits on his capacity to take the public in directions in which it does not wish to go. Presidents have rediscovered this fact of political life many times. A recent and highly conspicuous example was President Clinton's failure to mobilize public support for his health-care program. But if a president does not know where he wants to go, he is not leading, and if he is not sensitive to public opinion, his leadership is not democratic.

In my observation, the most common mistake of political leadership is that of starting from the wrong place. If in tackling a major issue, the first things the leader does are to determine the views of other key players and interest groups, study the polls, and develop a formula that looks as if it had a good chance of proving acceptable, he is beginning in the wrong place. He will never know what support he might have won for the solutions that best address the merits of the issue.

The leader who, having begun in the right place and developed a clear idea of where he wants to go and why, has given himself the best possible chance of persuading others that he is right. He will undoubtedly have to make adjustments along the way on the basis of assessments of what is required to win the support of others in a position to block his efforts. He may also have to reckon with the impossibility of overcoming public opposition unless he makes significant concessions. But the necessity for making compromises that will advance the prospects of achieving the right result is a very different thing from yielding before the battle lines are drawn. Knowing when and how to balance these consid-

---

[4] The chart on page 77 and what is said there, particularly about the role of a strategy in providing the framework for public debate, is directly relevant here.

erations is, of course, the reason why politics is the most difficult of the arts and the noblest of the professions.

The practice of politics in a healthy democracy inevitably tends to be centrist. That is because the grist of the democratic process consists of a complex mix of incommensurable values, conflicting ideas, and competing interests. All of these ingredients are continuously exposed to a Darwinian kind of testing that eliminates or subordinates those least rationally compelling or emotionally appealing.

Although, as previously noted, this competitive struggle is not a zero-sum game, it does result in acute tension among its most irreconcilable components. Such tension, however, can be beneficial. In fact, the phrase "creative balance," which became the title of my previous book, alludes to the mutually reinforcing state of tension that enables such apparently conflicting aims as liberty and equality, individuality and community, or innovation and conservation, to achieve their optimal fulfillment. Where, on the other hand, a limited resource must be allocated—as, for example, in developing a budget, appropriating money, allocating personnel, using persuasion, or spending time—practical necessities demand a compromise somewhere in the range between divvying up, a hybrid, or a blend. But where, as in the case of a new proposal, action is not propelled either by some urgent requirement, powerful interest, or widespread popular demand, the proposal will be deferred, shelved, or killed.

In each of these cases, of course, public opinion plays a key part. We see its most ephemeral impact in the utterances influenced by the incessant sampling of current opinion. At a more mature stage, the public debate may lead to the kind of near consensus that Daniel Yankelovich and others have called "public judgment." And when the system is working well, the outcome, as Madison foresaw, is "a coalition of a majority of the whole society" which, like the parallelogram of forces I learned about in elementary physics, yields a resultant that genuinely serves the ends of "justice and the general good."

Given these elements of the democratic process, any major shift in political priorities can achieve permanence only if it is able to win mainstream support. A conspicuous case in point is the complete assimilation within a decade or two of all the New Deal's significant reforms. Unless such support emerges, the very forces that propelled the shift will generate counterforces that eventually recover lost ground. Indeed, it is interesting to note how quickly this happened to the more extreme components of the "Revolution of '94."

An ideologically driven revolution goes against the grain of the democratic process. Ideologies seek to impose their own dogmas and exclude or suppress opposing views. Ideologues are united by a creed rather than an interest (though, as in the case of economic philosophies, the creed may also serve interests). Thus, where political parties are ideologically based, as in Europe during most of the post–World War II period, wide swings in policy can result from changes in party control of the government. In the United States, by contrast, where each of the major parties is forced to be a broad-based coalition, this does not happen.

Time is on the side of all the mixing, reconciling, and consensus-building that takes place in a democracy. The process makes it difficult for stark alternatives to maintain their tyranny. Clarity of analysis is an invaluable tool, but it is better at defining differences than at devising solutions. Michael Wines of the *New York Times,* for example, has brilliantly contrasted the conservative conviction that "what makes a civil society is . . . each individual's freedom to pursue his own happiness—and learn from the pain of his mistakes" and the liberal belief that government should "set a minimum standard for civilized society, then raise the oppressed and the needy to that level." Others have categorized governmental functions as if federal and state roles were mutually exclusive. Similarly, the issue of affirmative action has been portrayed as an inescapable choice between a color-blind society and the perpetuation of racial animosities.

The way I look at things, tough-minded analysis should precede but not impede persistent attempts to reconcile unavoidable moral claims. When "don't just stand there, do something" initiatives are disappointed, the appropriate response should often be, not their abandonment, but their redesign and redirection. In the case, for example, of social services, Richard Harwood has good reason to point to "searing reports on inner-city pathologies unredeemed by generations of social policies and social workers." Yet a great many dedicated and underpaid people struggling with impossible caseloads and excessive paperwork nevertheless manage to give a lot of significant help to large numbers of people. And yet as I have good reason to know, there certainly are ways of improving such services.

When it comes to distinguishing a federal function from a state or local function, the determinative factor, as previously noted, can often be whether some group, liberal or conservative, feels strongly enough about the urgency of its cause to demand federal action. Two well-known examples are voting rights, as to which federal action has achieved enormously successful results, and crime, as to which it's not obvious that overriding the federal structure makes any sense at all. In the latter case, indeed, I join with the CATO Institute in deploring the congressional disposition to deal with crime by "making every local problem a federal problem and every local crime a federal crime."

When the democratic process is functioning ordinarily well, it gives every person and every group who feel strongly about something (except, perhaps, for the looniest fringe) an opportunity to be heard. Such individuals and groups are quite justified in believing that if they organize well enough and work hard enough they can have a real impact. And since the chief end of democracy is to confer this feeling of efficacy, democracy's value does not depend on the efficiency of its performance. That is also why the citizens of our own unique democracy have so consistently been willing to tolerate its messiness.

Some outsiders are less tolerant. Our disorderliness offends, for example, "soft authoritarians" like Lee Kuan Yew, who as prime minister of Singapore inspired and led that city-state's extraordinary development. In November 1992, Lee, then Singapore's senior minister, gave a speech in Manila opining that "what a country needs to develop is discipline more than democracy. The exuberance of democracy leads to undisciplined and disorderly conditions which are inimical to development." When I paid a call on him in 1992, he immediately launched into a reprise of this theme. Suppressing the impulse to respond in kind, I asked if he was familiar with the dialogue in hell in Shaw's *Man and Superman*. He was. "I hope, then," I said, "that you and I will someday have time for that kind of dialogue."

If such a dialogue ever does take place, I would expect Lee to stress the individual's responsibilities toward the family and the community. He would also argue that administering appropriate discipline to troublemakers enhances the quality of life for the responsible and law-abiding majority. Of course, to the extent that Lee Kuan Yew and other "soft authoritarians" (notably Mahathir bin Mohamad, prime minister of Malaysia) are merely saying that individual rights ought not to be indulged at the expense of the community, few people would take issue. But moral teaching is one thing, and governmental coercion is quite another. Indeed, the official enforcement of conformity to community values is likely to give the body politic a degree of rigidity that inhibits its ability to accommodate change. Besides, there is no reason to believe that Confucian discipline makes people any more community-minded than they are in the United States. On the contrary, at last count ninety million American adults were devoting an average of more than four hours a week to voluntary service, and three out of four American households gave an average of $880 a year to charity.

But to say that believers in democracy should be willing to pay some price for its messiness is not to say that efficiency is unimportant. Even to survive, the democratic process must be able to satisfy three requirements: First, it must be able to give its citizens a sense of meaningful participation. Second, it must be fair to everyone while at the same time reaching out to those in need. And third, it must be efficient enough to be capable of meeting adequate standards of performance. In all three respects our system is under serious strain at present. These are the sources of the current dangers to which I referred at the outset of this essay. Several preceding essays have attempted to diagnose their causes and to suggest curative measures.

With regard to the first requirement, an essential element is leadership that sees the projection of goals, the creation of choices, and the shaping of priorities as the building blocks of consensus. Equally essential is greater effort by us the people and our elected officeholders to be honest with each other. As you may remember, that is a theme stressed in another essay. All I can now add is that sticking to the facts and pursuing the merits will yield as a bonus the satisfaction of confounding the cynics. As Mark Twain said, "Always do right. This will gratify some people, and astonish the rest."

But how far is the prudential axiom "Honesty is the best policy" applicable to politics? The pressures to say what has to be said can be remorseless, and I cannot be sure that if I were in a bind like the situations of Theodore Roosevelt and George Bush cited in my essay on ethics in government, I would have acted any differently. I am sure, nevertheless, that in politics, as in business, intelligent calculation will almost invariably lead to the same result as morality and integrity. The present climate of cynicism, moreover, has disgusted so many people that the politician who is perceived as telling it like it is could well gain more in public confidence and esteem than she lost by challenging commonly held preconceptions. This last is a conjecture I would dearly love to see put to the test. If we are ever to be committed to leveling with ourselves, we need politicians who not only will meet us halfway but also will set an example that encourages this pledge.

The previously mentioned measures to reduce the number and complexity of political choices at the national level include structural simplification, decentralization, the devolution of functions to state and local government, and selective privatization. By making governmental choices more accessible and intelligible, these measures will also enlarge the opportunity for citizen participation.

The second requirement, that of fairness and compassion, is integral to democracy's role in a society that affirms the equal worth of every person. A democracy succeeds to the extent that its citizens share and enjoy dignity and respect. These things are impossible without fundamental decency, which, at the end of the day, rests on the moral foundations discussed in my essays on the need for a sense of worth and ethics in government.

As to the third requirement—the achievement of results—the breakdown of trust, the growth of cynicism, and the accumulation of hostility toward government underscore the essentiality both of greater congruence between promise and performance and of maximum feasible effectiveness in the use of limited resources. My most useful suggestions for corrective action can be found in my essays on government overload, the management of bureaucracies, and the performance of public service.

Things will not be perfect, of course, even if all my prescriptions are accepted as correct, supplemented by others still to be invented, and then carried out to the letter. But a determined effort to put them into effect would at least give us a clearer sense of what we were up against and why. And the more clearly we understand what we have to face, the better able we are not only to decide how to cope with it but also to take whatever may come. For the capacity of human beings to adapt and endure is indomitable. Were it not so, human society would long ago have yielded to discouragement or been destroyed by envy. But to adapt and endure, we need as individuals both to have hope and to believe in ourselves. And we must retain a measure of loving concern for one another.

Every American who cares about this country—every one of us who is proud of what it has achieved and looks forward to what it may yet attain—shares responsibility for keeping its values alive.

Index

Index

Index

Index

Index

Index

Organization for Economic
    Cooperation and Development,
    232, 236*n*
Organization of American States
    (OAS), 183
Ornstein, Norman, 69
Otis, James, 11
overload, 52–80
    arts and, 66–67
    devolution and, 71, 73
    environment and, 55–56
    growth, complexity and, 54–56,
        59, 68
    health-care system and, 57–58,
        62–63
    incompatible demands and, 61–62
    leadership and, 75–80
    media and, 65–66
    mistrust of government and,
        52–53
    politicians, politics and, 69–71
    presidency and, 78–80
    priorities and, 71–72, 76, 78
    privatization and, 71, 74–75
    remedies for, 71–76
    self-renewing cycle and, 76–77
    simplification and, 71, 72–73
    standards, conventions and,
        66–68
    systems and, 56–59
    termination and, 71, 74
    unrealistic expectations and,
        61–64
    war on poverty and, 59–61, 62
    women's status and, 67

Packard, David, 218
Pascal, Blaise, 44

Payin, Emil, 47
peace enforcement, 157–87
    air power and, 177–78
    criteria, priorities and, 176–77
    and end of Cold War, 161–63
    escalation and, 180
    function of, 160–61
    Gulf War and, 159–60, 161,
        162–63, 166, 170, 172–73, 178
    international law and, 184–85
    intervention and, 164
    "King's Peace" and, 185
    media and, 175–76
    nation-building and, 182
    negotiated solutions and, 184
    "new humanitarianism" and, 164,
        165–66, 167, 169–70, 175, 180,
        184
    rapid deployment force and, 181
    realpolitik and, 167–69
    regional organizations and, 182–83
    rogue regimes and, 166
    sanctions and, 177
    UN and, 159–61, 164–65, 172,
        175–77, 179–81, 182, 184, 185–86
    U.S. leadership role and, 163, 165,
        170–72, 178, 186
Perot, Ross, 9, 69, 263
Personnel Management Project of
    1977, 99
Peru, 217
Peterson, Roger Tory, 106–7
Phelan, John, 152
Philip II, King of Spain, 128
Philippines, 30, 200, 218, 231, 232
Phillips, Kevin, 21–22
Platt, Thomas C., 209–10
Plaza, Galo, 182

280

Index

Index

Index

Index

About the Author

B orn, raised, and educated in the Boston area, Elliot Richardson has played an extraordinarily wide range of roles in government and politics. Trained in the law, he has practiced in Boston and Washington and served as U.S. attorney, attorney general of Massachusetts, and attorney general of the United States. In the Eisenhower administration he handled legislation for the Department of Health, Education, and Welfare, and as lieutenant governor of Massachusetts, coordinated the state's human services program. In the Nixon administration he was under secretary of state, secretary of Health, Education, and Welfare, secretary of defense, and attorney general. Under President Ford he was ambassador to Great Britain and secretary of commerce. He served for nearly four years as head of the U.S. delegation to the Third United Nations Conference on the Law of the Sea under President Carter.

Since then he has been a member of the Washington office of a major New York law firm and has been involved in a variety of public and nonprofit assignments, including service as the president's representative to the Philippine economic development program, as personal representative of the secretary-general of the United Nations for the Nicaraguan elections, and as a member of a United Nations humanitarian mission to Iraq after the Gulf War.

Elliot Richardson is best known for having resigned as attorney general of the United States rather than carry out President Nixon's order to fire Archibald Cox, the special prosecutor appointed to investigate Watergate. Mr. Richardson's resignation led to what is still called the "Saturday Night Massacre."